Thomas Hobbes

Twayne's English Authors Series

Arthur Kinney, Editor

University of Massachusetts, Amherst

TEAS 559

TITLE PAGE FROM HOBBES'S *LEVIATHAN*, 1651.
CORBIS/Bettman.

Thomas Hobbes

Conal Condren

University of New South Wales

Twayne Publishers
New York

Twayne's English Authors Series No. 559

Thomas Hobbes
Conal Condren

Twayne Publishers
1633 Broadway
New York, NY 10019

Library of Congress Cataloging-in-Publication Data

Condren, Conal.
 Thomas Hobbes / Conal Condren.
  p. cm. — (Twayne's English author series ; no. 559)
 Includes bibliographical references and index.
 ISBN 0-8057-1697-1 (alk. paper)
 1. Hobbes, Thomas, 1588–1679. I. Title. II. Twayne's English author series ; TEAS 559.

B1247.C66 2000
192—dc21
               99-054906

This paper meets the requirements of ANSI/NISO Z3948-1992 (Permanence of Paper).

10 9 8 7 6 5 4 3 2

Printed in the United States of America

To
A. D. Cousins
&
Damian Grace

Contents

Editor's Note

Almost since its initial appearance, the *Leviathan* by Thomas Hobbes has been the most important work of philosophy and political science in English literary history. While Hobbes's ideas profoundly affected such later writers as Locke, Hume, Rousseau, Kant, Hegel, and Freud, his writing, keenly aware of classical rhetoric and the uses (and dangers) of figures and tropes, laid an important literary foundation for such authors as Pope, Swift, and Coleridge. *Leviathan* remains that unique work that is as important to the study of English literature as it is to the fields of political science and philosophy. Yet, as the distinguished political scientist Conal Condren explains in this seminal study, *Leviathan* has often been misread, because those who study it fail to place it in the context of Hobbes's other thought and writing. To set this record straight, Condren examines first the central areas of Hobbes's works—in philosophy, religion, law, rhetoric, history, poetry, and social science—that contributed the ideas and perspectives as well as the style that culminates in *Leviathan*. This extraordinary book, like the work it analyzes, crosses the boundaries of many fields of study, but the interdisciplinary approach yields a richer and far more accurate understanding of Hobbes's greatest literary work and measures as accurately as we now can his place in the history of Western culture.

Arthur F. Kinney

Preface

There may be worldly resistance to yet another book on Thomas Hobbes. Over the last generation his work has attracted ever-increasing attention. In what is often thought of as an age of genius in science, philosophy, and literature he stands out as a figure of extraordinary interest and intellect. This having been recognized, there has grown a veritable Hobbes industry especially since the Second World War. The result has been at least two valuable introductory studies, Richard Tuck's *Hobbes* (London: Oxford Univ. Press, 1989) and A. P. Martinich's *Thomas Hobbes* (New York: St. Martin's Press, 1997). Although they have not been used in writing this study, they complement it. So why something else?

First and probably sufficiently, Hobbes's absence in a series such as this is a serious lacuna. He was not only a brilliant and provoking philosopher but also a superb writer. Indeed, in some universities *Leviathan* has been a compulsory English literature text. He was also a master of Greek and Latin. Secondly, the wealth of Hobbes scholarship has taken on new directions and the contexts in which his work can be placed have been transformed. Topics such as religion and rhetoric hardly touched on in traditions of inquiry preoccupied with political philosophy—as those terms are more or less understood—have now assumed centrality. Thirdly, his correspondence has only recently been made fully available and new works putatively by Hobbes have confidently been attributed to his pen.

In the light of this general situation the scope of this work is in one way exorbitant, in another quite modest. It is ambitious in trying to give an overview of a whole oeuvre. This cannot be done by attempting the gist of each of his works in turn, for his abiding interests were carried through and sometimes modified from one work to another in what seems to be almost an interlaced structure of thematic variation. Further, in the context of the aims of this series, it did not seem appropriate to rehearse each of his failed attempts to square the circle, or prove the vacuum impossible, the nuances of which are certainly beyond my competence. We must hope he really was wrong. Rather, I have attempted instead to give a conspectus of Hobbes's views on a range of topics at various times expressed through overlapping groups of his works and this has meant some mention of most of them. Where I think a position is pretty stable I have illustrated from different articulations of it but where there was significant change I have tried to make its nature clear. In different chapters then, some works will assume greater significance than in others.

In another way, however, the scope of this study is modest. It cannot pretend to a thorough account of any of the works discussed and its attempts at contextualization are perforce perfunctory. I have aimed only at providing a way into and a partial context for the individual items of Hobbes's extensive output. There remains a distinct unevenness of attention; *Leviathan*, as befits its title, looms large enough to threaten stranding everything else on the shore. But this may require only partial apology, as *Leviathan* is the book above all others for which Hobbes is read.

Such a study cannot be a summary of received wisdom but equally it should not be too idiosyncratic. Thus I have used most chapters to address what I take to be myths about Hobbes, often derived from reading all or part of *Leviathan* in isolation. In some cases, such myths may have been sustained largely because they make teaching a most demanding writer easier—an understandable fault to which introductory studies are most prone. In other cases, myths might still be adhered to because of established scholarly authority, and occasionally a myth survives because its interest exceeds more plausible readings.

The overall plan might, in fact, seem to be eccentric. There is no discussion of Hobbes's political theory. Of course, Hobbes was much concerned with what we now call politics. He claimed with typical gauntlet-slinging bravado that political science was no older than his book *De cive* (1642, 1646) and certainly *Leviathan* belonged to a loose genre of academic public law theory called "politica." Yet like many people of his day, he did not systematically rely on the political as a distinct and cohesive realm of experience. When he wrote of politics it was not unambiguously what we might expect and it often carried the sense of policy, administration, and prudential judgement, matters less for a philosopher than a sovereign to consider. In fact, what we see as his political theory was largely distributed between discussions of what he saw as philosophy, religion, rhetoric, and law. And there is much that is political to be found in his philosophical attempts to understand "man." I have thus used Hobbes's own modal understanding of intellectual inquiry as a guide to the organization of this book. From a modern perspective, this may seem odd, but we do need reminding that the political as a distinct form of human experience capable of generating theories and philosophies of its own, of being studied in its own right, would have seemed redundant to many in the seventeenth century familiar enough with words like "politics." It may well be, though this is not the place to argue it, that the technically anachronistic classification of Hobbes as a political theorist has created many of the problems that have been taken as his failings and inflicts unnecessary difficulties on his corpus.

So, after giving a brief outline of his life, in chapter 2 I have provided an overview of his understanding of science or philosophy, his general sense of intellectual modality, and his practice as a writer on science. Chapter 3 turns to the most persistent object of his scientific attentions other than mathematics, his understanding of mankind and the causes and mechanisms of socialization. Chapter 4 deals with the pervasive problem of religion, for Hobbes understood the drive to religious belief as fundamental to society, its misuse central to its crises. Chapter 5 concerns his changing understandings of law and sovereignty partly as answers to the problems of religion. Chapter 6 deals with the particularly difficult issues of his understanding and practices of rhetoric, history, and poetry. Chapter 7 covers the ground of the previous chapters as they are captured in *Leviathan*. Chapter 8 deals first with the characteristics of his philosophical and literary style, which themselves help explain problems of reception and interpretation. It is here that I finally turn to what is very much a brief interpretative afterlife.

As I am largely expounding the views of Hobbes and his contemporaries, I have used the masculine pronoun. Despite its potential ambiguity in subsuming or excluding the feminine, this seemed better than massaging Hobbes into a more gender-friendly shape.

Acknowledgments

My thanks are especially due to Professor Arthur F. Kinney for the invitation to write for TEAS and for his patient and astute handling of a manuscript of often Hobbesian convolution; to Sarah Brown for attentive and sensitive copyediting; to Averil Condren for the index; and to the students in my Hobbes seminar, 1997–1999.

Chronology

1637 *A Briefe of the Art of Rhetoric* published. "Ship Money" case occurs. Young earl comes of age and disputes inheritance with mother.

1638 Newcastle becomes tutor to Charles, Prince of Wales.

1640 Fails to be elected to Short Parliament for Derby. Writes "Latin Optical MS." *The Elements of Law, Natural and Politic* finished. Parliamentary attacks on earl of Strafford, flees to Paris.

1641 Disputes with Descartes begin, largely through correspondence.

1642 *De cive* published in Paris. Civil war takes place in England.

1643 Writes *Anti-White*.

1645 Newcastle and Sir Charles Cavendish withdraw from the civil wars.

1646 Appointed mathematics tutor to Charles, Prince of Wales. Writes *Of Libertie and Necessitie* (published 1654). Writes "A Minute or the First Draught of the Optiques" (incorporated into *De homine* [1658]).

1647 Falls seriously ill.

1649 Charles I executed. "Engagement controversy" begins.

1650 Pirated edition of *The Elements of Law* published. Falls ill again. *The Answer to the Preface before Gondibert* published.

1651 *Leviathan* published in April. English translation of *De cive* published as *Philosophicall Rudiments Concerning Government and Society*. Charles II defeated at Battle of Worcester and returns to Paris. Hobbes presents MS of *Leviathan*. Banished from exiled royalist court.

1652 Returns to London in February.

1653 Oliver Cromwell becomes Lord Protector. "Barebones Parliament" attacks universities.

1655 *De corpore* published.

1656 *Questions concerning Liberty, Necessity & Chance* and *Six Lessons to the Professors of Mathematicks* published.

1657   Hostility to *Leviathan* mounts. *Markes of the Absurd Geometry, Rural Language, Scottish Church Politicks, and Barbarisms of John Wallis Professor of Geometry and Doctor of Divinity* published.

1658   *De homine* published. Oliver Cromwell dies.

1660   Restoration of Charles II in May. Newcastle retires from public life. Royal Society formally founded.

1661   *Dialogus physicus* published.

1662   *Mr. Hobbes Considered in his Loyalty, Religion and Reputation* published. Continues attempts to square the circle.

1666(?) Writes MS of *Dialogue Between a Philosopher and a Student of the Common Laws.*

1666   Bill in Parliament makes possible trial for heresy. Possibly begins work on the *Historical Narration Concerning Heresy* and the *Historia ecclesiastica carmine elegaico concinnata.* Fire of London occurs.

1667   Latin translation of *Leviathan* published in Amsterdam.

1675   Leaves London for the last time for Devonshire estates. Probably begins the translations of Homer.

1678   *Decameron physiologicum* published.

1679(?) Writes advice on hereditary succession.

1679   Charles II forbids publishing of *Behemoth.* "Exclusion Crisis" begins. *Thomae Hobbesii malmesburiensis vita* published. Dies at Hardwick Hall.

Chapter One

Thomas Hobbes: A Brief Life

Birth among Rumors

The crowned head of Spain prayed in the Escorial during the spring of 1588 and calculated the costs of the invasion fleet he would urge so eagerly to England. Meanwhile, in a tiny Wiltshire village Mrs. Hobbes, the curate's wife, lay in her bed and contemplated the impending crisis of the arrival of young Thomas. He was unusually impatient to be about the world, bustling in prematurely on Good Friday, 5 April.[1] As the old Hobbes would later telescope events, "My mother brought forth twins, both me and fear."[2] Rumors of invasion were probably heavy in the soft west-country air given a world of slow and erratic news, but that Phillip II's planned armada caused the birth of Thomas Hobbes is an unlikely tale. It is nevertheless a prescient myth, rehearsed from John Aubrey to the present and encapsulating more about Hobbes than his mother. He would develop a complex awareness of causation's perverse patterns and of poetic and metaphysical association. Hobbes came to believe that myth, rumor, and superstition were as important in understanding human behavior as the reality behind the stories. He elevated fear to a pinnacle of explanatory saliency: it drove human action, its exploitation sustained society; but uncontrolled, it corroded civilization. The fear of unnatural death generated by the armada was a quintessentially Hobbesian fear.

Hobbes's native village, Westport, was close by the market town of Malmsbury. The area was thick with members of the Hobbes clan, quite typically spanning different strata of society. He had rich uncles in trade, but his own parents were poor; his father's curacy of the nearby village of Brokenborough afforded few resources.[3] Superficially Thomas seems to have been only a little like his father. Hobbes senior was intemperate and given to drink and gambling. Hobbes junior could be rash in argument, yet he was financially adept and careful of his health. Hobbes's father was the kind of cleric who united all factions of the English church; he was not the sort they needed. With him, wrote Aubrey, a little learning had gone a long way and in 1602 he was in trouble for neglect of duties. In the following year he was fined for slandering another cleric. A year later, he beat the man and, adding sacrilege to violence, did so in a churchyard. He was excommunicated and obliged to run away, dying "in obscurity beyound London" (Aubrey, 227).

Thomas Hobbes would turn running from danger into something approaching a civic virtue (*Vita,* ll. 27–28, 2). He certainly united otherwise bickering priests against him, but he had a remarkable capacity for personal friendship that crossed the barriers of belief and violence. Nothing provides better support for Aubrey's lively picture of Hobbes—as witty, good-natured, and generous—than the depth and diversity of friendship that would enrich his life. Long before his father fell into the obscurity of disgrace, Hobbes had made perhaps the first of his friendships, rescuing him from the worst aspects of his environment.

He was educated locally by Robert Latimer, an apparently remarkable teacher for whom Hobbes retained affection and who would eventually be rewarded with Hobbes's father's position at Brokenborough (Aubrey, 228; Malcolm, 15–16). Hobbes excelled at Latin and Greek, and because of the largesse of his Uncle Francis, a wealthy glover, he was sent to Latimer's old college of Magdalen Hall, Oxford, in 1602. It was a poor, strongly Reforming or Puritan college, but it is impossible to tell what impact if any it had on Hobbes. Like many people of talent he may have gilded the lily by exaggerating his laziness and may similarly have enhanced his hostility to university teaching to fit with his later views. Like many who have crafted justifying images of their own lives, Hobbes saw a unity that the otherwise fragmented evidence does not entirely support (*Vita,* 3, 18). His perception of the university, prejudicial and distorted, is nevertheless clear enough: Hobbes had no time for the Aristotelian philosophy taught, and he delighted instead in poring over maps and catching jackdaws (Aubrey, 228–29; Malcolm, 16). The cartographic skills would serve him well.

The Cavendish Connections

Hobbes's options were probably limited to the pursuit of a clerical career, if he took his M.A., or to something more precarious given the right connections. He chose the latter course. He was recommended to William Cavendish by the college principal, Sir James Hussee (Aubrey, 229), and from 1608 he was employed by Cavendish as tutor to his son, also named William, a man of about Hobbes's own age. Hobbes's position began as a combination of servant, secretary, and companion (Malcolm, 17).

As he was to spend most of his life in the ambit of the Cavendish family, it is important to say a word about them. They had great wealth centered on lands in Derbyshire, Nottinghamshire, and Yorkshire. They were descended from Bess of Hardwick, countess of Salisbury, who became probably the richest woman in England after Queen Elizabeth. Her wealth had been accumulated by living long and marrying often and upwards; Hobbes would eventually die at what had been her principal residence, Hardwick Hall. Meanwhile, he went riding and hunting with his tutee. The young men shared intellectual interests and in 1614 went on a grand tour through France to Italy, where they learned Italian. After their return, Cavendish translated Francis Bacon's *Essays* into Italian with some help from the author. It may be from this time that Hobbes also came to know Bacon while doing some secretarial work for him, although the acquaintance has usually been dated later (Malcolm, 18). He may also have collaborated in the last edition of Bacon's *Essays*. In 1620 the young William Cavendish produced a series of Baconian essays of his own, the *Horae subsecivae,* several of which have now been plausibly attributed to Hobbes, including an essay drawing on the visit to Italy. The elder Cavendish, Hobbes's employer, was a member of Parliament in 1614 and 1621 and, typical of many rich aristocrats, was involved in trade and speculation. Through him Hobbes became a shareholder of the Virginia Company in 1622, which paved the way for his financial independence. Hobbes's tutee had kept up his contacts from the Italian tour and it is likely that Hobbes was similarly as well informed, probably becoming familiar with the important antipapal writings of the Venetian Paolo Sarpi (1552–1623) and his *spirituale* and Marsilian antipapal ideas (Malcolm, 19–20). William Cavendish the younger inherited his father's title to become the second earl of Devonshire in 1626 but died in 1628, leaving his young son—yet another William—as the third earl (1617–1684) and in appalling debt.[4] Hobbes then took a sort of interregnum service with one of the Cavendish circle, Sir Gervase Clinton (1587–1666), travelling with his son to Europe but avoiding Italy because of war there.[5] It was during his service to Clinton that Hobbes published his translation of Thucydides (1629), with excellent maps of his own devising and dedicated to the young third earl of Devonshire. On his return to England, Hobbes reentered Cavendish employment: Christian (1595?–1675), the struggling widow of the second earl, needed a tutor for her son. Thus Hobbes would be teacher, then friend, to successive earls of Devonshire. The clear advantages to Hobbes in entering Christian's service were familiarity, friendship,[6] and convenience; tutoring a young boy left him more time for his own work.[7] The earl was only of grammar-school age, a time when rhetoric was traditionally taught, so Hobbes produced his *Briefe of the Art of Rhetoric*.

From this time a sense of Hobbes's circle begins to emerge. He became close friends with the cousins of the Devonshire branch of the Cavendish family: Sir Charles (1591–1654), a mathematician; William Cavendish, eventually first duke of Newcastle (1593–1676); and their associates, such as Robert Payne (1595–1651). It was around 1630 that the *Short Tract on First Principles* was written. It survives only in the hand of Payne and its authenticity has recently been doubted (Malcolm, 25). This synoptic set of propositions seems nevertheless to have been Hobbes's work and evidences his early thought as similar to but formulated in ignorance of Cartesian theory.[8] As such it lies behind the later disputes between Hobbes and Descartes, each equally jealous of his own independence of mind. Hobbes would remain close to Newcastle, whose interests were wide and who wrote on matters of policy in ways that illuminate Hobbes's own views. For a while Hobbes was also associated with an overlapping group around Lucius Cary, Lord Falkland (1610–1643). The attentions of what is called the Great Tew Circle were probably more centered on matters of religion, morality, and law. Aubrey describes Falkland's house of Great Tew near Oxford as being like a college.[9] Falkland, himself a man of highly tolerant and inquiring disposition, would become an equivocal supporter of the king in the civil wars and he may well have committed suicide in battle. He admired Hobbes greatly but was certainly responsible for propagating a theory of sovereignty Hobbes would find particularly obnoxious. William Chillingworth (1602–1644), central to the Tew environment, was a brilliant intellectual theologian given to extraordinary skepticism. He changed religion on several occasions, swayed by the negative force of his own arguments. Edward Hyde, later earl of Clarendon, was another member of the circle and a moderate supporter of Charles, but he survived in exile and became one of Hobbes's most trenchant critics. The war would divide people on many fault lines.[10]

In 1634 Hobbes went to Europe again, taking responsibility for the broadening of the young third earl of Devonshire's horizons. But Hobbes's own mind seems to have been focused firmly on matters of science, encouraged by the Parisian connections provided by Newcastle.

Thus Hobbes became an important part of a long-standing group of French clerical mathematicians, not least Marin Mersenne (1588–1648), who became one of his closest colleagues. During this time Hobbes also made sympathetic contact with Galileo. He returned to England in 1636 with the joy of study apparently overcoming "all other appetites."[11] In 1637 the young earl came of age and although Hobbes remained formally employed by the Devonshire branch of the family, he was fairly independent and able to spend much of his time in Newcastle's ambit at Welbec Abbey with its considerable library (Malcolm, 24). For a while this may have been wise, as Hobbes was caught in the middle of a dispute between Christian, who had rescued the estates from financial disaster, and her son, who suspected mismanagement.[12] For all Hobbes's energies, no manuscript material survives from this period excepting sporadic correspondence alluding to his work and the disputed *Short Tract*. The earliest certain piece is the "Latin Optical MS" (c. 1640), largely preoccupied with Cartesian theory. It refers to an earlier "section" and was probably a draft of what was to appear in *De homine* as the second section of Hobbes's tripartite scheme of human knowledge. So it seems that by the outbreak of the British civil wars the general structure of Hobbes's philosophy had been clarified and subdivided. The first section of his elements of philosophy would be *De corpore* (1655); the second *De homine* (1658); and the third *De cive* (1642). The impending crisis in Britain probably encouraged Hobbes to work most on *De cive,* which would be printed as a contribution to debates on sovereignty, civic liberty, and religion.

Civil Wars and the Flight to France

With hindsight it seems that from 1637 Britain was sliding to civil war, and although many were surprised that the crisis of rule came to war, there was nevertheless a fear of the sort of violence that had been endemic to Europe even before Hobbes's birth. Charles I, king since 1625, had ruled without Parliament from 1629 and in doing so had touched very raw nerves with respect to religion, taxation, and law. In 1640 he had been forced to call the Short Parliament, to which Devonshire wanted Hobbes elected for the seat of Derby as a partner or agent in the Commons (Malcolm, 27). Charles needed to raise money and was met by a host of fears and veiled threats concerning his policies, especially with respect to religion. He dismissed the impertinent Parliament but was forced to call another, the Long Parliament that would outlive him. Both houses of Parliament were divided and full of shifting alliances but overall were more hostile than they had been before, and to Hobbes the issue seemed to be one of sovereign control or chaos. In 1640 he wrote *The Elements of Law*, designed to clarify all such issues in general rather than in particular. It was intended for circulation among friends and supporters of the king. According to the dedication it was written at the request of Newcastle, who had been appointed a tutor to the young Prince of Wales in 1638 and as a major court figure was central to the consolidation of the royalist cause. Hobbes's formulation of issues of sovereignty may have been general enough, but he was pinning his colors to the king's mast. Noel Malcolm suggests that throughout 1640 Hobbes may have been thinking of moving to Paris; it was financially viable and the intellectual life of Paris exerted its own pull (Malcolm, 27–28). In November, however, antiroyalist attentions turned to those defending absolute monarchy. As such interest could lead to imprisonment and as Hobbes was unusual in systematically defending such a doctrine, he decided to flee.[13]

So it was from Paris that Hobbes had *De cive* printed, a work that established his fame more securely than had the widely circulated *Elements of Law*. In 1644 fragments on optics, "Opticae liber septimus," were included in Mersenne's compendious collection on mathematics, *Univerersae geometriciae*, and Hobbes provided a short metaphysical preface to his friend's work on the physics of ballistics.[14] While the ballistics hummed in Britain, Hobbes made more scientific and lifelong friends, notably Pierre Gassendi (1592–1655), a significant materialist skeptic who shared Hobbes's distaste for Aristotle, and the Huguenots Abraham Du Prat (1616–1660), Samuel Sorbierre (1615–1670), and Thomas Martel (1618?–1679/85?). His preoccupation with logic, science, and explanation is indicated by the long, unpolished *Anti-White* (1643), and his correspondence to England sustains a similar attention. But in 1645 Newcastle and his brother Charles arrived in Paris. Newcastle encouraged Hobbes to write first on problems of free will and logical necessity, published later as *Of Libertie and Necessitie* (1654), and then systematically on optics, resulting in *A Minute or the First Draught of the Optiques* (1646) (Malcolm, 30–31). Despite this, Newcastle's arrival also brought the war to Hobbes's Parisian world. Newcastle had been the king's chief commander in the north of England but had become frustrated with royalist personalities and policies. After the disastrous defeat of Marston Moor, Newcastle walked out in a huff and headed for Europe with a few friends and his brother, also a senior commander. It was, I suspect, an action that was to haunt Hobbes and inform the writing of *Leviathan*. As the situation deteriorated for Charles I, an exile community was created in Paris and to this the young Prince of Wales, Newcastle's tutee, was sent. Hobbes was appointed mathematics tutor to the prince and so was brought into the intense, insecure atmosphere of a guttering court. He made new friends, despite the tensions and severe illness during 1647, and kept up his old close ones at home; but royalist Paris did not suit him or his plan of work.[15] Mersenne died in 1648, after which Gassendi left Paris; little wonder Hobbes was considering a return to England, having written to Devonshire to that effect in 1648.[16] Charles I was executed in February 1649 and, like all in Europe, Hobbes was looking on a brave new world. In May 1650 he informed Robert Payne that *Leviathan* was largely written. It was during this time, when he was ill again (Stephen, 41), that he also wrote an important short study on poetry, *The Answer to the Preface before Gondibert*, a tribute to one of his newer friends, William Davenant (1606–1668), who would later found the English Opera. A partial pirated copy of *The Elements of Law* was printed as *De corpore politico*, presumably as a contribution to the enlivened debates about obedience and sovereignty stimulated by the execution of the king, as was an anonymous English translation of *De cive* as Hobbes's *Philosophicall Rudiments*.

Leviathan was published in 1651 and while this, too, was taken into the debates on allegiance, Hobbes presented a manuscript copy to Charles II. The intention was no doubt innocent, but the timing was inept. Charles II had invaded England with a Scottish army and on 3 September was beaten soundly and swiftly at the Battle of Worcester, Oliver Cromwell's crowning glory. Charles fled the field, making an ignominious if romantic escape back to Paris. Things had never looked darker for the royalists. *Leviathan*, relatively uncluttered by royalist sentiment, carried more than a suggestion of accommodation to the emerging order and, retrospectively, this suggested an admiration of the ascending power of Cromwell. It was also virulently anti-Catholic. Christian Cavendish would have understood; she may have aided Charles II's escape after Worcester, but she encouraged a grandson to marry into the Cromwell family.[17] Hobbes, however, was banned from the exiled court around Charles II's Catholic and embittered mother Queen Henrietta-Maria, and without the clerical support of his old friends, he was vulnerable. Sections of the Catholic clergy then apparently tried to have him arrested. Hobbes jumped from the fire back into the frying pan.

"A Mind to Be Home"

Hobbes was settled in London by early 1652 and once more into the protective bosom of the Cavendish family. Again his circle expanded, this time to include the great physician William Harvey (1578–1657). More surprisingly among his friends were the Catholic philosopher Thomas White, whose *De mundo* Hobbes had attacked in his *Anti-White;* the highly influential parliamentarian lawyer and scholar John Selden (1584–1654); the Cromwellian educational reformer John Hall; and the Independent Henry Stubbe (1632–1676) (Malcolm, 33–34). The breadth of Hobbes's friendships is striking, but the common threads seem to have been scientific and literary interests, anticlerical sentiments, and a propensity to heterodoxy presupposing a high level of toleration for differing views, an echo perhaps of Great Tew from before the war.

Gradually, however, during the Cromwellian interregum, hostility was focused on Hobbes. When it was suggested in Parliament in 1653 that the universities should be disestablished, Hobbes's distaste for them had to be taken seriously, for *Leviathan* provided forthright rationalizations for such dissolution. The universities were largely clerical organizations and so defense of the institution and the clerical office came together. Meanwhile, Hobbes was wrongly rumored to have married[18] while he was finally finishing the first section of his philosophy, *De corpore* (1655), a work to which he had been wed for many years.[19] *Leviathan* was attacked in print and even mathematical differences between Hobbes and the Oxford professor of mathematics, John Wallis, descended into acrimony. Hobbes, supported by Henry Stubbe, may have gone too far in claiming that there was a Presbyterian conspiracy against him, but there is no doubt that if he had a rare gift for friendship, he was also adept at uniting groups hostile to him. The Catholic Church, the Church of England, the Presbyterian Church, and the universities all fashioned a demonized Hobbes to their liking. Despite this, the scientific writing continued and in the year of Cromwell's death, 1658, Hobbes printed the third section of his philosophy, *De homine;* the earlier optical work with all its geometrical garnish was finally incorporated into a single argument.

The Insecurity of the Restoration

Ironically all this hostility was less a problem for Hobbes under Cromwell's regime than it would be under the restored monarchy, which he welcomed in 1660. For despite the image of a raffish free-thinking court, of oranges and theaters, wit, gaiety, and corruption, Charles II's rule was to become systematically oppressive. Once Charles II sat properly on his throne, the duke of Newcastle retired from public life, but not before giving his ex-tutee a long letter of often-brutal advice about how to keep his position. In some respects a Hobbesian document, it urged selecting bishops for their loyalty and capacity to enforce royal policy.[20] Charles was indifferent to much religious policy, as long as the Church of England helped control his kingdom. So a pious, insecure, and sometimes vindictive episcopacy made life uncomfortable for Independents, Nonconformists, and Catholics as well as Thomas Hobbes, whose books would be ritually burned by the hangman. Part of the problem was his acceptability at court. Charles, erratic in most things, sometimes paid Hobbes a handsome pension and gave him easy direct access (Malcolm, 36); Charles came to love *Leviathan,* for enthroned he could see himself in its pages. And so, as Malcolm states, attacks on a mythic image of Hobbes could often be surrogates for chastising the court itself for an immorality and irreligion Hobbes never displayed (Malcolm 35; see also chapter 8, "Beyond Britain to the Modern World" in this volume). Against that sort of encoded animus to "Hobbism," defense was difficult, but he did his best in public with *Mr. Hobbes Considered in his Loyalty* (1662)[21] and *Considerations on . . . the Reputation of Thomas Hobbes . . .* (1680).[22] Between the publication of these works Hobbes invested much of his private energies in preparing the grounds of defense against charges of heresy by writing his subversive history of the term and the *Historia ecclesiastica,* a somewhat Sarpian or Marsilian poetic dialogue on the history of the church.[23] Hardly surprisingly, Hobbes was not fully accepted in the scientific circle that became the Royal Society. This was no doubt a disappointment, for he spoke highly of it according to Aubrey (Aubrey, 237).[24] By contrast, his reputation on the Continent was high and secure. This by no means rested on *Leviathan,* but his modified translation of that work into Latin in 1667–1668 did him no harm outside Britain.

Throughout this time and until just before his death, Hobbes's energy was remarkable. According to Aubrey, Hobbes was abstemious, given to regular habits and exercise. He played tennis until he was 75 and rarely got drunk, but when he did, he drank enough to vomit. Part of the secret may have been in his singing for the good of his lungs, loudly and badly in a room well away from everyone else (Aubrey, 234–35).[25] This was not difficult to arrange, for most of his time was now spent with the Devonshire side of the Cavendish family, sometimes in London until 1675, and in the great establishments of Chatsworth and Hardwick (Aubrey, 237). Newcastle may have begun to retire from more than public life when Charles II was restored in 1660, and although he and his young wife Margaret could cut a spectacular, and to Samuel Pepys, shocking display on occasion, after her death he was no longer a pattern of patronage.[26]

The True Philosopher's Stone

In his last years Hobbes suffered from Parkinson's disease, necessitating an amanuensis. He wrote a history of the civil wars, *Behemoth,* which Charles II declined to let him publish for its inflammatory consequences, and translated Homer into English verse. Just before his death Hobbes destroyed many of his papers. He died at Hardwick on 4 December 1679, having suffered a stroke.[27] He had been known to loan money to his employers when there was a shortage of cash and, Aubrey states, given how charitable he had always been, having a thousand pounds to disperse to nephews in his will was remarkable. To this the earl added some extra (Aubrey, 236). Hobbes's burial, like his birth, comes with a fitting rumor. Having designed his own almost self-effacing epitaph, he toyed with an alternative. As Malcolm aptly notes, it expresses his wonderful sense of humor (Malcolm, 38). Perhaps it also displays the burning courage to rage against the dying of the light. It is said to have read: "This is the true philosopher's stone."

Chapter Two

The Nature and Scope of Hobbes's Philosophical Science

The Myth of Discovery

Aubrey relates how one day Hobbes, waiting alone in an Italian library, started to glance through an open volume of Euclid's *Elements*. Looking at an improbable conclusion he was lead to an earlier proof. Doubting that and being given to "emphaticall" oaths, he turned back to yet another until he was not so much convinced as, "By G—," converted to science (Aubrey, 230). The book formed a neatly circular hole on a straight road to Damascus. The story cannot be taken as literally true;[1] but too good to discard, it is held to symbolize a truth: sometime in adulthood, Hobbes became converted to scientific inquiry that dominated the rest of his life. He turned his back on the humanist study of his youth to become a part of the scientific revolution. Thus his life can be taken to encapsulate the shift from the Renaissance to the dawn of scientific Enlightenment. With a sufficiently selective sense of teleology he may be imagined to have devoted himself to advancing some cohesive project of modernity.

The problem with Aubrey's story, however, is that being so obviously mythical it lulls us into a sense of false security. Certainly Hobbes did develop a passionate love of science and held Euclidean mathematics to be an epitome of excellence. Yet the neat line of development is highly problematic. Most generally, the very idea of the humanistic Renaissance being superseded by scientific modernity would have been rather alien to Hobbes and his contemporaries. More specifically, he drew no distinction between philosophy and science and throughout his life retained a deep interest in what we might call the humanistic (Reik, 190). Moreover, the very term "humanism" is notoriously unstable; Hobbes was decidedly hostile to humanism as a cult of admiration for Cicero and his world, but this cannot be said of the fashionable Tacitean humanism of his youth, which remained consistent with his scientific

11

interests.[2] As for Hobbes's own science, it was marginal to the empirical mainstream, and his mathematics, resiliently dependent upon ancient and Renaissance conceptions, gradually became old-fashioned. Above all, Aubrey's story does not account for Hobbes's most famous work, *Leviathan,* rhetorically ornate and lacking scientific austerity. It is a work that needs explaining but to do so in terms of any straightforward trajectory towards the modern world requires that we trade only in superficialities.

It will be helpful then, to start with an overview of Hobbes's understanding of science, presented with a further qualification. Hobbes, as Aubrey also remarked, was a man whose mind was never still. There is, however, a general shape to his understanding. *De corpore* provides his most extensive and considered statement on the matter; it is a conspectus of the principles of philosophy, discussing, inter alia, method, definition, concepts of time, place, causation, movement, and sense. It deals first with what would now be called deductive argument and then considers inductive studies.

Method and Scientific Knowledge

Most broadly, Hobbes took science to be the application of the correct method for the appropriate subject matter. This may seem bland, but it does emphasize that science was identified above all by procedure. Like his onetime employer Bacon (1561–1626), whose promotional rhetorics for science were to have such long-running significance, Hobbes believed that correct method was necessary to minimize the barriers in the way of ascertaining truth. Like Bacon, he understood scientific method in terms of causative accounts of matter in motion.[3] And also like Bacon, Hobbes believed—though without the edifying optimism of the Baconian vision—that science brought with it power over the world. As Hobbes asserted,[4] most of the advances in humanity's existence were due to science. Procedure it might be, but he took it for granted that science would improve the lot of humanity (*De corpore,* 1.1.7); hence there is no distinction between science and technology. Nevertheless, with the principal exception of his civil science, Hobbes's emphasis was not on practicalities but procedures.

Under these circumstances, it is not surprising that Hobbes drew no distinction between science and philosophy—despite his provoking hostility to philosophers and book learning. The philosophers he criticized were, he believed, bad scientists; their book learning the cluttering weight of authorities, which was, as Bacon had also insisted, bad method. The distinction between science and philosophy was being made during Hobbes's lifetime, but slowly and on an ad hoc basis.[5] It is this distinction only later rigidified that has consigned Hobbes to the realm of philosophy, for he was not principally an experimental scientist. He was, in short, concerned with what might establish something as science, how securely we might know anything at all. The fundamental point was to achieve a universal understanding by the imposition of a certain sort of description upon the world. We need first to look at the components of such a description and then refine them in counterpoint to what Hobbes took to be delineating forms of knowledge.

Science or philosophy, he claimed explicitly (*De corpore*, 1.1–2), is sound knowledge of effects derived from causes and conversely knowledge of causes reasoned from known effects. In this way Hobbes often gives the impression that he held to a symmetrical or biconditional relationship between the two processes; that is, argument can move indifferently from cause to effect or vice versa. Yet he could also be most insistent that there are two different methods involved. Reasoning from causes involves movement through a series of definitions we have made ourselves; it is, roughly speaking, deductive. Reasoning from effects evolves from our experience of natural appearances (*De corpore,* 1.4;25.1), and so it is far more inductive. Neither process of ratiocination (*De corpore,* 1.1) could be equated with the mere accumulation of information. Science was not a matter of simply discovering or gathering the facts and then theorizing about them. In this way, Hobbes's views differed starkly from some of Bacon's more thoroughly inductive proclamations.[6] Despite some methodological variation, for Hobbes the most fundamental science was a matter of establishing and demonstrating universally from first principles. To do this required what he called acts of privation (*De corpore*, 2.7.1), attempts to imagine all the incidentals of the empirical world annihilated. This was clearly the sort of imagination more immediately relevant to argument from causation than from the appearances of effects. Argument from causation was, Hobbes believed, potentially more reliable and so some specific forms of science might be given to higher degrees of certainty than others.

In all cases, however, science strove toward systematic, demonstrable generalized understanding of causes and consequences. As Paolo Sarpi had suggested, what we see as contingent and uncertain is largely our ignorance of causes. This had become a widespread view by the seventeenth century, but Hobbes also argued that although the contingent is therefore always necessary with respect to its causes, things may properly be seen as contingent with respect to each other (*De corpore*, 1.6.10). Contingency is restricted to where there is no shared causal chain. The work of science for Hobbes, then, was to minimize our sense of contingency and uncertainty through methodical reasoning, one consequence of which would be an enhanced control over our lives and the world.

Skeptical Materialism and Causation

If a number of distinctions we now make with respect to science are unhelpful in understanding Hobbes, one later distinction may be worthwhile. Hobbes and his contemporaries drew no consistent line between the study of reality (ontology) and how we know it (epistemology). Ontologically speaking, he was a materialist. The only appropriate subject matter for science is material reality and its movement. The universe is nothing more than matter in local motion. And it was mechanical causation, what had been called efficient causation, that interested Hobbes.[7] Indeed, collapsing a whole range of distinctions common to medieval philosophy, he held all causation was efficient (*De corpore*, 2.10.7); a cause was the power immediately producing some movement (*De corpore*, 2.10.1). But for Hobbes, muscular tissue was no less mechanical than a wheel, an eye a mechanism like a watch, and vice versa. Images and imagination were mechanical. The mechanical or the material was what was capable of causal explanation. Whatever moved was subject to change and so came within the purview of philosophy.

Yet if ontologically he was a thoroughgoing materialist, epistemologically Hobbes sounded a little like a phenomenologist, even, some have thought, rather like a Hegelian.[8] This was quite typical of his circle and was a view in the most general terms dating back to the pre-Socratic philosophers and rhetoricians. What we think of as reality, he maintained, is comprised by the internal images of the world beyond us (*De corpore*, 1.7.1). Truths, then, must be of propositions: "we compute nothing but our own phantasms."[9] Hobbes believed this proposition to hold even for what we might consider the eradicable realities of space and time. He defined space as "the phantasm of a thing existing without the mind simply" (*De corpore English*, 1.7.2). A moved body similarly left an image of its motion in the mind and this led to the definition of time as "the phantasm of before and after in motion" (*De corpore English*, 1.7.3). It was the structure of these internal images that enabled man to explain and to predict and it was in turn such reliable anticipation of causes and effects that gave man power over the world. The point was simply illustrated very early and in terms remarkably suggestive of Hume's later theories of morality: we experience fire as hot, but the heat we feel is within us, "in the coal there is no such thing," and so the qualities we take to be inherent in the world are attributes of the sentient. "And this is the great deception of sense, which also is by sense to be corrected."[10] As he was to put it in the *Decameron physiologicum* (1678)[11] our theories are the results of the effects of material reality acting on the mind. This makes Hobbes a rather odd empiricist, and it renders the notion of causation problematic and potentially solipsistic. So he provided what he clearly hoped would be strict criteria for the use of the notion of a cause: that it is not absurd, and that we can infer material phenomena from its postulation (*Decameron physiologicum*, 254).

There is, nevertheless, a prescient ambivalence in Hobbes's notion of causation. Much of what he wrote attributes a logic of causation to the movements of matter themselves, a conventional enough view: causes were necessary and sufficient antecedents of events in nature. Yet because of Hobbes's theory about what we actually do know, our own internal notions, and his belief that philosophy is a specific methodical ordering of mental impressions, Hobbesian causation can be construed as itself a mental construct, part of a philosophic description. In this way, his understanding is suggestive of the revolutionary skepticism of David Hume, who held that causation was our recognition of patterns of constant conjunction and we could not show it to be any more than this. Hume's fundamental analysis of causation is still widely accepted, but right or wrong, it can be seen as an attempt to resolve the difficulties in the suggestive ambivalence of Hobbesian types of theory. Hobbes's own appeal to absurdity as a criterion for judging posited causal relationships does seem little different from an appeal to the authority of experience, which for Hobbes could not be scientific. Further, as material phenomena could be invisible, his dogma that we must be able to infer material phenomena from postulated causes might easily lead to causative reasoning being supported by the invention of invisible entities, such as phlogiston. This kind of reification endemic to materialist analyses was something Hobbes was very keen to avoid.

Overall, his understanding of causal analysis and of science was always seeking a passage between the Scylla of a reliance on experience and facts as raw, undisputable data and the Charybdis of an internal solipsistic world. One persistent motif in Hobbes's work that may be seen as a way of overcoming this difficulty was to evoke a sense of shared community by appeal to the experience of the reader, and to this end he offered immediate and graphic illustrations of his formal propositions. He resorted to something superficially like a Wittgensteinian notion of showing. Thus if Hobbes was a materialist, he was not a materialist in the philosophically optimistic idiom of Marx; neither was he really an empiricist or a positivist. He was too profoundly skeptical. Hobbes's science was largely a matter of the imposition of methodologically uniform linguistic or mathematical sense upon the world—a view not unlike Newton's, Kant's, and later Einstein's. It was only the communal nature of this activity that stood as a guarantee against a deep uncertainty about everything. Hobbes's skepticism was both a philosophical principle and a problem to be overcome as much as humanly possible. As I shall suggest in chapter 8, his attempts to do this brought his philosophical and literary styles into close if contingent conjunction.

Definition, Resolution, and Composition

If science was an understanding of causes and consequences, its truths being the truths of propositions, a great deal depended on establishing a properly defined and shared vocabulary. A good deal also rode on how the vocabulary was used to study problematic phenomena. Hobbes would call method in science the shortest way of discovering effects by known causes or vice versa (*De corpore*, 1.6.1). It was an economy of calculation. Both definition and what is called the resoluto-compositive or the analytic-synthetic method are important to Hobbes's understanding of science and each shows it to be philosophic and indeed humanistic, if not even in some respects medieval. The first expression of the centrality of definition and some notion of resoluto-compositive method is found throughout a long document now published as *Le critique du De mundo* but called the *Anti-White* (c. 1643). It was a rough-worked treatise on the theories of the Catholic philosopher Thomas White,[12] but the difficult task of integrating the dimensions of scientific inquiry into a coherent method was something Hobbes never really laid aside, and which therefore has led to varied reconstructions of his position.

But from the *Anti-White* onward, Hobbes's theory of definition was certainly relatively stable. He presents an extreme belief in definition as nominal rather than real; definitions, in short, are never of genuine phenomena, they are of words. It was in *De corpore* 1.6 that he defined nominal definition most succinctly and set down most extensively his arguments for its significance. He referred to it as a sort of speech (*De corpore*,

1.6.14) directly about other words. These, he claimed, were but marks by which we could recall our inventions (*De corpore*, 1.6.11) and shape and stabilize the images or phantasms of the mind. Definition must seek universality, exclude incidental features, and eradicate equivocation (*De corpore*, 1.6.15). He suggested, however, a vital qualification to the criterion of universality. The word "hyperbole" in geometry and rhetoric may legitimately be given different definitions (*De corpore*, 1.6.15). Hobbes thus believed that definition legislated only about words and their interrelationships within discernible spheres of discourse.

The main features of nominal definition are important in understanding his discussion of political concepts, or signs. So, for example, by definition "subject" entailed the corollary term "sovereign" and vice versa. Subjects without sovereigns, sovereigns without subjects were therefore definitional impossibilities, for each was defined in relation to the other. So too with words like "good" and "bad" (*De homine*, 2.11.15). Again, his views here were not eccentric, though they could be put to provocative use. Hobbes's understanding of definition can strike us as remarkably modern but had been generally derived from medieval nominalism, most famously associated with the logician William of Ockham (d. 1348). The Ockhamist and scholastic doctrines that informed Hobbes's whole conception of science were that language is an arbitrary sign system, and that universal terms are no more than abstractions aiding the organization of particularity (*Elements*, 1.5.2). So, it is the analysis of the perceived similarities between phenomena we call horses that justifies the general classifier "horse." To think of the concept of horse or man in general as real is a delusion, a confusion of what would now be called signifier for signified (*Elements*, 1.5.6). The labeling functions of language are therefore seen to be central. When Ockham had developed such views, he flew in the face of a more realist, ultimately Platonic orthodoxy. This had held that we were entitled to call certain phenomena horses only by virtue of their conforming to a prior universal concept, idea, or paradigm of the horse. Thus although Plato was among the few ancients Hobbes admitted to admiring, their theories of definition were strongly opposed. The realist/nominalist polarity with respect to definition is probably fundamentally unsatisfactory, but it still has a lingering relevance; for example, in debates between methodological individualism and holism in the social sciences.

Be this as it may, Hobbes was brought up in a world in which forms of nominalism held sway, and he remained a part of that scholastic milieu. Indeed, his nominalism could be expressed with extremity.

When dealing with the putative origins of language in *De corpore* (*De corpore*, 1.2.4), he held that God's naming all things was itself an arbitrary process, but at least once Adam had been taught to speak, language had some divine warrant. Pat Moloney notes, however, that in the Latin edition of *Leviathan*,[13] when Adam is held to be self-taught, the divine sanction for human language all but disappears.[14] For Hobbes, speech is the most important purely human accomplishment. It is an arbitrary act of making on which all other achievements depend; our own language, as in the case of geometry, can potentially be understood with certainty because we fashion it.[15]

Nominalism seemed also to fit well with an emphasis on material particularity, for no thorough-going materialist can grant a real existence to the very concept of a horse prior to the act of naming particular horses, let alone give it an explanatory value. Hobbes would have had no truck with what still passes for popular explanation, as when people say that nature does this or that. In this sense, the general term "nature" is just an extrapolation from the particulars needing explanation (*De corpore*, 1.6.13; *Elements*, 1.5.6). Hobbes's conception of material particularity was taken so far as to make him quibble with the master Euclid on the understanding of the concept of a geometric line: as it had a physical manifestation, it was formally subdivisible (*Six Lessons*, 211).[16]

Nevertheless, although Hobbes held definitional labeling to be fundamental to philosophy, he did not believe that language was just a matter of labeling in ever greater degrees of particularity. In *The Elements of Law* (*Elements*, 1.13) he wrote largely of language as expressive and active, its primary function being to manifest our conceptions from which follow other functions concerned with affecting others. In different ways he also recognized its expressive, persuasive, aesthetic, and performative functions. In the *Anti-White* (*Anti-White*, 106–7), for example, he identified four legitimate functions of language and associated each with a distinctive sphere of intellectual activity: poetry celebrated, history narrated specific facts, rhetoric produced action, and philosophy, aiming at universality, demonstrated truth (*Anti-White*, 106).

It is in this context of scientific or philosophic reasoning that he stressed the crucial role of nominalistic definition designed to expurgate ambiguity and equivocation (*Anti-White*, 106–7). And because he accepted the variable nature of signification, he also explored the social dimension of scientific activity and thus of language. Public agreement on systematic word use and a capacity to teach it were the sine qua non of cumulative knowledge, the enterprise of science. Ironically he chose a highly equivocal term, demonstration, to embrace both the propositional and social nature of science. He defined demonstration as the proper derivation from combined definitions (*De corpore*, 1.6.16). In his manuscript notes to *De corpore* he called it a sequence of reasoning from properly formed syllogisms (*Anti-White*, 473). Yet he also referred to demonstration as teaching (*De corpore*, 1.6.11). When we demonstrate, defined words become public signs. (*De corpore*, 1.6.11); and so demonstrable can additionally mean teachable, what can be shown or even made manifest (and so be impressed upon the experience of others). Often it meant what could be argued both from cause to effect and vice-versa and what could be synthesized from analysis (*De corpore*, 1.3.20). The nuances Hobbes gave to the term do not always amount to inconsistencies, but they do conspire to give a false impression of the coherence of Hobbes's theory of science. This takes on generally firmer shape when we turn to Hobbes's notion of analysis integral to demonstration.

Definition made possible the analysis and explanatory synthesis, the demonstration, of problematic phenomena. Hobbes's understanding of science has often been taken as an application of what is called the Paduan or resoluto-compositive method. Broadly this was the belief that explanation required first the analysis of something into its smallest definable parts and then a resynthesis into a new satisfactory whole. This itself was a strongly nominalistic theory, reinforcing the familiar prejudice that the smallest material components are somehow the most real (human beings are *really* just molecules or a handful of chemicals and a bucket of H_2O). On such a view, explanation first requires the search for the minute. Hobbes would well have appreciated the desire to split the atom as a quest for a greater understanding of reality and would, if for different reasons, have stood optimistically behind Rutherford and Cockcroft, for he believed it possible to split the Euclidean point (Grant, 112). The association with Padua was with the medical school of the university whose methods had been most famously codified by Jacopo Zabarella in the sixteenth century. But again, in a world of such fluid intellectual relationships, it is misleading to see Hobbes directly in line with Zabarella and it is certainly anachronistic to impose an exclusively scientific cast on the method.

Analysis and synthesis could mean many different things. The Paduan variation was strongly Aristotelian and empirical. Hobbes's understanding often sounds more like Galileo's. This was a mathematical procedure, formulated partly as a critique of Zabarella, providing a model which might be extended to other phenomena.[17] Paduan method also owed much to traditional principles of rhetorical and grammatical analysis and something to the structure of the scholastic *quaestio*, in which a general issue was subjected to a series of questions producing ever more refined distinctions, prefatory to reformulating, and solving the initial problem.[18]

What Hobbes seems generally to have taken from overlapping understandings of analysis and synthesis was a sense of the biconditionality of explanation given properly defined terms; one should be able to demonstrate by being able to move in either direction, from postulated cause to consequence or from consequence to cause. In either case, one should end up with something affirmed, cohering with what we accept, or something to be rejected because of absurdity. However, Hobbes's own insistence that in some respects analysis from causes and analysis from appearances are asymmetrical (see the previous "Method and Scientific Knowledge" section) means that even here the ground is apt to slip beneath our feet. A degree of certainty in demonstration cannot be indifferent to how we proceed if one procedure is definitionally assured and the other seeks assurance from appearances determined from beyond us.

With these general comments on Hobbes's overall vision of science we can now see why he admired Galileo and Harvey so much and why it was Euclid's geometry that lay waiting for Hobbes in Aubrey's story. Galileo's mathematics provided a model of biconditional analysis and synthesis. He had provided a hypothetical mathematical explanation of matter in movement. In particular, a projectile was seen as moving along a path that was itself broken into specific horizontal and vertical moments. Having plotted the trajectory, he reversed the analysis to show that the flight was the sum of the different motions.[19] All final causes were rendered redundant, violations of William of Ockham's philosophical injunction never to postulate entities beyond necessity. More generally, mathematics, Galileo had held, was the language of God and nature—hence the encouragement to extend mathematical methods of analysis in the quest of elusive certainty. In several senses of the word, Euclid provided Hobbes with a paradigm of demonstrable, definitionally certain knowledge. Harvey, though more Paduan than Galileo, had used analysis and synthesis to demonstrate a most symbolically suggestive anatomical truth—that the heart pumps blood around the body—by moving from appearances to causes.. He had taken a problematic identity and (so his argument was presented) had analyzed it into its smallest parts and hypothetically reassembled them so that the whole made new sense: the tubing running through the body and attached to the heart is explained if we hypothesize that the blood is pumped around the body by the heart. Only this conclusion made sense of the problematic structure that dissection revealed: the valves and diminution of vein size as they ramified away from the muscular heart. Only this solution fits with what experience shows, that blood does not seep or fall from a wounded body but spurts as if pumped, and blood ceases to flow when the heart is not beating.[20] The work of Harvey, Galileo, and even Euclid was consistent with nominalistic, Ockhamist theories of definition, labeling, and perhaps even generalization. Predominantly, then, for Hobbes science or philosophy (by his own definitional procedures and theories) can be nothing more than the exercise of its methods, dependent upon proper definition. Geometry and arithmetic existed as paradigms of this process. This is not to say, as he has sometimes been misread, that he foolishly wanted to reduce all forms of inquiry to geometric propositions. It is only the method hitherto best displayed in this particular science that matters. As he insisted (*De corpore*, 1.6.7), it is possible to write scientifically about the causes of commonwealths without any knowledge of geometry at all.

Sense Beyond Science

In his more polemical moods, as in *Six Lessons to the Professors of Mathematicks* (*Six Lessons*, 181–356) and *Markes of the Absurd Geometry, Rural Language, Scottish Church Politicks, and Barbarisms of John Wallis Professor of Geometry and Doctor of Divinity*,[21] Hobbes was wont to give two unfortunate impressions—that all that was not science was nonsense, and all that was not Hobbes was not science. He could be goaded into extremity. Nevertheless, he could be responsive to criticism, as his correspondence now shows; and characteristically, as his published work has always displayed, he did not simply divide the world of learning into science and superstition or sense and nonsense. His association of different language functions with established forms of discourse shows that he had a distinctly modal understanding of the world. Here he exhibited some of the ambivalence of post-Hegelian idealists, who partly for that reason have found him congenial. Philosophy or science was at once a superior form of understanding; yet at the same time, other legitimate modes of discourse had rules, procedures, and goals of their own and so could not simply be reduced to, or be replaced by, philosophy. Demonstration was superior to celebration, but demonstration made poor poetry. To one side of recognized forms of discourse and science lay all the confusion, superstition, and false learning for which Hobbes castigated his real and imagined enemies, past and present.

In order to frame Hobbes's understanding of science, then, it is necessary to say something provisionally about the forms of intellectual activity that helped give it shape and a place in the world. The most significant of these will be the focus of the following chapters. Characteristically, although not invariably, Hobbes's discussions of discursive forms were couched in terms of the responsibilities and latitudes allowed to those engaged in them. He was apt to write of intellectual offices such as that of the poet, historian, or rhetorician. He had what might be called an "official conspectus" of the world. This is true of his analyses of philosophy also; they slide persistently into accounts of what a philosopher should or should not do.

Hobbes provided different specifications of nonscience in different works. Such looseness possibly arose because what mattered was less the fixed status of a field of study such as astrology than the question of whether it could be reformed or approached scientifically or had any nonscientific rationale. Medicine is absent from his various tables of science. This is not as odd as it might seem. William Harvey was a physician, but Hobbes admired him for his methodical anatomy; medicine would have been meaningless as anything but science. Crucially, however, theology, formally speaking, is beyond the scientific pale. For Hobbes it could not be science because however definitionally rigorous it might seem to be, its subject matter is immaterial. There was precious little in the way of an office for the theologian, except perhaps to keep quiet and pray. Theology was at its worst vacuous, as he put it in the *Historia ecclesiastica* (*Historia ecclesiastica*, ll. 19–26, 349; ll. 470–74, 362), a means of creating parasitic faith and priestly domination. At its best, what we say of God is an expression of piety, not a pursuit of science. By the same token, Hobbes had little truck for much Cartesean science because of its emphasis on the soul. As Tom Sorrell succinctly points out, in Hobbesian terms both Descartes's *Meditations* and the first part of *The Principles of Philosophy* were not philosophy.[22] More generally, Hobbes had no time with any science that was thought to lead to theological conclusions, excepting his own negative ones (see chapter 4, "The Mystery of God"). For Hobbes the soul was material or nothing, an immaterial substance being a sheer absurdity, a belief that has erroneously reinforced the myth of Hobbes's atheism (see chapter 4). As I shall argue, religion was important to him, but as a problem arising from the study of moral and civil science and so subject to scientific analysis.

Hobbes insisted, moreover, that history is not science because it is little more than a reservoir of particular facts (e.g., *Anti-White*, 106). These facts can be about the natural world or about the workings of human agency (*De corpore*, 1.1.9). In the first case, the natural historian is an under-laborer for natural science. Hobbes himself undertook a little of this, writing a natural history of comets (*Anti-White*, 151–53). Although certainly recognizing its potential, he gave it a very subordinate status because it was so difficult to control and was largely dependent upon individual observation, transmitted through the vagaries of descriptive language or commonly accepted on authority (*Anti-White*, 152–55). Human history, by being an artificial expansion of experience, is certainly important as an aid to prudence, the art of making sense of experience, but this is not properly science. For experience, he insisted, allows no universal, scientific conclusions as philosophy should (*Elements*, 1.4.11). He nonetheless undertook a good deal of broadly historical work throughout his life. Looking at it we will see that Hobbes's attempt to exclude history from science was not as simple as his general proclamations might make it seem.

Poetry may be both morally improving and a means of generating delight—and Hobbes was never far, even in old age, from the delights he received from Homer. He also wrote poetry, in the highly symbolic country house genre, and wrote his *Historia ecclesiastica* in verse and possibly also a poem on the movement of the earth around the sun (*Anti-White*, 439–47).[23] It would, however, be wrong to expect the poet to give certain propositional knowledge of causes and consequences. The necessary gifts of imaginative inspiration could be seen as entailing what Hobbes regarded as philosophical abuses of language, of which there are many in "De Motibus Solis"; yet as we will see, he contradicts this view.[24] So too, rhetoric has ambivalent status in his work. At times it is classified as science, at other times it is evoked as a contrast to help delineate philosophy and the philosopher's responsibilities (*Anti-White*, 107). More than once it is viewed as the enemy of sound reasoning and civil society. Law was also a field of study of which Hobbes became deeply suspicious. If parts of the *Horae subsecivae* are indeed by Hobbes, he moved from a confident faith in common law to the view that common lawyers undermined the authority of the sovereign. Law properly understood is a major part of what he sometimes called the science of justice,[25] his political theory.

The scope of this political theory focused mainly on subjects also considered in various additional capacities or offices being governed by sovereigns, but at times it also alluded to the relationships between such sovereigns. The analysis of all this comprised civil and moral science, the science of justice. How were such phenomena explained, in what ways were men as material objects moved to form states, in which ways might these institutions themselves be transformed and dissolved? Such issues were to occupy much of Hobbes's time, precisely because, as he sometimes claimed, it was his task to convert the inchoate fields of moral and civil inquiry, advocacy, and disruption into science. Their place in a table of sciences was thus very much dependent upon his own ongoing energies.

Yet on what we have of his scientific activities, civil and moral science might only be insecurely located within the domain of the truly scientific. It is sometimes uncertain whether Hobbes held his analyses of political bodies to have been as scientifically pure as his theories of natural ones. If so, the bulk of his major work failed to deliver the scientific goods. Conversely, it may be that his understanding of civil science was metaphorically derived from the language of mechanical philosophy, in which case the trajectory of scientific endeavor is of only partial relevance to what he did and why he is now read.

Optics and the Sections of Science

Hobbes's intellectual ambition is seen clearly enough in his confidently advertised masterplan. Sometime during the 1630s he formulated a program he called (in Euclidean vein) the elements of philosophy: body *(De corpore)*, man *(De homine)*, and citizen *(De cive)*. From fragmentary evidence in letters, it was clearly the culmination of a period of intense work and darting curiosity, but as the sections were published out of order it is impossible to be sure how far what we have corresponds to the original conception. Hobbes's notion of the branches of science was itself an expression of his theory of science, for he sought to show that an explanation of human nature also explained civil society. The emphasis on human nature as causative was not, as Richard Tuck has pointed out, as self-evident as it has been taken by modern commentators who are prone to assume that all political theory must be derived from a theory of human nature.[26] Hobbes's plan of scientific inquiry focusing on humanity included a great deal that the refinement of a concept of science would later exclude, a point true even for his persistent interest in optics, a study full of symbolic resonance.[27]

Since antiquity, images of sight and light had been taken as a synecdoche of all the senses and of understanding. Even now, colloquially, our language of intellection is permeated by terms from this one area of metaphorical expansion: we see the point, mental incapacity is dimness; conduct may be shortsighted. Hobbes inhabited a world in which solving the problems of light and vision could be construed as opening the door to human understanding. Spectacles were in common use; the telescope had been invented by none other than Galileo; the theater was using optical illusion; the nexus of speculation and human improvement was nowhere a greater source of scientific optimism than in optics. No sense was of greater significance than sight for those who would see into the human mind: And seeing this or that was a favorite Hobbesian construction.

Optics seemed specifically congruent with Hobbes's understanding of science, and over his long life probably did much to reinforce his scientific doctrines. It relied greatly on geometry to plot the pathways of light and to map impressions and their impact on the eye. Jan Prins proposes that optical speculation first suggested to Hobbes that all natural phenomena could be reduced to the local movement of matter.[28] Analysis of light offered a model that guided his scientific work (Reik, 71–72). The exemplum behind much of this from the *Short Tract* onward seems to have been the Galilean analysis of the projectile. It also encouraged the view that explaining sense impression, especially that of sight, was little different from explaining distinct inner motivations similarly affected by external movement of matter. This was to prove a long-standing homology, perhaps not systematically challenged until Wittgenstein's critique of Freudian motivational theory. Hobbes had a good deal in common with Descartes, who approached a similar set of problems from an adjacent perspective, but materialism was a sticking point. Hobbes's early work, the *Tractatus opticus* (c. 1640), was a reply to Descartes's theories of vision and a nonmaterial mind. Following this Hobbes wrote but did not publish the *Tractatus opticus* II (1644) and then *A Minute or the First Draught of the Optiques* (1646), to be printed partially in *De homine*. Much of the *Anti-White* was also taken up with optical issues.

Generally, according to Prins, Hobbes's views constitute a mechanical rereading of scholastic and Aristotelian theories with some insistent departures. He took over the traditional notion of species, which he redefined as material corpuscles. He insisted that all motion was local, contrary to Descartes, and that sensible qualities could not be real (Prins, 129–39). Indeed, in keeping with his skepticism, Hobbes developed in the *Optiques* a notion of double mediation, for he pointed out that the image created on the retina had to be different from the impression on the mind not just because it was inverted but because we cannot see our own retinas (Prins, 146). From the *Anti-White* onward he held that the heart, not the head, was the seat of sensory perception, a view made plausible by considering the ramifications of Harvey's circulation theory. In isolation, this alteration could be taken to indicate the dated nature of Hobbes's optical work, but in the context of seventeenth-century science it remained an important point of departure for nearly all optical theories seeking an alternative to Descartes.

Hobbes helped bring about a change in perspective in optics, drawing attention in a way appropriate to his whole understanding of philosophy to the position of the observer.[29] As Miriam Reik remarks, Hobbes's optics and much beyond it jelled around the belief in "the subjectivity of secondary qualities." It was, she claims, a crucial moment in the development of early modern science (Reik, 71). Indeed, it is mainly in his optical studies that we see Hobbes approaching engagement with the burgeoning experimentalism of his age. Now that Hobbes's correspondence is fully available we can see an extra dimension of this interest. There is an unpleasant exchange with Descartes, and an ongoing process of reflection, correction, and reformulation in a series of letters, first with the Cavendish circle, then predominantly with his friends in France. As Malcolm notes, letter writing was a major means of scientific inquiry and must have given substance to Hobbes's strong sense of science as a communal cooperative activity, progressing because communicants do share language: French, Latin, and, underpinning both, mathematics.[30]

Mathematics

It is to be expected, then, that most of Hobbes's mathematical work was in geometry, ignoring the gradually developing and more socially useful field of statistical probability and rejecting the contaminations of algebra. His mathematics went hand in hand with his optics; the controversies with which he became embroiled over the former spilled into the latter, and from there into the fields of study with which his name has ever since been associated.

As a mathematician Hobbes was courageous beyond the confines of competence, and he was no match for his Restoration bête noir Wallis, he of the rural language and Scottish Church politics. Hobbes thought that he had squared the circle (several times); Wallis, among others, showed (several times) that he had not, and from 1657 Hobbes and Wallis entered into an unsavory, increasingly vitriolic exhibition of name-calling. It was Hobbes's reputation as a mathematician that declined before his eyes. He also spent much time and ingenuity on proving that a vacuum was an impossibility (*De corpore,* 4.26; *Dialogus physicus*). Such energies were unable to compensate for poor timing for vacuums were being created. Hobbes did not just reject but seems to have had no grasp of what was being so brilliantly pioneered by his contemporaries: the use of algebra in geometry that resulted in its being established as a field of mathematics in its own right. He comes across as something of a self-taught geometric recidivist, convinced by the ancient authority of Euclid. But again, one needs to stress that algebra was being pioneered. Seventeenth-century mathematics was subject to considerable turmoil, with an uncertain place in higher education.

Under such circumstances, an overtly rhetorical dimension to the promotion of mathematics is only to be expected. Mathematics held out tantalizing promise of certainty, but cases usually had to be made for the value of specific forms, techniques, and operations. While there were those who saw potential in algebra, others saw mathematics mainly as an aid to alchemy and magic, and quite a few like Hobbes held firm to the greater explanatory rigor and demonstrable certainty of traditional geometry. This was a vital consideration when the specter of skepticism loomed so large. So Hobbes's partial grasp of what was going on was typical of an age of great if coordinated energy. Nevertheless, it seems that he may have been the first to prove an important similarity between parabola and spiral and, precisely through his attempts to square the circle, he raised a range of issues that led others to important discoveries (Grant, 124–26). The controversies Hobbes generated at the nexus of philosophy and mathematics probably had some part in changing the status of the new disciplines. Leibniz, the coinventor of calculus, had considerable respect for Hobbes, not least for the suggestiveness of the characteristic Hobbesian association of reasoning with calculation. That is a proposition that now lies behind much cognitive science and has made Hobbes a topos in fields of study undreamed of by him (see chapter 8, "Beyond Britain to the Modern World"). And it is here that Hobbes's greatest importance lies—not in the minutiae of mathematical calculation but in his grasp of the significance of the preconditions of arithmetic and geometry for the possibility of certain knowledge (Grant, 126).

Science and Skepticism

As I have hinted, Hobbes, like so many of his contemporaries, was preoccupied with the problems raised by skepticism. This hardly cohesive phenomenon took several quite distinct forms and so in one way or another could seem totally invasive. In its academic phyrronistic form, skepticism maintained that all propositions could be contradicted. In its more informal, pervasively Montaignesque variety, it amounted to the questioning of the grounds for our sense of certainty about anything, but in order, as Tuck summarizes, to achieve wisdom through the exposure of harmful belief. It is this sense of skepticism that partially blends Hobbes's science with what Tuck calls his Tacitean humanism (Tuck, xiii–xiv). In its manifestation as rhetorical probability theory, skepticism was the doctrine inherited from Aristotle that in practical life arguments could always be for and against, *ad utramque partem.* Added to this was the problem of Jesuitical moral probabilism, particularly significant and controversial in the England of Hobbes's youth, yet underexplored in this context of argument. This was the view that any course of action might be morally justified because none was more than probably valid and any might be supported by some plausible authority. In short, there was a heady and destabilizing mix of practical and purely theoretical issues under the auspices of the heading of skepticism.

Of course, if there is nothing beyond the reach of skepticism, both certainty and the value of doubt are destroyed. Hobbes himself was a great epistemological skeptic, as I have suggested, and he made a mighty show of exposing harmful beliefs. Polemically he did all he could to undermine argument from any authority, which with its cornucopia of competing texts only created unnecessary doubt and confusion. Ironically, however, it was his understanding of geometry and arithmetic as models of reasoning that might seem to rescue both skepticism and a small island of certainty. Geometry could give rise to certain truths because it was nothing but a deductively created system of names and rules for their use and these the philosopher could internalize and then demonstrate. To understand it was to have access to certainty, relatively free from the equivocations of all that we did not create and arbitrarily predetermine. Hence Hobbes's distinction between the fully deductive certainties of geometry and our explanations of the natural world requiring hypotheses. Thus although in the *Short Tract* he had formulated his optical theories with the propositional certainty of geometric conclusions, in the *Tractatus opticus* his revised arguments become hypotheses.[31] Hypotheses, however, could always be redescribed, so natural science remained haunted by the rhetorical doctrine of *ad utramque partem.* Formally, at least, phyrronian skepticism might be seen, but stopped at the geometer's gate.

Now this sense of geometry's paradigmatic status may explain Hobbes's frustrations in his flawed mathematical practice—for his relationships with Wallis flew straight in the face of his utopian vision of scientific inquiry. That the disputes were over geometry must have made things particularly galling. No wonder he tried to explain mathematical differences in terms of ad hominem conspiracies and religious intragigence; no wonder he did not want geometry being cluttered or diluted with the suggestive uncertainties of algebra, one of Wallis's errors. Geometric reasoning in its safest, most self-contained form, then, became an ideal by which to measure our grasp of the world and that itself he used to dramatic explanatory and polemical effect.

Arithmetic had a similar if not more primordial status, and Hobbes used it to make his point about scientific reasoning. Arithmetic is calculation made possible by our use of an interrelated set of arbitrarily and relationally defined terms; numbers and functions are labels making sense only by mutual association. The meanings of "$+$" and "$-$" are relationally defined and we calculate by adding and subtracting, breaking down large wholes into constituent parts and building larger totals from the combination of small numbers. Science, then, a point used to polemical effect in *Leviathan,* is epitomized in a proposition no more complex than "$1 + 1 = 2$". All this is casting accounts. It is of practical value, and it can be taught and the truths it might give are a function of conventional agreement on the meaning of the marks we call words. The polemical use of such arguments aside, Hobbes genuinely believed that all reasoning itself could be analyzed as being nothing more than such computation, just subtraction and addition in simple or complex forms (*Anti-White,* 463).

Entangled with this sense of the power of arbitrary interrelated sign-systems was the notion of the intimate knowledge endowed by creativity. That which we make we know. Traditionally, God was taken as standing in this privileged relationship to the whole of creation, but for Hobbes, who averred to this omniscience only occasionally, human knowledge was much more limited. We can know ourselves, use our minds to examine our minds; and, through our creative capacity to fashion language, we can make definitions that might establish a form of knowledge immune from the extremes of skepticism. Certainly, Hobbes believed, we know ourselves as we do not know things external. Knowing in a sense makes them ours. In a remarkably casual sense, these features of sure scientific knowledge are brought together in a typically

Hobbesian definition of the circle in need of squaring. In *De corpore,* (*De corpore,* 1.6.13) he defined it as "a figure made by the circumduction of a straight line in a plane." A geometric concept is thus described in terms of human endeavor and artifice (Hanson, 618).[32] So making, as defining, is a form of knowledge, and so too perhaps are the social relations we create, for they also are the consequences of human artifice. As we will see, all these themes will be of pervasive importance to understanding *Leviathan.*

Chapter Three

Mankind and the Transition to Society

Myths of Egoism, Liberalism, and Tyranny

In a rare point of agreement with Hobbes, Alexander Pope wrote the famous lines, "Know thyself, Presume not God to scan, / The proper study of mankind is man."[1] Hobbes's philosophic eye was turned largely on human beings, but less as systems of material tissue, liquid, and bone than as social creatures and as individual organisms composed of competing passions and emotions. His conception of science strongly suggested that these aspects of human existence needed to be related to each other. As a materialist, he held that human capacities for passion and reason were, no less than anatomy, explicable in terms of solid flesh and its melting. More specifically, as has been suggested (see chapter 2, "Optics and the Sections of Science"), Hobbes's optics were intended as a contribution to the physical study of the human animal as well as to the broadly psychological and epistemological dimensions of what it is to be human. The problem of "man," then, needs isolating before we can move to his more specific preoccupations with religion, law, rhetoric, and the creation of opinion.

Hobbes's brilliant and protean image of humanity has given rise to several suggestive but reductive myths. The first, purely Epicurian reduction is the belief that Hobbes was a psychological egoist—that is, one who held that human beings only act from selfish motives in order to gratify desire. This picture provides the Hobbesian topos in rational choice theory; it is in essence Hobbesian man as *homo economicus*. The need to qualify it will be outlined shortly. The second myth is that Hobbes's emphasis on individuality makes him some sort of liberal or protoliberal. The third myth is that Hobbes advocated the untrammelled, tyrannical power of the state. These impressions sit ill with each other and will be discussed only at the end of this chapter. They need to be addressed in the context of Hobbes's theories of the individual simply because he saw a causative relationship between individual and state. This was expressed most powerfully in Hobbes's depictions of a natural condition and the agreement among individuals to abandon it for the security of life in a commonwealth. The Hobbesian social contract will thus provide a point of transition to the discussion of what Hobbes saw as the substantive problems of political society.

Moving Matter and Imagination

All living creatures for Hobbes are but constellations of matter in motion; they are all simply a part of material reality. He was never much interested, however, in the aspects of life that made humans just animals. The problem was in what manner humans might be differentiated and what this might explain about our social life. He began *De cive* by specifying four faculties of human nature—strength, experience, reason, and passion. All are more or less shared with most other sentient creatures and are spread sufficiently among humans to give us a rough and highly significant equality. The sorts of belief with which he took issue are still current today: that human beings are different from animals in being rational, having immaterial souls, and in being social, rather than being merely instinctive, herding creatures. Hobbes eroded or reconfigured such apparently absolute points of difference to make the question of human nature problematic, not least for the polemical twists he would give his arguments. Occasionally when dealing with salient features of humanity he slipped in a satirical barb so that the uncontestable became uncomfortable. Only human beings, he remarked in chapter 5 of *Leviathan,* are capable of absurdity, of which philosophers have a near monopoly. This was a wonderful inversion of the pompous nostrum that the philosopher's is at once the least bestial and most elevated of human life forms. For Hobbes there was no such summum bonum (*De homine,* 11.15), and so the philosopher's life could hardly provide a normative image of human fulfillment.

Hobbes distinguished vital from voluntary motion. Vital motions are those such as pumping blood that we share with other animals; so too in plants the sap rising in the spring is a vital motion in the forest. Voluntary motions are predicated on sense impressions and involve some intention and discrimination. Here we can see something of the wider significance of Hobbes's interest in optics. As I have suggested (see chapter 2, "Optics and the Sections of Science"), the sense of vision was widely taken as paradigmatic of sense and understanding, and although this begs a number of questions, a conception of sight clarifies the salient features of Hobbes's theory of sense impression and voluntary motion (*Elements*, 1.2.4). Only material reality can be seen; light itself is corpuscular material in motion that when striking the retina gives a mental impression of the original material. All such impressions, pointedly called phantasms, are for Hobbes ultimately derived from some original (*Elements*, 1.2.4; *De homine*, 2.1). Inevitable derivation involves relative distortion; the image is not the object, and often it takes a good deal of education for us to realize this (*Elements*, 1.2.4; *De homine*, 2.1–3.). Our understanding is a constant process of manipulating and storing such images, the variety of which is itself a condition for our being sensible of anything. There must always be a "perpetual variety of phantasms, that they may be discerned from one another" (*De corpore English*, 1.25.5). In more than one passage there is the suspicion that Hobbes is the metaphysician of Plato's cave, that allegory of delusion in which isolated prisoners can do little more than guess at the sequences of images being put before them.[2]

Endeavor

Hobbes's notion of endeavor broadly complements the theory of sense impression. He gives, however, three distinct meanings to this word: as a will to engage in action, as appetite, and, most generally, as a feature of any interaction in the world.[3] In one main sense, endeavor is acting upon discernment, and, superficially, it is in such voluntary motions of decision that we are most clearly separated from other animals. We have stronger faculties of reason and experience. Sense impressions are themselves of different sorts. Some we are insensible of, some are the focus of attention, and some we are self-consciously aware of receiving. In short, we are intermittently reflexive creatures and this is where our reactions to impressions, our endeavors, are most distinctive.[4]

Additionally, however, Hobbes described endeavor in terms of appetite and aversion (*De homine*, 11.1–2), what had been called the faculty of passion.[5] Animals also have sense impressions and, we may plausibly infer, are capable of voluntary motions. They may certainly be seen to manifest endeavors in appetites and aversions (*Leviathan*, 6). Like us they can be habituated to certain forms of behavior in response to patterns of impression. But there is a large difference in degree of voluntary motions in a human and a dog, not least because the mechanisms explaining our voluntary motions are more complex. They include bodily constitution, experience, and habit, as well as social circumstances (the goods of fortune), the authoritative opinions of others, and our sense of ourselves (*De homine,* 13). Consequently, the capacity for diverse socialization is much greater than for animals. So vital motion is a common ground for all other movement in living things. The more significant actions of endeavor are in modifying the vital motions, the more human or humanlike those actions become. Yet if Hobbes often considered it as a self-conscious reaction, he also more widely wrote of endeavor as the process of interaction among phenomena, thus further undermining it as a defining feature of human beings. As he would put it in *De corpore,* ". . . in all sense of external things there is mutual action and reaction, that is, two endeavours opposing one another. . ." (*De corpore English,* 1.25.10). This is to evoke a world not unlike the Aristotelian one of constant teleological interaction.

Freedom, Necessity, and Language

The concepts of endeavor provide a variable context for the more specific acts of willing. Hobbes was decidedly unusual in arguing that free will and determinism are compatible (Gert, 172). He discussed this most fully and controversially in *Of Libertie and Necessitie.*[6] He insisted that human actions could at once be free, as voluntary motions, and determined, as causally explicable. In *De homine* (*De homine,* 11.2) any tension is peremptorily resolved by calling the will the last appetite to lead to a given action. Seen thus, the will is only a privileged link in a causal chain. To refer to free will was therefore not to predicate the will itself as undetermined but to say something about the liberty of the actor: as Hobbes urged both in *Of Libertie and Necessitie* and in the earlier *Elements,* part of the confusion around discussions of free will arose from the semantic mistake of reifying the word "will." It is not a thing or agent from which acts proceed, but only the act of willing, "the *last act of our deliberation*" (*Libertie,* 275); "a man can no more say he will will, than he will will will . . . which is absurd and insignificant" (*Elements* 1.12.5). Again, "he is *free* to do a thing, that may do it if he have the will to do it, and forbear, if he have the will to forbear" (*Libertie,* 240). The will, in short, might be called nothing more than a verbal noun, and liberty is found in any situation immediately prior to a willed decision to modify it. A creature that endeavors discriminates between what it takes to be physically possible actions. The fact that all actions may retrospectively be explained causally (that is, just thinking scientifically) is quite in agreement with the proposition that human beings are largely free in their actions. Pretty consistently Hobbes's emphasis was on freedom *properly* understood as the absence of external impediments to endeavor, or the will to do (*Anti-White*, 337; *Leviathan*, 14; *Libertie*, 275), whereas internal impediments signified a lack of power, not freedom. Free will is the conversion of any desire or appetite into an endeavor. The action may be fruitless or disastrous, the options psychologically unpalatable, but, strictly speaking, such considerations do not make us less free in acting.

In such trains of argument Hobbes brings together two important features of his philosophy, the understanding of science as unrestricted method and the penchant for resolving problems through semantic analysis. And, like many modern linguistic philosophers, there was a tendency to assume that the unraveling of a poorly formulated problem was itself a solution. That is not always so, and Bishop Bramhall (1594–1663) was convinced that Hobbes was really avoiding the problem of freedom and causation. There was a lot at stake in the debates between them, for the issue had metaphysical, theological, and political dimensions (Gert, 172). While not disputing the value of science, Bramhall wanted to quarantine certain areas of human experience as noncausal and in which the will could operate. Thus he would confirm the theological doctrine that humans were free and insulate God from the accusation that he was responsible for evil. Hobbes's modal conception of science was bound to find this arbitrary and unsatisfactory. Because science is a perspective on the world as a whole, it must predicate in terms of causation, but this is logically unconnected to our existence as free, endeavoring creatures—a position it was difficult for Hobbes to sustain. As will be explained more fully in chapter 4, for Hobbes God had nothing to do with the issue in any case, since science can say nothing about immaterial divinity.

The political dimension of Hobbes's doctrine has recently been discussed by Maurice Goldsmith and Quentin Skinner, taking up a hint from Roland Pennock. They have pointed out that the consequence of Hobbes's notion of liberty is to subvert the issue of political freedom.[7] This whole matter will be taken up again in the specific discussion of *Leviathan* (see chapter 7). It is sufficient simply to note here that freedom was an issue in Hobbes's day because people saw it as both precious and easily endangered. Such understandings of freedom were reinforced, or generated by, spacial metaphors of the sort Bramhall employed. Freedom was a sphere limited and potentially threatened by restrictions of various sorts; thus it needed vigilant policing, lest it be eroded. Such

metaphors of a reified freedom or liberty are still part of the small
change of political rhetoric, as is the belief that some societies are free
and others are not. But for Hobbes liberty was a ubiquitous feature of
being human. It is a dimension of movement, a descriptor for action;
only confusion and special pleading render it politically contentious. As
he argued in *The Elements of Law* (*Elements*, 1.15.13), an agreement made
out of fear is as valid, as freely made, as one generated by greed. They
are similar motivations for what is still voluntary action. This doctrine of
motivational irrelevance was later used by Hobbes to legitimate conquest and has a particular resonance in *Leviathan* (see chapter 7).

The relative significance of voluntary motion *inter homines* has itself a
material cause in the human capacity for language. The centrality of
language for Hobbes has already been canvassed and in its destructive
potential will need to be considered again (see chapter 6). For now, the
important point is that for Hobbes, the fact of language explains our
enhanced capacity for voluntary motion. Our abilities to store and label
our phantasms; to form and project a sense of being; to read and understand authoritative opinion that might guide us are all fundamentally
linguistic (*De homine*, 13). It is language that mediates and makes sense
impressions useful. Up to a point this may be done privately. When we
name something, wrote Hobbes, we use a word "taken at pleasure to
serve for a mark, which may raise in our mind a thought like to some
thought we had before" (*De corpore English*, 1.2.4). Here clearly is a sense
both of the arbitrariness of naming systems and the internality of understanding by association. He immediately adds that once a name is pro-
nounced to others it may be taken as a sign of what was in the speaker's
mind. Words are signs (*signa*) of our conceptions, not the things themselves, and by no means all signs purport to name something (see also
Elements, 1.5.2). And it is the conversion of marks into signs that makes
language public, partially shared, and always expressive.

It is this perhaps more than anything else that differentiates us from
animals. Cry and signal as they may, emitting noises of fear, lust, and
pain, they do not label or use language creatively (*De homine*, 10; *Elements*, 1.5.1; 1.13). Understanding is "conception caused by Speech"
(*Leviathan*, 4.30). But more than this, language is for the sake of action
and the use of language is a form of endeavor that alone enables us to
become social beings (*De homine*, 10; *Elements*, 1.5; 1.13). As I have suggested, despite Hobbes's emphasis on language as labeling, it is really
our own self-created dimension of what it is to be human. In short,
judgment and prudence are shaped by language, which is thus the prin-

cipal medium of understanding, communication, and action. If Hobbes was a materialist, he was above all a linguistic materialist.

Appetite and the Limits of Self-Interest

Human beings, then, exist only in free action and explicable behavior. The potentialities for movement are constrained by vital motion within the organism and conditioned by constant interaction with the external world, causing internal phantasms that are processed by language as opinions, notions, and conceptions, the expression of which in a system of signs is itself linguistic and semiotic action.

All this indicates that human behavior is decidedly less than random, even if it is at once all caused and largely free. On a spatial axis, it suggests an image of the human animal perpetually located between isolation and social existence, among but not with others, a feature of our condition ameliorated but not eradicated by civilization. For Hobbes perception and experience are ultimately individual, a conception reinforced by his belief in language as initially private, an inner silent system of marks. Language as a sign system, however, is social; it is the basic if imperfect means of modifying the isolation of living solipsistically. On a temporal axis, Hobbes made it clear that a sense of time is essential to human action and identity. Like animals we live in the present. This present he called sense, but we have recollections of past experience, called remembrance, and these we use to project anticipations of the future; thus we live between a power past and acts to come (*Elements*, 1.4.7–10; 1.8.3).[8] And again, it is language that greatly enhances the potentialities of our situation, sometimes with dreadful and delusory results. Hobbes's theories of science also invite a closer examination of the patterns of causation that might explain this uncertain but more or less predictable identity.

Hobbes became controversial not just because of his materialism but also because of his sense of the causes of human action: voluntary movement is largely a matter of the attempt to satisfy appetites arising from pleasure and to avert anticipated pain, the ultimate form of which is death (*De cive*, 1.7), a point heightened in *Leviathan* by the qualification "unnatural" death. Put so synoptically, such a description of movement would fit a large part of the animal kingdom, but Hobbes used it to generate a whole series of definitions of human qualities and emotions called "mental movements" (*De corpore*, 1.6.6). This vision locates Hobbes in a broadly epicurean tradition of thought, but the notions of pleasure, pain, appetite, and aversion should not be taken too narrowly; they constitute the whole faculty of passion. It may seem that, superficially, pleasure and pain are the poles between which the human animal moves in a constant process of calculating or reasoning about the imponderables of action. But for Hobbes, pleasure and pain were not the objective points of reference that a notion of polarity might suggest. In typically nominalistic fashion he argued that pleasure, what we label as good, is whatever we might have an appetite for. Questing after it is anticipation of felicity (*De cive*, 3.31; *Elements*, 1.7.2–3). We are never permanently satisfied and, indeed, frequently there is more pleasure in anticipation than in the acquisition or achievement of what we seek (*Elements*, 1.7.6). Physical or emotional pain is what we label as bad and thus seek to avoid. Death, of course, is an objective terminus although, he held, to no correlative good (*Elements*, 1.7.3). Strictly speaking, however, it is not death's sting but the internalized fear of it that explains so much of our behavior. Fear, he emphasized (*De cive*, 1.2), is a certain foresight of future evil, not simply being frightened, a point he would reiterate in chapter 13 of *Leviathan*. Although we need a concept of both for either to have meaning, good and bad are then not objective universal realities but are the consequences of naming in relation to our motions and perceptions—specifically, our hopes and fears, beliefs, or opinions (usually) as to our interests (*De cive*, 3.31).[9] Milton gave Satan a distinctly Hobbesian voice when he was cast from Heaven: "So farwel Hope, and with Hope farwel Fear, / Farwel Remorse: all Good to me is lost; / Evil be thou my Good."[10] Goodness is but the quality in something that pleases (*Elements*, 1.7.2).

Attention to these general postulates and only to Hobbes's more synoptic statements about mankind provide the main evidence for his psychological egoism. In terms of these still simple propositions, however, Hobbes described a whole economy of moral discourse that qualifies consistent psychological egoist principles. General dispositions toward or away from something when habitual are called manners, or mores. What are seen as good manners are called virtues, those deemed evil are vices (*De homine*, 13.8). Fear is aversion in the belief that harm will come from the object of the fear; hope is an appetite accompanied by optimism (*Leviathan*, 6). Delight is appetite presently enjoyed; annoyance, a failure to avert a perceived ill (*De homine*, 11.1). Glory is a joyous imagination or an image of one's own power; vain-glory an unjustified indulgence in one's power or situation. Despair is appetite without hope. Shame is grief for the discovery of some defect of ability (*Leviathan*, 6).

Although these are all clearly self-regarding, they do not in themselves constitute the unremitting selfishness often attributed to Hobbes's conception of humanity. Additionally, there are emotions including benevolence, good will, and charity that for Hobbes are desires for the good of others; while indignation is anger at injury done to another. Human beings, at least once socialized, are capable of all of these as well as self-sacrifice and generosity, love as well as lust.

Hobbes's discussion of lust is only ambivalently self-centered, for it consists in the twin desires to please and be pleased (*Elements,* 1.9.15). Sexual love arises in a need that at least renders its origins self-regarding (*Elements,* 1.9.16). Yet having claimed this, Hobbes turned immediately to discuss love as charity, commenting on Plato's depiction of the selfless love of Socrates for Alcibiades, as a form of completion in the other. His concluding comment is skeptical, but there is no claim that in principle other-regarding virtues are really selfish, an easy if nullifying move for consistent psychological egoism. Rather, he drew attention to the social conditions that could create such a mutually advantageous relationship and allow what he suspected was the masking of sensual love with a pretense of honor. It is indeed the crucial factor of socialization that so complicates any simple dichotomy between selfish and selfless behavior for Hobbes. It is to an aspect of this that we must now turn, for just as he saw the individual human animal as explicable in terms of its constituent parts and their vital and voluntary movements, so he believed his hypothesized vision of human nature explained society, its generation, responsibilities, and collapse.

Images of the Natural Condition

Where Hobbes tried to imagine unsocialized adults he tried to picture them without the benefits and habits of society, in order, as it were, to see what difference living in society makes to us. He may be seen as attempting a scientific act of privation in erasing the full details of existence (*De corpore,* 2.7.1; see chapter 2, "Method and Scientific Knowledge" in this volume). What he did was to describe the psychological features of a generalized man in such a way as to make it seem rational, if not causally inevitable, that such people will form a political society, contracting or agreeing among themselves to give their manifest powers of self-preservation to another or others for the sake of protection. That voluntary movement of human matter constitutes the barest bones of Hobbes's infamous and continually discussed theory of social contract.

Hobbes did not invent social contract theory. In a world heavily populated by lawyers, by theologians much interested in covenants with God, and in which people could figuratively purge themselves of an old world by sailing to a new in order to fashion a fresh society, images of contract were likely to be pervasive. The whole language of natural conditions and presocial states had been in periodic use since antiquity. Cicero, for example, in describing the world before the civilizing impact of the orator, sounds not unlike Hobbes,[11] while the discovery of the Americas had given a newfound plausibility to notions of such a natural condition. Images of the natural condition are found in Shakespeare's *The Tempest,* which blended an ancient topos with physical immediacy; and with great symbolic resonance they shape the heath scene of *King Lear* (act 3, scene 1). Indeed, rather than its being a theory, social contract is best seen as a subject matter common to diverse idioms of theorizing. Sometimes the point of argument from contract is simple, but in the case of Hobbes it is highly ramified. It should also be stressed that Hobbes lived in a world in which the Garden of Eden was taken to have existed literally and so notions of contract had an uncertain relationship with the alternative explanation for how man became a political and social creature. Hobbes's understandings of the natural condition sat ill with the Edenic myth as his contemporaries understood it, and he felt obliged to recast the meaning of Genesis to fit his theories (Moloney, 242–43).

If his natural condition was a source of religious controversy, it also exhibits his faith in a resoluto-compositive method of science. Hobbes attempted three main formulations of the natural condition in *The Elements of Law, De cive* (expanded in the second edition of 1646), and most vividly in *Leviathan,* modified in his own Latin translation of 1668 (*Leviathan Latin,* 99–102).[12] In these accounts, both the status of the image within his theory as a whole and its specific content vary, so he seems never to have been entirely satisfied with previous formulations or to have been content to use contract imagery for any single purpose.

Perpetually, Hobbes's contract hovers uncertainly between being a purely hypothetical model describing certain human propensities and being an abstraction from immediate social experience. As a consequence, the criteria by which to judge the adequacy of his accounts are themselves slippery. Should the model be tested against experience and evidence, or should it be more austerely judged in terms of the coherence of its postulates?[13] How far is it about a generalized concept of man? How far about men and women wandering vulnerably over the weather-ravaged heaths of civil war with only the remembrance of sovereignty urging them to peace? Further, his was always a highly problematic enterprise if seen as scientific, not least because of the difficulty of treating as independent variables (appropriate to any resoluto-compositive method) what are only formally distinguishable features of human beings in society. This will be seen most obviously in the ambivalent status of language in Hobbes's accounts of the natural condition, which in this regard seems no more satisfactory than more established Edenic myths of social formation.

Despite the changes in his accounts of the natural condition, there are four common threads in his model of humanity: that it is man's less social propensities that have most explanatory power; that the contract is between individuals per se and does not involve any government as an agent; that Hobbes was not attempting a description of all human beings; and that society must be seen as a fragile civilizing force. Something needs to be said about each of these entangled themes in turn.

The Paradox of the Antisocial

First, Hobbes held that the explanation and justification for civil society lies in mutual recognition of our less social and most primitive passions. This was to proffer a deliberate paradox contradicting what he took to be the conventional view that humans are naturally social, and it assumed most significance in De cive (De cive, 1, 2; 5.5). There is a certain unfairness to Aristotle's position intimated in citing out of context the famous tag that man is by nature a political animal (De cive, 1.2). Nevertheless, there remains in the Hobbesian paradox a certain family resemblance with Edenic explanations of society—it is because man has fallen and been cast from Eden that society becomes necessary. The Edenic myth is also in part a story of gender relationships; it cannot be understood without dealing with man and woman. In De cive 2.9 Hobbes provided a clear alternative arguing that there is no natural right of men over children. The mother's power is original. The specific point was to counteract strictly patriarchal theories of political authority, which held that the relationships of a father to his family provided a natural and uniquely legitimate pattern of civic authority. The more general force was to emphasize just how much what might seem natural was socially structured. This could be affirmed, however, only by introducing into the natural condition features of social relationships he would later ostensibly exclude.

The exclusions, however, were never complete and the most problematic was not gender but language. Simultaneously, language as a public sign system provides an enabling condition for society; yet to function thus, presupposes some sense of society. As he insisted (*Elements*, 2.10.8; *De cive*, 6.1), salient terms such as "mine," "thine," "right," and "virtue" will have no established meaning in a natural condition, and so may "beget controversy" (*Elements*, 2.10.8). This is also at one with Cicero's account of preroratorical authority. The less socialized image of man in chapter 13 of *Leviathan* does not so much solve this difficulty as occlude it by simply saying less about language except in more manageable contexts. Despite Hobbes's shifting to a less socialized creature in *Leviathan*, he still needed some vestige of the social in shared language to provide a condition for the transformation of man into citizen. This leaves us with a sense of arbitrariness and petitio principii. Leaving this problem aside, Hobbes's image does have considerable explanatory power.

Human beings seek what they deem good and avoid what they deem bad, but recognize each other as sufficiently similar and sufficiently equal in power to assume or create a state of uncertainty and competition (*De cive*, 1.3).[14] Above all, they seek self-preservation and may be taken to be prepared to exercise all means to this end (*De cive*, 1.8–9). Hence there is extraordinary freedom because there is little security, and thus constant fear of what others might do in the exercise of liberty. Every man's unlimited liberty, each one's right to whatsoever he wants, is effectively no liberty at all (*De cive*, 1.11). This may be seen to exemplify the important logical point Hobbes was to make later in *De corpore* (*De corpore*, 1.25.5; see chapter 3, "Moving Matter and Imagination" in this volume). There must be a variety of images in the mind in order to discern any one distinctly. An unrelieved phantasm of liberty can hardly be discerned or valued, but there is also a more injunctive force to Hobbes's argument. A world populated only by bearers of equal rights is intolerable. Experience, imagination, and a degree of rationality lead men to compromise, to accept a mutually diminished and more recognizable liberty for a greater sense of peace. This requires an agreement among those in the state of nature to put their safety in the hands of one or some group, and give that group the requisite powers of protection. This contract transforms a natural condition of war to a state of peace. Civilization is artificial peace, not natural war (*De cive*, 1.12).

From Association to Office

The second point Hobbes stressed is that the contract is one between men in the natural condition, not a contract between them and a governing body. The contract creates the office of government. To consider a government a contracting party presupposes its prior existence, a contradiction in terms. Here Hobbes is logically more consistent than he is with respect to the generation of language. Again, however, it is not just logic but an injunctive corollary that was significant for him. The insistence on a contract between individuals had the political force of subverting conventional notions of contract that, by imagining rulers as parties to a contract—as affirmed through something like a coronation oath—were formulated as a means of holding them accountable to the requirements of their office. By contrast, Hobbes would have us believe that in creating a sovereign we do not simply delegate certain provisional powers—that is, loan them under the fixed terms of a contract—but give them over. We alienate our rights from the natural condition.

The vocabulary through which this process is described varied as Hobbes grappled with the implications of what he wanted to establish and undermine. Initially (*Elements*, 1.15.3), he wrote of divesting and relinquishing a right and of transferring it to another. When a man transfers something without any expectation of reciprocity it is a free gift (*Elements*, 1.15.7).[15] But this was not a satisfactory description. Most gifts involve reciprocity and Hobbes's men give rights for protection. So the contract and the promise to obey the contract is a covenant (*Elements*, 1.15.9). For Hobbes's purposes, one surmises, this was to prove too close to a conventional notion of contract between people and sovereign. He therefore needed to tread a narrow pathway between metaphors of gift and trust.

In *Leviathan*, this process of creating a sovereign through transfer or alienation is couched as a matter of authorization, a refinement from earlier versions of the theory and one maintained in the Latin version (*Leviathan Latin*, 131).[16] The sovereign is whoever is authorized by the individuals to protect them, and it is the act of authorization that creates political obligation to obedience (*Leviathan Latin*, 132). The oaths that might follow such acts of promising are only forms of words displaying the prior commitment, adding nothing more sacrosanct to it. This dismissive attitude also plays its part in displacing the conventional language of governmental limitation; the specific significance of the coronation oath or any other public "engagement" is discounted as a sticking point in changing allegiance. When we authorize, we do not just loan portions of our natural power; we invest a power, creating an artificial man who acts as if he were all of us. There is created, as it were, a power of attorney. Probably the majority of modern scholars find the arguments unsatisfactory for a combination of political and logical reasons. Politically, Hobbes's doctrine is at least disconcerting and ill-suited to an age of democratic temper. But as Hobbes would no doubt remark, not liking is hardly refuting. Logically, however, it is uncertain how far a notion of authorization confuses issues of alienation, and it is doubtful how far alienation coheres with Hobbes's notion of mankind. For some scholars it is questionable whether there has even been a "contract."[17] As Roger Coke, one of Hobbes's contemporaries, also argued, Hobbes's concepts of willing and endeavor sit ill with his notion that people can will to stop willing and let another will for them.[18] If willing to will is absurd and insignificant, as Hobbes put it, is willing not to will more sensible? Jean Hampton has gone so far as to say that such total alienation is not only impossible, but Hobbes himself relies on a contrasting fallback position little different from more qualified theories of contract in which the sovereign is just an agent of those needing protection (Hampton, 224).

What the emphasis on authorization does, however, is to make clear that the shift from the natural condition to political society replaces the centrality of power with the overriding importance of authority; it exchanges an unrestricted liberty with more limited rights and liberties given and secured by authority. In Hobbes's day the semantic relationships between power, authority, and liberty were not as they are now. Frequently power was seen as a moral right, often opposed to force, and certainly the language of authorization was chosen to suggest a hedge of moral legitimacy for the sovereign when Hobbes was giving his sovereign a remarkable capacity to enforce, to exercise what we would call power. If this is described as a matter of authorization, the control appears to be the delegated action of those who are to be controlled, the ruling body an authority because they will it.

To put the matter another way, Hobbes's authorized sovereign is a representative in the sense of standing for the represented rather than being accountable to them. Again this might seem strained to us, but Hobbes was using a long-standing medieval notion of representation, ironically found in its extreme form in the doctrine of transubstantiation, rejected so roundly by Protestants like Hobbes. Nevertheless, in terms of seventeenth-century usage, irrevocable representation of the Hobbesian kind was quite intelligible and there were a number of thinkers who reserved the term "representation" for it, using words such as "officer" to express a notion of accountable representation or the representation of qualified trust.[19] Hobbes does this also; the agents and advisers to the representative, the sovereign, are entrusted, accountable officers. In this way it may be disconcerting to note that Hobbes and the Levellers, so often seen as the radical heralds of modern representative democracy, posit the same semantic relationships. Nowadays such irrevocable forms of representation are largely restricted to the sports field where players represent a town or a state.

Nevertheless, although there is no contract to which the sovereign is a party, the sovereign arising from the agreement assumes an office no less than the individuals who consent to become subjects. And it is in this pervasive sense of reciprocal office, not contract itself, that Hobbes provided the sense of limitation which seems to be lacking if we take his notions of alienation or authorization in isolation. Indeed, it fleshes out the fuller import of authorization. That is, what Hampton identified as Hobbes's fallback position, the acceptance that the sovereign has some obligations, some purpose and is entrusted to that end, is a misconstrual of Hobbes's description of the function of the office of rule. There are not two positions but two stages in the argument in all Hobbes's formulations of the contract, one concerning the origins of the mutually related offices of subject and sovereign, and one specifying their reciprocal functions once established (Hampton, 224).

An office for Hobbes and for all his contemporaries, including those who used representation in the same irrevocable manner, was a role or area of responsibility carrying rights only for the sake of fulfilling duties. Almost all conceptions of social activity, including intellectual ones such as writing poetry or philosophy (see chapter 2, "Sense Beyond Science"), were seen in terms of office-holding or office abuse: priests, lawyers, rulers, nurses, parents, spouses were all understood in terms of areas of responsibility, of having rights contingent upon duties. In fact, Hobbes is unusual among social theorists in going so far as he does in specifying people as individuals rather than in terms of overlapping spheres of office-holding, and this perhaps is an underlying source of difficulty. All rights given to the sovereign stem from the protective office of rule. Among those rights is, as it were, the metaright to decide what does come within the exercise of the office, what can be done in the name of protection (*De cive*, 6.13; 7.12). Whoever has such a right must be the source of sovereignty; its possession makes the ruler absolute. The worrying point for Hobbes's contemporaries was that such a self-limiting sovereign was a judge in its own cause and potentially tyrannous. As tyranny was abuse of office, the sovereign was immune from the accusation from the outset—exactly the conclusion Hobbes wanted drawn.

Hobbes's critics have never been slow to point out that the sovereign's metarights of self-definition and self-legitimation effectively give it absolute power in a modern sense as well as in a seventeenth-century sense of being without legal limitation. The other side of the equation, however, is that it can never be given absolute authority, despite Hobbes's final theory of contractual authorization. We cannot authorize self-destruction—that contradicts the very reason for entering society in the first place. As he put it in *De cive*, we submit only for security and if that cannot be had, a man cannot be assumed to have submitted himself to anything (*De cive*, 6.3; see also 2.18). By absolute power, then, we should not understand Hobbes as having meant powers totally unrestricted any more than the authorization or transfer of right is unlimited. Rather, "absolute" meant unfettered in the exercise of the protective office. In practical terms this is not much consolation, but it does remove theoretical difficulties that have been seen by taking authorization and alienation in conceptual isolation rather than as aspects of a definition of office.

What should now also be clear is that Hobbes's theories of what it is to be a human being, always a semi-isolated creature mediating images of material reality, meant that the senses of fear and security are inevitably motions internal to the animal itself and its judgments. To repeat, fear is our own sense of some future evil (*De cive*, 1.2). Strictly speaking, then, as Coke perceived, and as Hampton has elaborated, we cannot will not to will. More specifically, in Hobbesian terms, we are so constituted that we cannot authorize anyone to provide us with security; we can authorize them only to do all that is possible to create an impression of security within us. This is a distinction Hobbes persistently elides without ever denying. Its importance may be seen by way of a contrast with Machiavelli, whose views on the generation of fear and love were familiar enough to Hobbes's circle of friends and with whom Hobbes is too frequently and neatly associated. In *The Prince*, Machiavelli recommended that, if necessary, a prince should strive to be feared rather than loved, for love is capricious and arises from the reaction of the lover to the loved one; fear is generated from outside and so is a tool in the hands of the prince. Thus reliance upon fear gives the prince more security. In terms of Hobbesian psychology, Machiavelli's dichotomous options are both naive and arbitrary. Fear and love are equally motions of the mind, so neither can be a simple instrument of rule. Indeed, in the business of government, too much emphasis on the power of the sword is bound to be counterproductive, especially for Hobbesian individuals well capable of the excess of passion called "madness" (*Leviathan*, 8).

It is probably from this continuing sense of the asymmetry between external reality and processed impression that Hobbes insisted that the sovereign's *office* itself entails a constant endeavor to give not bare protection but a continuing sense of comfort (*Leviathan*, 30). As David Johnston has rightly stressed, it is the sovereign's task to persuade us to fulfill our subject duties to live in peace and do as we are told.[20] For Hobbes it was not some objective truth or reality that drives and explains our conduct, but our opinions and expectations (*Elements*, 1.12.6); yet he persistently wrote as if peace and security could be objectively established by the sovereign. So the fundamental difficulties for Hobbes's absolute sovereign arise less from a tension with his psychology than from a dissonance with his epistemology and ontology. As fear and security are internal secondary qualities, it is difficult to see how far we can authorize another simply to replace one with the other. Hobbes's reductive notion of irrevocable representation marking the origin of the office of rule sits no better with his sense of the functions of the office and with his metaphysics than does a notion of transubstantiation.

A Model of Humanity or a Metaphor for War?

It is clear that in his various formulations of the natural condition, Hobbes was not attempting to describe or attribute uniform characteristics to all human beings. He was in fact much criticized on this score because of the forcefulness of his paradoxical formulation of the matter.[21] Despite his writing globally of man, the logic of his position does not require even most people to conform to his description. A small minority will do, a point captured in Locke's apparently more benign image of the natural condition, a social state from which arise inconveniences still necessitating political rule. Basically, the issue for Hobbes was what explains most about the generation of society, the social or asocial propensities of the human animal. He believed it was the latter, because fear of systematically selfish behavior is enough to make the situation of the natural condition intolerable. Anticipations can become self-fulfilling prophecies. The state of war lies not in open conflict, any more than bad weather is the occasional shower; it is a continual lowering expectation (*Leviathan*, 13). Just so: hope of felicity drives us from it. A civil condition, as he insisted in amending *De cive*, is not just a matter of people coming together but being bound in some sense of mutual association. It takes very few to disrupt it. Hobbes certainly did not see all human beings as conforming to his account of "natural" man. Indeed, *Leviathan* is dedicated to the memory of one, Sidney Godolphin, whom Hobbes considered an exception to his general description. He asks of the reader only an effort of introspection: read thyself, to see if the cap fits. As Hobbes pointedly and aptly remarked, when we lock our doors we accuse mankind no more or less than he does through his words (*Leviathan*, 13; *De cive*, 1.2).

Misunderstanding of the philosophical limits of Hobbes's account of natural humanity has nevertheless been encouraged by his own use of his theories. He was not averse to looking for societies that might approximate to his hypothetical model of behavior, nodding knowingly in the direction of the American Indians and the Amazons (*De cive*, 1.13; 9.3); and in what may have been an ongoing discussion of the issue, Jean Peleau (1627?–1672?), one of Hobbes's enthusiastic correspondents, suggested that a state of nature even existed within some societies.[22] Hobbes's response is not known, but he had clearly failed to make clear that, as modern commentators put it, the social contract was a *purely* hypothetical thought experiment. Hobbes was not that pure a philosopher. There is also little doubt that the lurid description in *Leviathan* was fashioned to connote the horrors of the civil wars through which he lived in order to convey the overriding necessity of settling the country in peace. Indeed, civil war was probably a close enough analogue for his persuasive purposes. If this is so, it dispenses with most of the difficulties that have been seen in his theory, though it makes it altogether less interesting; fundamentally a prose rendition of Lear's heath, a "scatter'd kingdom" subject to "conflicting wind and rain," a world of exposure and insecurity of "division" "covered with mutual cunning" (*King Lear*, act 3, scene 1).

The Fragility of Human Artifice

If certain drives have explanatory force they did not constitute the totality of Hobbesian human nature; for as he was often at pains to stress, we are in many ways socialized and our most universal categories of value and self-description are given great variety of content through social mediation. Theft and murder may be universal crimes, but what is meant by such terms depends upon the diversity of civil laws (*De cive*, 6.15). So much of what we may project as natural, such as the primacy of the father in family structures, may be only the result of internalizing social mores. Social virtues, as David Hume would more consistently call them, were, for Hobbes, artificial; that is, they are socially shaped and conditioned. They are no less virtuous or genuine for that, he often seems to say, but they have simply been mislocated when people project them as part of some preexisting moral order abstracted like grammar from the language rules of the day.

If we seek to move beyond the most general formulations, however, Hobbes's position is variable. His nominalism can leave the distinct impression of value terms like "good" and "evil" being arbitrary abstractions from the particular circumstances of social life. Yet he also explicitly adhered to a faith in natural law that was manifested in particular societies. Natural justice for Hobbes was, in most moods, sheer fantasy, but at the same time, only "the fool" says there is no justice (*Leviathan*, 15). In *The Elements of Law* (*Elements*, 2.10.8) he claimed, in his most nominalistic mood, that even the appeal to right reason is little more than the individual's sense of reason and not a common standard giving access to eternal verities. In *De cive* he claimed that justice consists of the attempt to follow the laws of nature (*De cive*, 3.30). That is an altogether less nominalist position; and in *Leviathan*, although remaining as suspicious of appeals to an objective reason, he still imbued his natural men with a fugitive sense of some higher law in relation to God; they can recognize by reason and are obliged to obey a natural law forbidding self-destruction (*Leviathan*, 14; *Leviathan Latin*, 102). In such comments we have perhaps necessary if ever fainter echoes of Eden, for above all, the Garden was an image of ideal earthly unity between man, woman, and God where all God's requirements were directly and incontrovertibly accepted, where a relationship of office between God and his creatures was for a while unproblematic. Such modifications as Hobbes made in his formulations of the natural condition were entangled with his slippery understanding of law (see chapter 5) as much as with his needing to leave natural man with a residue of social attributes.

The overall force of his argument about the natural condition, however, remains clear enough: when we destroy society, we destroy not only peace but civilization, all its advantages and virtues (*Leviathan*, 13). Any notion of a prepolitical social sensibility was for Hobbes illusory; at best it was the decaying sense of what political society had achieved. He wanted always to insist that unless there is a political society to offer security at a price, we are so constituted as to make life intolerable for ourselves. In a word, we needed to be taught the virtues and habits appropriate to our office as subjects; as the office was not natural, neither were its necessary attributes. It was thus part of the reciprocal office of the sovereign to educate us in subjection. It was no easy task when so many subjects, misunderstanding concepts such as liberty and obligation, failed to understand their status or recognize the proper ambit of sovereignty. It was for Hobbes not liberty but civilization itself that is the fragile creation of human identity, which at the same time makes us fully what we are.

But what is the relevance of this to a world in which peoples were far more likely to be conquered or invaded than they were to sit down and contract with each other to invent a sovereign? Hobbes drew a distinction between sovereignty by institution and by acquisition, only to minimize its significance. It is here that the doctrine of motivational irrelevance is turned to immediate political effect. The vanquished may quite properly and rationally seek protection from a conqueror, and that they do so because they fear for their lives does not make their consent less binding or less an expression of liberty. Oaths may well be broken, but as Hobbes insisted, they only expressed a promise for a purpose and so were contingent on circumstances—a doctrine that saw.him unceremoniously called a casuist.[23]

In this way, Hobbes sought to put origination in conquest on the same footing as sovereignty arising from willing consent. This is consistent with his overriding belief that any civil society was better than none, but it was also more immediately pragmatic. Recognizing that most regimes began with some act of violence, paradigmatic cases of which were Rome's foundation in fratricide and the Norman Conquest, Hobbes was reluctant to leave any trace of a casuistic rhetoric that might reactivate violence in a long-settled society. As some of his contemporaries were already saying, time legitimizes rule. Most pressingly, from 1651 his own society could plausibly be seen as conquered and founded on blood. Here his doctrine had a multiple effect. In its earliest formulations, it affirmed the legitimacy of a monarchy that had descended from the Norman Conquest; yet when it too was overthrown, it gave some vestige of legitimacy to the fledging regime to be dominated by Cromwell. If accepted, Hobbes's doctrine also gave grounds for honorable peace for those who might otherwise hopelessly destroy themselves and delay a fully peaceful settlement for all (see chapter 7).

Between Individual Liberty and Tyranny

I began this chapter alluding to the myth that Hobbes was a psychological egoist, but have left out two further misconceptions I noted about his vision of humanity. Thomas Hobbes's notion of scientific method is partially at one with what is called methodological individualism, a multifaceted and nominalist doctrine that claims, inter alia, that the individual is both the source of social explanation and the reality behind social constructs. In recent years one trend in Hobbes scholarship has been to see him as an individualist, eliding this with being in a political sense a liberal individualist. This accommodating slippage is technically anachronistic. Liberalism was not any sort of political category in the seventeenth century. To project it onto such a distant past has required first assuming that our ideological categories must have a transhistorical relevance and then proving the point by redescribing would-be liberals and protoliberals in the language of modern liberalism. In Hobbes's case, it depends on converting what for him was a condition of human existence into a contingent set of values fostered by some sorts of society and not by others.

Liberalism is a doctrine that values individuality and freedom because these are seen as contingent and easily threatened features of our world. In modern formulations, individuals are above all rights-holders and so the function of society is construed as protecting individual rights and minimizing interference with them. Liberals believe such societies can meaningfully be called free. The result, of course, depending on how one applies such notions as minimal interference, is to designate a wide variety of arrangements liberal. Hobbes, however, saw individuality fundamentally as a predicate of individuation; individuals are what you can separately count. So too with freedom, as I have suggested. For Hobbes it was less a jealously guarded value—and he saw it as highly dangerous when used in this fashion—than a feature of most of our endeavors. If nearly all individual actions are as free as they are determined, it can be a confused enterprise to worry about protecting freedom or seeking to maximize it. For Hobbes, the laws are only artificial chains; we remain free to break them. When provokingly making such claims, he was attempting to subvert a rhetoric of political freedom by debasing the currency of its use. He was not struggling toward any idea of negative or positive liberty.

The corollary of which he was adamant was that it is nonsense to call some societies free and others not. If on such grounds Hobbes might be called only a protoliberal, it is difficult to see who would not be. This is not to say that in practice Hobbes was indifferent to what he and others would have called liberties; they were simply not the focus of his understanding of individuality. This is partly why, as we shall see, it has been difficult for scholars to decide how far he favored religious toleration (see chapter 4). More than this, Hobbes, like all his contemporaries, saw individual rights as contingent upon the duties of and constrained by office. Once people became socialized, rights arose because of the diverse requirements of embedded responsibilities. This pervasive presupposition cuts across modern political doctrinal classifications, attempting to co-opt appeals to freedom such as liberalism with its emphasis on a deontology of rights and republicanism or communitarianism with their emphases on the freedoms of participation.

By the same token, seeing him as hostile to liberalism involves many of the same sorts of misconceptions; historically speaking, we do have to resist the Gilbertian assumption that every child born alive is either liberal or conservative. Hobbes certainly would have had no objections to a modern liberal state if it really could provide mutual security and keep the peace; he was, after all, insistent that democracy is a proper form of government. With the same proviso he would probably be as happy with a dictatorship.

It is this frequently casual attitude to the specifics of legitimate political forms that helps explain how by turns Hobbes can be commended for being liberal and condemned for encouraging tyranny. The problem, however, might be of our own making. It is all too easy to confuse what a general doctrine subsumes with what it justifies. It is additionally difficult for us not to read the ominous power of the twentieth-century state back into his notion of a polity and the ramshackle reality of seventeenth-century politics to which it alludes. We look in vain for what might be adequate guarantees of individual liberty against tyranny in Hobbes's state; but the absence of such guarantees against the abuse of office does not amount to the advocacy of abuse. In this respect, at least, he was exploring the logic of his own postulates about the individual motions of the mind and was reluctant to give sovereigns merely prudential advice. A very powerful state, which is not the same thing as a highly governing state, was, he believed, needed because of our individuality; but because of it, the state will always be precarious. He would persuade us that civilization itself requires the virtues of individual obedience. Certainly Hobbes thought that states were altogether less secure than they have proven to be. It is in a way technologies of violence undreamed of in his philosophy that do most to make his vision of sovereignty look like an irresponsible relic.

One reason for his perception of fragility lay in the pervasive importance of religion. Because of their fear and curiosity, human beings were worshipping creatures. Religion is derived from the Latin *religio,* meaning to bind together, and as he had insisted in *De cive,* entails mutual bonds; the irony of religion's role in breaking asunder was not lost on Hobbes. Having placed his human beings on the cusp of society, it is now important to turn to this continuing and much misunderstood preoccupation of his work.

Chapter Four

The Problems of Religion

"... all the calamities of war and devastation"

Hobbes lived in an age of extraordinary religious turmoil. For most of his life England was an increasingly beleaguered Protestant outpost lapped by the tides of resurgent Catholicism. The Protestant world proved fissiparous under pressure. The Dutch squabbled with each other and with England; the British civil wars, Reformation Europe's last wars of religion, began with a Presbyterian Scottish invasion of Protestant England. They ended when Cromwell's pious army returned the compliment. During those central years of the century, there was such a profusion of sects that modern scholars remain as fully employed disengaging them as were their contemporaries. Dispute and diaspora: the Christian life could be that of the self-inflicted exile driven by the images of the deity, the devil, and salvation. Where the issues were so burning, so could be the stakes. Violence bordered on being a purifying virtue, but aggression was not exhausted by marching regiments under the gaudy standards of holiness. Governments could inflict exile, imprisonment, loss of a living, mutilation, and death. Pastors and sectaries, themselves suffering under the weight of authority, might systematically oppress in the name of truth by instruction, education, edification, and reform. Many might prefer to withstand the rigors of the law or the slings and arrows of hectoring correction rather than contemplate the toleration of opposing churches. But for the relatively open interlude of the Commonwealth, giving rise to brief hopes and fears of widespread toleration, the whole religious ethos of Britain was toward enforced orthodoxies. Heresiarchs sprang up like dragon's teeth. The predominant ideal was to reestablish such a uniformity of belief and practice that toleration would not be necessary.

In such an ambience, Thomas Hobbes never ceased to worry at the ironies and paradoxes of religious belief. The need for religion arose from the nature of humanity and yet did so much to destroy it; Christianity as a religion of peace was at constant war; the true religion furnished rhetorics of self-delusion, oppression, and ambition. Nothing generated so much controversy as the guiding word of God. "The controversies betwixt Rome and the Reformation are long since beaten out of the pit, by other combatants of their own brood" (*Libertie,* 233). We live in a world of "endless, and fruitless controversies, the consequences whereof are jealousies, heart-burnings, . . . factions . . . quarrels . . . and . . . all the calamities of war and devastation" (*Libertie,* 233). Meanwhile, abroad, "What stir there is between the Molinists and Jansenists about *grace* and *merits;* and yet both pretend St. Augustine!" (*Libertie,* 234). Even from the simple pronoun "THEE," remarked George Lawson in a particularly Hobbist tone, "we have chemical extractions of all sorts of governments" (Lawson, 168).

The Myth of Atheism

The problems in the way of understanding Hobbes's views on religion are considerable. This is partly because "religion" is too cumbersome a term,[1] and partly because modern commentators have tried to constrain the issue of Hobbes and religion to the preoccupations of a more secular age. The haunting question has been, "was Hobbes an atheist?" The belief that he was has been one of the more robust myths of modern scholarship, for some an expression of faith immune to evidence.[2]

The myth has been plausibly sustained by some substantial misunderstandings. First, the word "atheism" was multivalent and often different from the modern meaning of having no belief in God, or of denying God's existence. Predominantly, references to atheism were accusative extrapolations from specific religious doctrines.[3] Erastianism, for example, was the doctrine that the civil authority should arbitrate religious dispute and where it was thought necessary it should control all public expressions of faith. This was articulated by the Dutch Calvinist theologian Thomas Erastus (1524–1583) and could be branded as atheistic because it might lead to the situation in which an unbelieving or unchristian civil authority forbade the expression of religious belief. Barroom logic perhaps, but by such argument was Hobbes dubbed the "Turkish philosopher" for his civil ecclesiology seemed to open the way for justifying Christian allegiance to a hypothetical Islamic magistrate.[4] Hobbes became an Erastian, but that is not to render him any more atheistic in a modern sense than many devout clergymen. In the end, when the issue became acute, he stopped well short of being a "Turkish philosopher."

Atheism could also be little more than an accusation of heresy.[5] Perhaps with Christendom, especially Hobbes's Britain being divided into so many competing churches, each defined by its own senses of heresy, the charge of heresy was losing its effect and so needed the more lurid dysphemism of atheism. In any event, when Hobbes's *Leviathan* and *De cive* were burned as atheistic in 1683, it was because of their heresies and lack of respect for ordered churches, not for their denial of God's existence (Springborg, 347–48). Fundamentally, the problem arose from the logic of enforced orthodoxy, from an insistence on public conformity in the hope of salvation. How can the arbiters of orthodoxy be sure of the conformist's sincerity?[6] The suspicion was only intensified when a conformist like Hobbes explicitly claimed that obedience is a virtue, conscience forever a closed book. He could only focus suspicions upon himself (Springborg, 369).

Atheism was additionally equated with anticlericalism. It was, according to Malcolm, a particularly English association and an insecure clergy that was most apt to make it.[7] Hobbes was openly anticlerical, but in a devout world the pious are most likely to pick at the imperfections of their priesthood; hence strong traditions of anticlericalism stretch well back into the Middle Ages. As Mark Goldie has remarked, religion was often seen as too important to be left in the hands of priests; secularization could amount to a Protestant sacrament.[8] It was in this way that, balancing the clerical conflation of atheism and anticlericalism, accusations of popery were also debased. From being claims about allegiance to Rome they became claims about the implications of some Protestant doctrines and practices that might lead back to Rome. So the charge of popery gradually became an expression of hostility to the presumed authority of any priest or pastor. It was an enmity Hobbes sometimes exhibited, in a willingness to associate the excesses of the Protestant clergy with those of the priesthood of Rome. Yet he was also capable of pointing out such eristic devices for what they were. In *Behemoth* (*Behemoth*, 2.61–62), he outlined the ways in which fears of Catholicism were used with increasing implausibility to undermine the monarchy. Most of his disparagement of religion was directed at the gentlemen of the cloth. Clerics handsomely reciprocated in kind.

Finally, John Pocock has suggested a further useful distinction between scientific and humanistic atheism. The latter was the accusation that all sense of God has been equated with human identity; the former was the belief that God had been totally excluded from the natural world and its explanation.[9] This latter accusation was certainly leveled at

Hobbes with considerable justification. This, however, was a theologically derived doctrine of materialist philosophy that did not amount to atheism in any modern sense. As an uncompromising materialist Hobbes also wrote in the Epicurian and Lucretian tradition by dismissing the very idea of an immaterial soul; heretical, no doubt, but it was a doctrine Hobbes shared with that most devout of seventeenth-century sects, the Muggletonians. Hobbes's correspondence, unusually private as it is, now further reveals how he was hardly viewed as an atheist by his close French clerical friends, some of whom were prepared to defend him publicly. Similarly, despite a chorus of disapproval in England, he had a number of admiring sectaries and religious Independents familiar with his most notorious work. On the evidence we have, if Hobbes was an atheist, so too that age of religion itself could be atheistic.

To make headway with Hobbes's religious views we need to distinguish at least the following: his arguments about the nature of God; his understanding of the causes and functions of religion; his ecclesiology, that is, his views of church structure and the role of priests in society; and his theories of biblical interpretation and the authority of the Bible. Infused with all of these was his pervasive anticlericalism, and although this will not be treated as a separate topic, it will also be worth isolating what Hobbes took to be the principal means of priestly usurpation of secular authority, the powers of defining heresy and of excommunicating.

Hobbes's beliefs about the nature of God and the causes of religion are most closely tied to his demarcation of science, but they are not unalloyed with vehement religious dogma. An early letter is symptomatic of his peculiar admixture of ratiocination and passion. Writing to William Cavendish in 1634, he remarked that he could hardly wait to get hold of Galileo's *Dialogues,* a work more likely to confound the Catholics than all of Luther and Calvin put together.[10]

The Mystery of God

Theology presupposes the existence of God. The issue in medieval and Reformation deliberation was rather what might be predicated of God, what and how certain were our sources of knowledge given the postulate of existence. The preoccupation of some seventeenth-century theologians with proving the existence of God was a response not to people who would disprove it, but to those theologians who consigned knowledge of God to a realm of faith. To demonstrate God's existence was to

reunite what skeptical logical theology of the fourteenth century had
made logically problematic. Broadly, there were those who held to a *kat-
aphatic* concept of God. That is, God's nature was in some way revealed
and could be understood, whether from the evidence of nature or divine
revelation or both. Conversely, there were those who held to an *apophatic*
conception, insisting that ultimately God is unknowable and that anything we say about or predicate of God is either an expression of piety or
an inadequate approximation. This understanding could, as with Sir
Henry Vane the younger (1613–1662), lead to a highly elaborate
metaphorical and impenetrably devout mysticism.[11] It was capable of
more logical exposition and in this form dates at least to the theology of
Duns Scotus (1264–1308) and William of Ockham (d. 1342?). They
were used with respect across later ecclesiological divisions and lay
behind Hobbes's theories.

Further grounding for Hobbes's *apophatic* notion of God can be found
in the later medieval doctrine of political averroism, or the two truths
theory. This was the proposition that philosophical and theological
truths could be different but in their own terms valid. Such radical
modality was initially associated with Siger of Brabant (1235–1282),
but most famously used by Marsilius of Padua (c. 1280–1346?). Among
Hobbes's contemporaries, both Bacon and Descartes had wanted to
keep theology and philosophy, faith and reason distinct, but Hobbes was
particularly insistent on the issue.[12] As he pointedly remarked to Bishop
Bramhall[13] God "is not a fit subject of our philosophy." This was no
mere opportunistic deflection. As early as 1640 in *The Elements of Law*
(*Elements*, 1.11.1), he had drawn the fundamental distinction between
affirming the existence of and giving attributes to God. In the *Anti-
White* he went much further. A major part of Thomas White's *De mundo*
had been devoted to demonstrating the existence of God, and Hobbes
proceeded to attack the enterprise as mistaken in principle and poorly
executed in practice. To reiterate, the point was not to prove the contrary but to show that White had overstepped the limits of philosophy,
misunderstood demonstration, and persistently slipped from affirming
existence to specifying qualities (see, e.g,. *Anti-White*, 367–72). Again
succinctly in *The Elements of Law* (*Elements*, 1.11.2), Hobbes claimed that
because God is incomprehensible it follows that we can have "no conception or image of the Deity." All talk of God loving, seeing, hearing,
knowing, signifies human incapacity or a sense of reverence (*Elements*,
1.11.3). The general argument about philosophy's limitations is reiterated in *De corpore* (*De corpore*, 1.1.8). Summarizing Hobbes's position, we

may say that God is beyond philosophy because uncaused, and philosophy deals with causation; and that philosophy's concern with demonstrating propositional truth precludes that which cannot be contained by propositions. It was this conception of philosophy that would lead to the accusation of atheism in the sense of making talk about the world godless. Yet Arrigo Pacchi has argued that such a notion of God is in fact necessary to Hobbes as a grounding for philosophy. Something is needed to cut the infinite regress of causal analysis (Pacchi, 180–81). As Hobbes remarked in *Of Libertie and Necessitie* (*Libertie*, 246), the "concourse of causes may well be called . . . the decree of God."

God, then, may not be known but there may be an imaginative evocation of some notion of divinity. God delineates philosophy, and not to realize this is for Hobbes both presumptuous and philosophically self-deluding. Similarly, talk about God may function as expressing piety, but if construed as being more than this it is confused. In a partial repudiation of what he took to be Descartes's attempted philosophical proof of the existence of God, Hobbes produced a striking metaphorical, and consistent, alternative. In a passage suggestive of Bede's powerful image of life as a sparrow flying from the dark briefly through the warm winter hall, Hobbes likened our legitimate conceptualization of God to a blind man's understanding of fire. Born in the dark, he may not know or understand fire, have no image of it in his mind, but realizes that something gives him warmth and so concludes that something must exist. To this mysterious source of warmth he may give the name fire, so too we give the name God to the object of faith or reasoning (see Pacchi, 180).[14] In all this, however, there is more than a matter of philosophical delineation. Hobbes also wanted to undercut what he took to be destabilizing appeals to God in public debate, and it played a part in undermining the assumed authority of priests derived from some assumed access to divinity.

Religion, Worship, and Conscience

Hobbes took religion to be a universal response to mystery. Arising from fear and curiosity, it is directly explained by the basic human passions. He was careful to distinguish individual piety from the organization and public expression of religious belief and it is the latter, the formation of churches around objects of worship in the hands of priesthoods, that concerned him most (*De homine*, 14.1). Organized religion, as he put it in *De cive*, treads a difficult path between atheism and superstition and is constantly prone to slide into idolatry (*De cive*, 16.1). This, of course, would give Hobbes ample opportunity to turn his general understanding to polemical effect. It also allowed him to develop the argument that religions have clear human functions, to satisfy inner needs and to foster peace. Again there is an implicit anticlericalism, for it is easy to claim that cults have been causes of civil disruption. The matter had a particular poignancy with respect to Christianity; at once, the true religion was one whose history was a contaminated narrative of priestly corruption, superstition, and idolatry. In the early *Discourse on Rome*, if the work is his, Hobbes provided the gist of a standard Protestant account of the consequences of the conversion of the Emperor Constantine to Christianity. What in one sense was a triumph for the true religion was also the beginning of the downward slide of Catholicism. Much later, in the *Historia ecclesiastica*, for example, he would repeat such a narrative of religious history, broadening his range to include the priesthoods of the Reformed churches.

Three points need making here. First, Hobbes was by no means distinctive in identifying a social origin and function for religious belief in general.[15] Secondly, from an inherited sense of the dual function of religion, and especially Christianity, came the specification of the double duty of the priestly office. With respect to the unique otherworldly responsibility of Christian priests, Hobbes held consistently that priests could do little more than inculcate piety by teaching and example. Above all, the office precluded pretensions to rule. As he remarked in a letter when giving advice on a potential tutor to the Cavendish family, the young man may be worth employing if he encourages piety "without superstitious admiration of Preachers."[16] The office of the priest should be as carefully circumscribed as it was important. Again, this suspicion arose within mainstream Christianity; it was channeled into Protestantism and was evident in the *spirituale* movement of Renaissance Catholicism.[17] The authoritative and delimiting text was one many others had also relied upon: "My Kingdom is not of this world."

Thirdly, if we turn to the socializing functions of priests, the encouragement of obedience and civil society—which had traditionally brought priests and rulers into some sort of symbiosis—it is easy to see how this could become a species of Erastianism. England had long had a quasi-Erastian tradition of rule. Henry VIII had assumed the functions of the pope more than he had departed from the theology of Catholicism. If he was not quite a priest-king, he gave an intensified sense to the Constantinian notion of a godly magistrate by implicating the priesthood in rule. Erastus's doctrines stimulated by the desperation of being on the losing side of a theological dispute in Holland were fundamentally an appeal to a civil magistrate to mediate in the interests of peace. Given English Reformation practices, they could be taken much further to become a doctrine of direct lay control with the priesthood being rewarded and fostered as a department of state.

Hobbes came to hold strongly to such a doctrine, indicative of long-standing habits of ecclesiastical preferment. His close friend William Cavendish, duke of Newcastle, expressed common views with a refreshing directness. In his remarkable letter of advice to Charles II just prior to the Restoration of 1660, Cavendish suggested that the priesthood as a class was always potentially hostile. To maintain the effective subjection of his people, Charles must therefore select and promote bishops only on political loyalty and administrative capacity. His church must be in his own hands (Cavendish, 14). Hobbes had come to believe exactly this. Episcopacy could be splendid as an adjunct to the sovereign's rule, but if bishops are not watched, he warned, they will "sliely slip off the Collar of their Civill Subjection" (*Leviathan*, 42.374). Theological qualms about the consequences of such a relentlessly secular treatment of the priesthood seemed not to have troubled Cavendish.

They had, however, troubled Hobbes, who in his early works had allowed some independence to pastors. In *The Elements of Law* (*Elements*, 2.6.2), he raised what he took to be a distinctly modern difficulty at the heart of establishing absolute subjection to a sovereign. What if there is a conflict of conscience between the commands of the sovereign and of God? It was a serious possibility, he insisted, where private interpretation of scripture is permitted or escapes the hands of civic authority (*Elements*, 2.6.2).

Initially he argued that, quite simply, the appeal to conscience is irrelevant because human laws are not "intended to oblige in conscience" (*Elements*, 2.6.3) but concern "actions only." In this sense, the conscience is known only to God, but it is action that is properly subjected to law because actions aid or undermine peace. As Christianity enjoins peace, there can be no licit appeal to obeying God before man. This distinction between conscience before God and action seems to be much the same as one that had been drawn by Marsilius of Padua between intransient and transient acts. It too had been developed in the context of an attempt to control the excesses of priests claiming to have authoritative access to the commands of God, and by the time Hobbes wrote, it was widely accepted.[18] The fundamentally Marsilian distinction drawn in

The Elements of Law is not one between public and private worship, for all public and much private worship constitute actions, transient acts between human beings. Because in this sense conscience is a purely inner sense of a relationship with God, it leaves no room for priests to establish any independent area of authority over people's lives. Yet later Hobbes referred to conscience in a broader sense of being nothing but a "settled judgement and opinion" (*Elements,* 2.6.12). This allowed him to state immediately that when a man has transferred this right of judgment to a sovereign, what is commanded in his name is his own judgment. So, by turns, conscience is inscrutable and openly transferable. This is more than an expression of the contemporary multivalence of the term; it illustrates the tension between Hobbes's image of the isolated human animal and the social being capable of authorizing, or irrevocably delegating, action to another (see chapter 3, "From Association to Office"). In *De cive* (*De cive,* 15.12), the terms of the argument would be shifted slightly again; he would draw a distinction between public and private worship (see also *De homine,* 14.8), but use it in much the same way as he used his concept of an intransient conscience. In both works, Hobbes's sovereign may in the interests of peace regulate all forms of human behavior that he, she, or they consider appropriate. This was a belief from which he would never waver, and it came to override his somewhat muted attempts to allow some independent voice to a properly constituted priesthood.

Despite a certain incoherence of meaning, then, the word "conscience" is used consistently to discredit appeals to it in public debate. To reinforce this general thrust, Hobbes drew a further distinction between fundamental and superstructural beliefs, more commonly referred to as the distinction between necessary and indifferent (*Elements,* 2.6.5). From the postulate that Christianity is the true religion, it was seen to follow that certain beliefs were necessary to salvation. Many others, admirable or tolerable though they might be, were indifferent. Two problems arose and dogged English sixteenth- and seventeenth-century religious debate. First was the question of the content of the fundamental and superstructural. Beliefs held necessary to salvation were those that could not be compromised and thus if threatened were the principal source of escalating social conflict. Not surprisingly, Hobbes always sought to minimize the content of the fundamental. In *The Elements of Law,* for example, he claimed quite simply that "there is not any more necessary point to be believed for man's salvation than this, that Jesus is the Messiah, that is the Christ . . . *that he is God's anointed*" (*Elements,*

2.6.2; see also *De cive,* 18.5). All else being superstructural was negotiable.

On a second crux hung the whole issue of toleration, comprehension,
and conformity. Should the realm of matters indifferent to salvation also
be independent of civil authority; or did indifference mean that which
the civil authorities should control? The heated dispute over the obser-
vance of the Sabbath and the right of the church to alter long-standing
regulations provoked a short letter to an otherwise unknown Mr. Glen
from Florence. Hobbes agreed with him that if a church could make
alteration to one of the Ten Commandments it was being treated as
merely human law, and that might encourage the view that any moral
law was alterable.[19] At much the same time, the Scottish Presbyterian
George Gillespie (1613–1648) was taking the bull by the horns, arguing that the very notion of the indifferent was unstable. If a belief is genuinely indifferent, then any church should be able to alter it at will, but
if a belief is taken as a sign of something further, as ceremony may be
taken as a sign of piety, then it ceases to be indifferent. It was in this
sense that the sacraments were commonly regarded as sacrosanct.
Appearing outwardly indifferent, they were taken as signs of inner
grace.[20] The notion of indifferency, in short, could be seen as opening
the door to Erastian control, widespread toleration (or anarchy depending on perspective), or even the unthinkable reversion to Rome.

This was how the matter would be conceived by the young John
Locke and his adversary, Hobbes's correspondent Edward Bagshaw, in
1660. Bagshaw saw indifferency as a warrant for toleration, Locke as
therefore requiring secular intervention in the name of peace.[21] This, in
fact, seems always to have been Hobbes's view, but with the important
proviso that kept the door to toleration very much ajar, offering hope to
sectaries and Nonconformists in appeal to the sovereign. By the mid-
1660s, Locke would want that door more fully opened.

So, according to Hobbes, it was the duty of the sovereign to control
the extensive realm of the superstructural insofar as the sovereign considered it a threat to obedience and civil society, but it was certainly not
the job of the sovereign's church to decide such matters for itself. There
was, then, no requirement to force conformity for its own sake and, as a
matter of simple fact, conscience in one sense could never be touched;
epistemologically, no human could know the conscience of another. In a
different sense, conscience, as settled opinion, came very clearly within
the sovereign's realm of judgment. The result was a form of Erastianism
likely to appeal to any group seeing itself as innocent yet oppressed by

priests. Consequently, Hobbes could be flexible and sanguine about specific church forms and ecclesiastical style.

He greatly respected the high church ceremonialism of Dr. Cosins
and could sound much like the Calvinist preacher William Perkins
(Sampson, 728–29). He befriended a whole cluster of French Catholic
priests, and had a warm correspondence with Independent Puritans
such as Bagshaw and Henry Stubbe; he regarded the Cromwellian
experiment with greater toleration reasonably well, yet conformed to
the requirements of the Church of England—all this without any necessary hypocrisy. Hobbes respected Dr. Cosins's ceremonialism as a legitimate if indifferent expression of piety and reverence for God, and if that
is what ceremonialism was it could hardly challenge peace and "civill
society." As he had expressed the matter more generally in *The Elements
of Law,* "no man is justified by works, but by faith only. But if . . . the
will be taken for the deed, or internal for external righteousness, then
works do contribute to salvation" (*Elements,* 2.6.10). He thus offered a
cautious Arminian modification of Luther's and Calvin's insistence on
salvation by faith alone. It was a common enough Church of England
view in his generation. If "works," that is ceremony and ritual as well as
more general actions, were enforced or regulated by the sovereign for
peace and civil society, clearly it was acceptable to Hobbes. In this way,
ceremonialism was one thing as it was an expression of royal policy but
quite another if a means to clerical independence and episcopal aggran-
dizement. If it became mistaken as a sure mark of salvation, hence carrying a whiff of popery, Hobbes could be as hostile as any plain Puritan.

What we do see is a gradual hardening of attitudes to bishops and
their sense of spiritual significance. In *The Elements of Law* (*Elements,*
2.7.8), he gave credence to the doctrine upon which bishops of all forms
of Christianity built their sense of independence, a claim to apostolic
succession. In later works, he resoundingly denied this doctrine. The
change was intimated just after *The Elements of Law* was written. In a
letter of 1641[22] relating an antiepiscopal petition gathered in Notting-
ham, he showed unexpected sympathy for the petitioners complaining
about the excesses of bishops. William Laud (1573–1645), Charles I's
ceremonially minded archbishop of Canterbury, did not regard his
church as a mere department of state and was highly jealous of its independence. Thus he was vulnerable alike to Erastian and more Puritan
suspicions of overreaching his office. In partial contrast, Gallican
Catholicism had shown itself theoretically quite amenable to a consigned place within the order of French government, or at least theoret-

ically affirmed conspicuous loyalty to the French sovereign, whereas English Catholics were tarred with the Jesuitical brush of rebellion in the name of allegiance to the pope. Independent sectarians were apt to be suspicious of priests in principle, especially the potential oppressions of the ordered clerical hierarchies of Episcopal and Presbyterian churches.

Hobbes's hostility to sectarian clergy stirring up sedition and disobedience in the name of obedience to God was unrelenting. Such men had been a principal cause of the civil wars (*Behemoth,* 1.22–26); but what concerned Hobbes was not inner belief or piety but transient acts disruptive of peace. By the same token, he accepted Archbishop Laud's piety and integrity, but similarly criticized his willingness to stir up religious controversy, claiming Laud misunderstood the limits of his office (*Behemoth,* 2.73). Mutual hostility to priestly hierarchy, however, drew Hobbes to men of sectarian disposition during the period of the Commonwealth, and insofar as they saw themselves as anything but threats to peace, they at least were apt to see Hobbes as providing a theoretical structure within which they might hope for toleration. Even Cromwell's chaplain, Dr. John Owen, apparently found *Leviathan* congenial, but for its indiscriminant anticlericalism.[23]

As Hobbes would eventually remark in *Behemoth,* "I confess I know very few controversies amongst Christians, of points necessary to salvation. They are the questions of authority and power over the Church, or of profit, or of honour to Churchmen, that for the most part raise all the controversies. For what man is he, that will trouble himself and fall out with his neighbours for the saving of my soul, or the soul of any other than himself?" (*Behemoth,* 2.63).

The consistency, then, of Hobbes's position lies not in adherence to any church form but to the Erastian function of its priesthood conjoined with strict adherence to the modesty of its otherworldly office. A church is not a priesthood; it is a whole community of believers (*De cive,* 17.20) that elects or decides upon its pastors, directly or through the sovereign (*De cive,* 17.24). Thus priests largely ratify church decisions. The same derivation of church from *ecclesia* appealed to sectarians and Congregationalists, for *ecclesia* seemed also to mean house, thus suggesting the primacy of the gathered, independent church no larger than its own congregation. *Ecclesia* could also be used to suggest the legitimacy or even practical desirability of a national church in the interests of peace. In *De cive,* Hobbes treated the church and city as coextensive, "for a Christian city and a church . . . are the same thing." (*De cive,* 18.13,

429), the city or *civitas* being a paradigm for any sovereign rule. Yet he also insisted that many cities cannot make a single church, the target being the papacy and its claims to ecclesiastical authority over Christendom. If "city" is read as the English more than the Latin *civitas* allows, then this was clearly appealing to Congregationalists. Hobbes's understanding of the *ecclesia* had one further negative function, to suggest that churches were very much human institutions and none could claim to be the kingdom of heaven (*Leviathan*, 42); all had priests as functionaries, teachers, and advisers and these, as priests, are equal. All additional arrangements, ranks, and rules are superstructural and legitimately under the auspices of the sovereign (e.g., *Behemoth*, 1.14) or, given the sovereign's silence, may be determined by the members of the church itself.

The Interpretation of Holy Texts

Two further preoccupations of Hobbes's religious thought follow quite naturally from this: the hermeneutic concern with the right to interpret holy texts and the mechanisms by which priests, ancient or modern, assumed their bogus authority to the detriment of civil society. Hobbes's interest in the private interpretation of scripture has already been noted (*Elements*, 2.6.2), and he was hardly unique in recognizing the political power that came with the authority to interpret texts. The more potent those texts, the greater the authority of those who wielded them, but sure command could be elusive for the printing press had brought about a cumulatively complicating set of hermeneutic uncertainties. Censorship might be established but was rarely effective for long, and forbidden books were the forbidden fruit of busy presses. Works such as the Bible, itself the surviving monument to ancient attempts to control what was stamped as the Word of God, were translated into vernaculars and spread beyond the complete control of priestly or civic elites. Part of what Hobbes saw as the modern problem of obedience to civil laws stemmed from such fugitive control (*Elements* 2.6.2; *Behemoth*, 1.21–22). Textual controversy always meant more "work for *printers*" (*Libertie*, 233–34). An analogous situation (see chapter 5, "Civil Law versus the Rule of Lawyers") occurred with respect to the authority of the law being in the hands of lawyers.

In many ways, Hobbes's simple and draconian view of biblical interpretation mirrors his image of civil law. Because Christianity has but a simple fundamental doctrine of belief necessary for salvation, much of the Bible is a matter of indifference. The whole Bible might be inspired by the Word of God, but it contains much *"Politicall, Historicall, Morall, Physicall* and others which nothing at all concern the *Mysteries of our faith.*"[24] What is of relevance to faith is what touches the necessity of obedience. In *De cive* he went so far as to argue that it is the sovereign who mediates the Word of God as it is relevant to the mysteries of faith (*De cive*, 17.12, 18). His sovereign was thus a godly hermeneutic prince in the Henrician Protestant tradition. Hobbes nevertheless expressed no hesitation in outlining what he took the laws of God to be (*De cive*, 16) and claiming that the Word of God is made clear in three forms: reason, revelation, and prophecy. These characterize God's relationship with the world in terms of political power. All this was done without any intimation that such a description was merely a metaphorical expression of faith and piety, as his other concept of God would seem to require.[25] His point, of course, was engaged, but what might seem to be the arbitrary invocation of God in Hobbes's religious writings was not, I think, a matter of inadvertence or simple confusion; it was a sort of "averroistic" appeal to two truths. In *De cive* he had claimed to argue both by faith and by reason, but there he had interwoven appeals to two distinct criteria that would be separated more clearly in *Leviathan*. One theme common to all Hobbes's excursions into the relationship between religion and the sovereign was the reclamation of the sovereign's hermeneutic domain, by showing in passing how priests had used the Bible as a means to their own usurpation of power.

"unpleasing priests" and Godly Princes

Hobbes was a man often at odds with priests; his works suffered an allegedly orchestrated campaign by Presbyterians and were burned at the behest of the Church of England's episcopacy. He was threatened with trials for heresy in a society that on several occasions came to the brink of making heresy a crime. Unsurprisingly, he had an acute interest in how priests had acquired the power they exercised. Much was explained by the specific word "heresy," which they could wield as a weapon; by their assumed power of excommunication, most generally by the deft exploitation of human superstition; and by mythologizing the past to their own advantage. If priests could claim apostolic succession, and so have the power of the keys of the kingdom of heaven, then their capacity to terrorize could far outstrip and undermine the sovereign's. These issues are taken up in various places. In chapter 42 of

Leviathan, Hobbes defined heresy as private opinion maintained obstinately in the face of official teachings of the civil magistrate. Conscience and heresy might be opposing descriptions for much the same thing. The main point was to refute Rome's insistence that it was the arbiter of heresy, its extirpation, the duty of kings.

In later work, however, Hobbes developed a more wide-ranging account of the word. Heresy was originally a Greek term meaning the taking or holding to an opinion. It was, he indicated in typical fashion, most characteristic of philosophers to develop opinions and in their competing schools heresy, as it were, assumed its variable but offensive shape. And it was the conjoining of Greek philosophy with simple Christianity that brought with it the incubus of heresy fit to be developed as one of the great tools of priestly control.[26] Tracing the history back to antiquity was no mere philological exercise. As Springborg has aptly noted, it seems strategically designed to diffuse debate by associating the essence of the charge with the pagan and philosophically arbitrary (Springborg, 352). At its heart was unchristian intellectual obscurantism; no wonder he saw himself as a likely victim. The preoccupation again crops up in the *Dialogue Between a Philosopher and a Student of the Common Laws,* where Hobbes rehearses arguments already noted. Heresy properly signifies a doctrine of a sect taken on authority.[27] Gradually shifting its shape, a term of reproach improperly became a sin (for no man errs deliberately), then a crime, the monstrous progeny of law. As a residue of papal pretension, heresy should have no force at law in England. By implication a heresy law is a form of popery.

In his Latin dialogic poem, *Historia ecclesiastica* (perhaps finished around 1666), Hobbes followed a broadly Protestant trajectory from the pure church of the New Testament to the political engine of the papacy, the crucial point being the conversion of Constantine and the gradual assumption of administration by bishops. The hierarchies of the church necessitated by the very success of the religion carried with them the seeds of corruption, a devious blend of grasping self-interest and intellectual chicanery. So, too, Constantine's praiseworthy conversion afforded ill-used opportunities to the bishops. With organizational power came an effective control over heresy, and the priestly class abrogated powers of excommunication to make the charges effective. The whole clerical edifice was built upon a supposed gift of power from Constantine to the church, the so-called "Donation of Constantine," known by Hobbes's day to be a forgery. Nevertheless, the Nicene Creed had been established, and something of the purity of Christianity was maintained by later Reformed churches. Hobbes did not publish the *Historia* but, notwithstanding his satiric vehemence, his views of church history were overall hardly so scandalous that they needed to be hidden. Andrew Marvell, for example, published a similar vision of ecclesiastical history. The full significance of Hobbes's views on heresy and church development are finally indicated by his abstracting some of the main themes from the *Historia* and the *Narration Concerning Heresy* and using them to explain the civil wars of his own country (*Behemoth*, 1.8–20).

Hobbes's attitude toward excommunication is predictable. In *De cive* (*De cive*, 17.26), he argued that pastors may provisionally remit sins but it is up to the church to judge repentance and that the church, not the priests, has the power of excommunication. The force of his argument is negative, that princes cannot be excommunicated by other princes, or one city by another. What would become more explicit in *Leviathan* is that the church (even if not originally called together by a sovereign) acts only through its representative, thus effectively excommunication is in the hands of the sovereign.

Between Conventionality and Revolution

Although Hobbes's views on religion were sometimes eccentric and provocatively expressed, it has been possible to indicate that they were responses to problems endemic to Christianity and were developed from a broad, late scholastic and Reformation Protestant tradition. To reinforce this point, a comparison between Hobbes and his critic George Lawson (1598–1678) is instructive, not least because Lawson was a long-standing and accommodating cleric in the Church of England, pious possessor of a hair shirt and never a candidate for accusations of atheism.[28] Lawson, like Hobbes, held to an *apophatic* conception of omnipotent God[29] and also had a minimalist sense of the beliefs necessary for salvation. He insisted on the same philological evidence Hobbes evoked that a church, an *ecclesia*, was first and foremost the community of believers, which he also thought might legitimately be a national church under one sovereign in the interests of peace. He held to the epistemological immunity of conscience, to priests as equal in serving Christ whose kingdom is *not* of this world. He too elaborated on the ease with which priests went beyond and abused office; as popes had done, so had Reformed bishops and others. Without bishops, he noted, there would be no popes. The conversion of Constantine proved a turning point in their acquisition of earthly power. Like Hobbes, Lawson developed a notion of representation as irrevocable. Yet Lawson too had respect for ceremony if it was an expression of piety, and he could accept ecclesiastical hierarchy if it were not dressed in myths of divine right. Like Hobbes he argued that salvation is through faith but works may help along the way. At the same time, he counted as his friends Independents and Nonconformists who were suspicious of priestly rank. He insisted too that most ecclesiastical arrangements were of human invention and were alterable since much came within the sphere of the sovereign's control whose duty was to maintain peace. He balked at allowing the civil sovereign hermeneutic control over the Bible, but was no less aware of the intense politics of biblical interpretation, remarking darkly, as I quoted at the outset, on the chemical abstraction of different governments from a mere pronoun. He denied being an Erastian and disliked *Leviathan,* but the similarities between the two men remain striking.

This is not to say that, except in the trivial sense of conforming to its outward requirements, Hobbes was a conventional member of the Church of England. It is to say that the church could be broader than we often think. It is also to accept that when all such propositions were given specific content, they could result in a variety of arrangements and potential injunctions. The devil, as they say, is in the details. Thus constantly in a Protestant world, hopes of ecumenical agreement, of toleration or comprehension, were dashed; a Hobbes could be persecuted while a Lawson went about his work in obscurity and peace.

Thomas Hobbes in his Erastianism may be associated with that strand of Protestantism that could place much faith in a godly prince. His sovereign looks a little like a priest-king. It may be that what fuelled the enthusiasm of some English Protestants for furnishing the sovereign with so many of the accoutrements of religious control was a fear of priests and ultimately Catholicism. Only a godly prince could be an effective bulwark against the pope. Predictably, the palpitations could be seismic when it was feared that the man in whom so much hope of protection was invested was selling the Reformation to Rome. Some had feared that Charles I was moving deviously in this direction, though Hobbes did not; many would become deeply suspicious of Charles II and Thomas Hobbes was silent. When, however, Charles's brother James, the heir apparent, disclosed himself to be a Catholic, destined to rule as a Catholic prince, the tensions between political loyalism, even an adherence to a principle of sovereignty and to ecclesiastical integrity, became extreme. The moves and countermoves around the attempts to guarantee the English Reformation led to the "Exclusion Crisis" of 1679–1683.

It is in the context of mounting unease over the counterposing commitments to sovereignty and religion that a late fragment of a Hobbes manuscript (c. 1678) should most probably be placed. Unsigned, undated, and in the hand of James Wheldon, his amanuensis, the work seems to be a partial response to a number of questions possibly raised by William Cavendish, earl of Devonshire. Hobbes, well aware of the full implications of his theories of sovereignty, is significantly circumspect in dealing with specifics. The crucial question seems to be just how inviolable is hereditary right. It is clear that for Hobbes the sovereign is effectively still divine, as the only mediator of God's laws. Yet although this hedge of divinity does not extend to any heir, no one can force a sovereign to disinherit a future ruler. This seems clearly to suggest too much of an impasse for Hobbes's interlocutor. It would certainly be deeply discouraging for anyone seeking Hobbesian reasons for ousting a Catholic heir to a Protestant throne. So Hobbes suggests that if a sovereign cannot protect through want of natural reason, thus ceasing effectively to be a sovereign, we had better wait until there is such a king. This untypical deflection intimates the unacceptable and impractical— wait for a Catholic sovereign before acting. It provokes an insistent reformulation of the issue of the right of succession. Hobbes, true to his theories of sovereignty, reiterates that no sovereign can be forced to exclude his own heir. There the Hobbes of *Leviathan* might be expected to stop, but he continued stating that although a living king cannot lawfully be deposed, a dying one "is ipso facto dissolved," the people relapsing into a lawless condition of war, "Which by making a King they intended to avoid."[30] It was a prescient equivocation explicable only on the assumption of Hobbes's full awareness of the heightening tensions over sovereign power and religious integrity. His earlier expressions of theories of sovereignty, and the accusations that he was an atheist or "Turkish philosopher" might have led us to expect a more uncompromising affirmation of sovereignty and its self-generation through an unqualified right of succession. As it is, we are left on the tantalizing cusp of law and lawlessness, a dying king ushering in a state of war in which parties can commit no injustice in determining a sovereign power once more. Where true religion is concerned, there is, in short, the suggestion of a semantic escape from the rigors of sovereign power and the necessity of its continuity. Within a few years of this, the ostentatiously loyal Cavendish family would be part of the revolution to oust England's new renegade godly prince. There were noticeably few people to justify it in Hobbesian terms.

Chapter Five

The Nature of Law

The Command Theory of Law

From the earliest writings attributed to him until late in life, Hobbes had an interest in law and different senses of law pervade his formal political theories. He variously wrote of law—natural, divine, or eternal, civil, common, and customary—taking an interest in lawyers and their strong sense of autonomy and standing. There are even occasions on which he seems, superficially, to mean by law the whole range of the humanly conventional and the socially contingent of which formal laws are a subset (*De cive,* 4). Predominantly, however, Hobbes is regarded as a legal positivist and as a command theorist—that is, one who thought that law is a matter of command and enforcement. Yet he did not hold that any enforceable command (such as "Your money or your life") was a law. Enforcement had to come from an authoritative command. Law, then, requires two things: an origin in some authority and a capacity to enforce. The two combined result in justice. This was to make central what we have since taken for granted, the process of legislation. The elaboration of such a view was what Hobbes regarded as the science of justice. Ignorance of it was social disaster.

The belief that Hobbes was, or became, a legal positivist and command theorist is broadly correct, but it does involve discounting some of what he wrote, and consequently some ambivalent statements about justice and reason. More specific and many animadverted issues have flowed from this, especially concerning the status of natural law in his political writings. One school of thought has held that natural laws are no more than prudential maxims for him, or codifications of what interested human reason can establish; another, that they are properly laws. The myth is that there is a simple and invariable position that can be grasped and that apparent exceptions need only explaining away. Loose ends, however, are likely because Hobbes shifted emphasis in dealing with the salient characteristics of law. All law might be command but the weight of his analysis would sometimes fall on effective and sometimes on authoritative command. Where it falls on the former Hobbes may be construed as a simple legal positivist; its weight upon the latter shifts the scales toward a deontology stemming from God's authoritative commands.

It is perhaps best to begin by asking what generally his references to law do in his theories and in counterpoint to what alternatives. Here I think the matter is straightforward: law is almost invariably invoked to help formulate or support his sense of sovereign authority against any sets of views or practices that he saw as endangering it. He was even apt to express his preferences for specific forms of government in terms of their agreement with the principles of legal sovereignty. Thus monarchy was superior to democracy because it was less easily divided and more plausibly seen as continuous. It was the principle of sovereign legality that was of paramount importance to Hobbes, but what this amounted to became highly contentious. He lived in a society that thought very largely in legal terms when it did not construe its problems in theological ones. In their own right, lawyers constituted an increasingly powerful profession and, additionally, some training in the law was common among the gentry who might have serious legal responsibilities as justices even without a formal legal education. Common law in particular was regarded as pervasively important to English society and a common law ethos could become a whole theory of the polity. Common law could be seen as authoritative reason revealed over time and properly intelligible only to those thoroughly inducted into its mysteries. So important was this attitude that even a monarch with as elevated a sense of his own office as James I could regard himself as living under the law.

At the same time, continental jurisprudence, in many ways antagonistic to common law notions, often discussed what we call politics as public law; *scientia politica* was close to coextensive with jurisprudence. In Hobbes's lifetime, common law and a more European Roman derived understanding of public or civil law vied for supremacy. The voice of continental civil law had been heard in Christopher St. German's *Dialogues betwixt a Doctour of Divinitie and a Student of the Lawes of England* (1523/32), in the much publicized writings of Jean Bodin, and then in a whole sequence of academic theorists such as Christopher Besold and Henning Arniseaus, all known in England. Bacon, although a common lawyer, was much taken with continental notions of codification and legal sovereignty.[1] The institution of Doctors Commons was the focus for such concepts of civil law. Common law was less given to accessible theoretical statements, let alone programs of reform. It was formed by a highly specialized language, the meaning of which was determined by lawyers and legal judgment. The consequence was that lawyers could assume an autonomy and significance that could put them at odds with royal command and the slowly increasing importance of legislation. Enacting a law was one thing, determining what it meant as law and applying it was quite another, and something lawyers claimed was their business to decide. Law could be seen as a challenge to the monarchy. There were in addition ecclesiastical courts for the purpose of executing canon law and controlling the church; despite the Reformation this too gave a residual independence to the clergy.

Characteristically, in public debate appeals to natural and divine law and to justice and reason, rights, and constitutionality were a means of counteracting or challenging the application of human laws. Thus at one and the same time, some sort of appeal to law and a whole penumbra of salient claims putatively embedded in law could be made in the name of legitimacy and stability, yet also they could be seen as a threat to society from within, depending on one's perspective and the case at issue. Hardly surprisingly, then, issues concerning the nature, extent, and content of the law became increasingly fraught during the seventeenth century. In its simplest terms one set of issues became how far political authority was and had traditionally been constrained and legitimized by law, or was reducible to what was accepted (by lawyers) as legal and constitutional; and how far political actors, above all the monarch, could properly exercise independence of the law in emergency or even in normal circumstances. Such imponderables were signaled by the pervasive legitimating language of prerogative right of rule, and were countered by accusations of arbitrary rule and tyranny.

Overwhelmingly, Hobbes's discussions of law need to be seen against this multilayered backdrop and were attempts to render law consistent or coextensive with sovereignty and to co-opt or undermine the surrounding semantics of justice and reason and the appeals to divine, natural, and common law against tyranny and arbitrary rule. Thus many of the statements about law that have caused difficulties can be explained, though not explained away, by the attempt to neutralize a wayward discourse of law. By the same token, as Margaret Sampson has suggested, Hobbes's hostility to the arts of casuistry derived from his sense that it amounted to a set of rules independent of and qualifying the authority of any established law (Sampson, 723).

In one of the earliest works only recently attributed to him, Hobbes subsumed all law under the notion of regulation, "So the true end of all

Laws is to ordain, and settle an order,"[2] a notion that presumably he would have taken to justify his own later attempts to restrict the idea of law to the sovereign's office of peace and protection. The "Discourse of Laws" was written without signs of the political urgency and sense of law-induced crisis that would mark so much of his mature work, and so it exhibits a more generous notion of law than we will find later. Human beings, it is argued, are rule-following creatures, but there is no sense that justice is a creature of the sovereign's law. It is rather "the true knot that binds us to unity and peace" (*Discourses*, 106). Such a statement could be rendered consistent with later views if he is read as meaning by justice only the sovereign's justice. But there are, Hobbes went on to remark, "certain fountains of natural Justice and equity, out of which has been taken that infinite variety of Laws, which several people have [adapted] to themselves" (*Discourses*, 112). This is at one with Hobbes's strong sense of cultural diversity, but the notion of law itself is extended in the very way that Hobbes would later consider potentially dangerous. Justice seems clearly to be given a primary status. Laws are derivative regulations.

There are three main forms of law, "every one stricter than the other" (*Discourses*, 110). Here strictness seems to mean specificity rather than genuineness of legal status, as he would later argue. There are natural laws; these we share with all creatures. There are the laws of nations, rules "which reason has prescribed to all men in general" and that are accepted as just (*Discourses*, 110). And there are municipal laws varying from country to country. It is these that provide us with peace and security and that stand as a protection against those who might oppress us (*Discourses*, 110). So, too, they may override bad custom, although Hobbes actually concludes the essay by claiming that ancient custom, *mos Maiorum*, differs only in name from a law having the same "power and authority" (*Discourses*, 119). Much of this was conventional enough, but it shows an uncertain distinction between law and custom and it opens the way to seeing the law, or a rule of law, as an independent protection against political dictates, and from there the elevation of the lawyer as a custodian and guardian of the body politic analogous to the physician tending the physical body (*Discourses*, 111). All law deserves respect, the common laws customarily handed down as much as the civil laws promulgated by some authority. Here the competing claims of the common and customary lawyer and the civil or Roman lawyer who saw municipal law in terms of statute and codification are being ameliorated without common law and custom being required to give an inch. If the *Three Discourses* is by Hobbes, there were considerable adjustments afoot.

Between Natural Law and Custom

In *The Elements of Law,* the natural law under which, according to the "Discourse of Laws," men and animals live alike, was now problematic. Some have considered law to be determined by the consent of most or the wisest of nations, others require universal agreement. Neither position, according to Hobbes, was satisfactory. Natural law is a law of reason, not consent (*Elements,* 1.15.1). This formed the prelude to arguing that it is rational to seek peace, and permitted Hobbes plausibly to extrapolate through his own reason a set of correlative laws of nature. Similar statements would shortly be found in *De cive,* where Hobbes would also equate natural and divine law, asserting that reason is given by God for appropriate action (*De cive,* 4.1). Further, our trying to live by natural law is itself just (*De cive,* 3.30). These and statements like them give a clear impression of law as somehow antecedent to society, universal, available, God-given, and entailing justice. It is from such statements that some modern commentators have developed a reading of Hobbes that sees all civil obligations as ultimately dependent upon God. For a few, ultimately, it is God's law that obliges us in all significant matters, which of course is to take us a long way from the "atheist" Hobbes.[3]

There is a good deal, however, that moves in a rather different direction. Most generally, law and/or justice as universal, antecedent, and independent conceptual realities requiring our application and interpretation of them, sits ill with the generally nominalist tenor of Hobbes's writing. Such universals should have meaning for him largely as abstractions from the particularity of legal arrangements. And indeed Hobbes did write of law in ways more consistent with his nominalist ideas of language and conceptualization. He wrote, fairly persistently, of natural laws, in the absence of effective command to obey them, as being prudential maxims urging peace. Hence natural law seems to be an abridgment of such practical wisdom. The maxims constituting it are, though rational, too often honored in the breach unless (until) there is a civil sovereign. In time of war, all laws are silent if we consider the actions rather than the minds of men (*De cive,* 5.2). That is, a sense of law or what is right may be internalized, but it fails to control or dictate behavior. Given his emphasis on command, this would seem to mean that in war, especially the war of *omnium contra omnes* defining the state of nature (*De cive,* 5.2), either there is no law or no effective law. The metaphor of silent laws may be a trifle operatic, but the general point is clear: if law were just a matter of effective punishment, natural laws could not be laws, at least in and for this world—and Hobbes would no more than hint piously at the reckonings of judgment day (*Elements*, 1.18.12). As he had remarked in *The Elements of Law*, because law is command, to speak properly the dictates of nature are not laws "in respect of nature," but he immediately restores some balance by adding that they are laws "in respect of the author of nature, God Almighty" (*Elements*, 1.17.12.93).

Hobbes insisted on reliability of punishment as a defining characteristic of law, but his position was never totally reductive. In *The Elements of Law* he distinguished three types of law—divine, natural, and civil in terms of origin of command or authorship (*Elements*, 2.10.6). This is not very satisfactory, for presumably divine and natural law have the same author. He then distinguished the form of law, its mode of promulgation, as being either written or unwritten. Again, this is fairly sketchy as it is not clear where case law can fit in. Thirdly, he distinguished global commands (e.g., "thou shalt not steal") from penal laws, specifying penalties (*Elements*, 2.10.6). This might seem to be merely a matter of detail. Some writers might also take this to conform potentially to the difference between natural and civil laws. There is a natural, universal law against murder but penalties for it are variable. Hobbes would sometimes give this impression in claiming that the sovereign mediated and applied natural law. But more significantly here, the distinction between types of law intimated what he would refine as two complementary features of law, authoritative command and enforcement.

The matter is further elaborated in *De cive*, where he argued that judgment and enforcement or punishment are complementary; it is roughly the difference between a rule and its application. The English translation renders the Latin terms as distributive and vindictive *(vindicativam)* (*Rudiments*, 215); but more importantly, Hobbes specifies the aspects of law as the two offices of the sovereign, *duobus legislatoris officiis* (*De cive*, 14.6.317). The sovereign then sets forth all rights and rules of conduct and propriety. For Hobbes this was largely a matter of contract law *(pactum)*, mutual agreements between people specifying rights and duties, and it is these that delineate offices. In society this necessarily requires mutual restrictions. When these are abused or confused, the sovereign then penalizes offenders in order to maintain rule.

There are a number of points to note from this. First, there are what Hobbes regarded as strict entailments of his notion of legal authorship—that the sovereign be undivided, for only thus could it speak with one voice about rights and punishments. A mixed or divided sovereignty where there is some principle of division of powers, a mixarchy, is a confusion of office. The institutionalization of potentially competing authoritative voices was bound to give conflicting judgments, thereby creating insecurity and conflict and so destroying the whole rationale of the state. The single voice of sovereignty must also be perpetual, for otherwise there can be no security in the future. Law is nothing without some assurance or anticipation of its continuing protection. It is, in a word, coextensive with society and its continuation. This is a point that he would reiterate and seem to wriggle away from at the very end of his life when asked to comment on a possible alteration to the succession (Skinner 1965, 218).

Secondly, his was a very formal and procedural notion of law, identifiable as law from its origin in the office of the sovereign. Thus again he remarked in his final manuscript fragment, what gives a constable a right to inquire into a person's behavior is not the fact that a theft may have been committed, but his office as constable (Skinner 1965, 218). This sense of legal formality also reinforced Hobbes's lifelong acceptance of the remarkable and legitimate diversity of human law, which in turn became part and parcel of a similarly procedural notion of justice and of rights; both arise from the execution of the law and are defined by the sovereign. The sovereign's right of punishment is the sword of justice (*De cive,* 6.5).

Thirdly, custom, however ancient, however rational, had no independent power or authority (*Elements,* 2. 10.10). These features of Hobbes's mature legal philosophy alike undermined appeals to justice and to some constitutional or natural standard beyond the sovereign as adjudged by lawyers or anyone else. Not surprisingly, Hobbes sided unequivocally with the civil Roman law tradition as opposed to the law of the common lawyer. His law was, then, civil law in a double sense: it is the law of the city, and as the city was emblematic of any political community in *De cive,* his terms of description encapsulate the priority of civil law in the more jurisprudential sense.

For Hobbes, civil law not only has a known author, the sovereign, but it is legislated, written, and codifiable and thus can give the security of knowledge to those who live under it. That is, the laws must needs be prospective; only the existence of general rules provide us with a reliable framework of obligations and liberties in which to conduct ourselves. This also requires some principle of intelligibility. If laws are not intelligible and available, ignorance of the law is legitimately an excuse for our behavior. The contrasts are implicitly with the English common law, which was not commanded but revealed or declared by judges more than it was legislated. It was resistant to codification and inscrutable, even if constantly adaptable. It was thus, according to Hobbes, incipiently inimicable to security and order. In this perhaps more than in the details of his theories of science, he came to believe, like Bacon, in the importance of codification for the support of sovereign rule. Common law, for all its difficulties, could make a plausible claim to be embedded in the customs and ethos of a people, appropriate to them, not arbitrary, to have been accumulating in wisdom. In short, common law could claim to be both rational and just. To many common lawyers such well-attuned virtues were altogether less obvious in the alien rigidities of civil law. Arbitrary and alterable, its justice no more secure than its source, the main problem with civil law might well be seen to lie precisely in its being no more than a tool of sovereign power.

Law and the Language of Justice and Tyranny

Hobbes, however, attempted to assuage such fears by embedding the very idea of civil law in the laws of nature, claiming that civil law could not command anything contrary to them (*Elements,* 2.10.5). Hence his natural law has the same legitimizing and stabilizing function for civil law as custom, sometimes called a second nature, could have in common law. He argued that as natural law requires that we seek peace, it therefore entails that we keep contracts, for there could be no peace without reliability of contractual agreements. The laws of the city are enacted exactly for the purpose of insuring contractual reliability and peace. Thus civil law is an expression of natural law (*De cive,* 14.10). The upshot of Hobbes's cementing civil law in natural law is to deny any form of appeal to a standard beyond the laws of the sovereign. There is no appeal to justice, for justice is defined by the laws of the sovereign. So there can be no legitimate appeal to natural justice, for natural justice is only available through civil law. The concept, as it were, is universal, but its content or range is socially and historically variable.

The doctrine that at once affirmed the universality of justice and natural law and denied their availability independent of civil law was one Hobbes was to repeat on numerous occasions. Time did not dim his insistence, although the details might be adjusted. In *Leviathan* he allowed a natural law appeal to equity but insisted that justice is a function of the sovereign's law. The qualification, however, did not hold. In

Behemoth he wrote "To obey the laws, is justice and equity, which is the law of nature, and, consequently, is civil law in all nations of the world; and nothing is injustice or iniquity, otherwise than it is against the law" (*Behemoth*, 1.44). Thus when in *De cive* (*De cive*, 1.4) he had maintained that but for law we are all equal, he was not suggesting a notion of law so broad as to include all forms of habit and social convention along with what might be authorized by a lawmaker. Rather, the emphasis was on the significance of not having a sovereign lawmaker. Everything we have that differentiates and associates us is dependent on the voice or silence of the law; take that away and we assume the horrendous equality of the natural condition.

By similar reasoning, Hobbes was insistent that there could be no valid accusation of tyranny leveled against the sovereign, for tyranny is either an abuse of office or ruling beyond the laws. There would be nothing to stop a sovereign determining that subordinate offices might be abused tyrannously, but such a term cannot be used to apply to a sovereign or system of government itself. For Hobbes there was properly speaking no such thing as a tyrannous form of government or system of civil law (*De cive*, 7.2–3). This was in part because private citizens have no access to an independent standard by which to judge the sovereign tyrannous, and the sovereign as author of the laws is above them (*De cive*, 12.1–3). We might imagine an example where a legislator, a Caligula, say, legislates to allow breach of contract as a general rule and arbitrarily plays with and exploits his subjects in a way that might seem clearly unjust and tyrannical. Does this mean, as Hobbes is easily misread, there is nothing anyone can do? It does not. Hobbes's position was that *if* such behavior truly undermined our peace and security, which as described it would, *then* effectively we would be returned to the natural condition because the peace by which society is justified would have been destroyed. As far as we were concerned, being in a natural condition, there would definitionally be no civil law or author of it and because by definition the authority would therefore not exist, it could not be a fit subject for the predicates tyrannous and unjust. As he remarked, "he whom men require to be put to death as being a *Tyrant,* commands either by Right, or without Right; if without Right he is an enemy, and by Right to be put to death; but then this must not be called . . . *killing a Tyrant*" (*Rudiments,* 177). If, conversely, the accused has a right to rule, "then the divine interrogation takes place." On what independent grounds do we judge good and evil? Do we have knowledge of good independent of civil law and the ruler's commands? The questions are heavily loaded, especially in the invocation of God, but what is easily overlooked is the fact that the point is as much about the protocols of the language of politics and law as it is about action. As he would put it briskly in *Leviathan,* tyranny is nothing but monarchy "misliked" just as, he added with balance, those "grieved under a *Democracy,* call it Anarchy" (*Leviathan,* 19.130).

This propensity in Hobbes's writing to move by definitional fiat might seem oddly cumbersome and tricky. Why not simply say that rulers can be tyrannical and we can destroy them rather than be destroyed by them? For manifestly Hobbes is not foreclosing on destructive action. The answer is partly a matter of Hobbes's sticking relentlessly to the sort of nominal definition so important in his theories of science (see chapter 2, "Definition, Resolution, and Composition"). Here it is simply exploited for polemical effect; it is to purge from the language the vocabulary around which arguments of what he regarded as sedition and rebellion (similarly prejudicial terms) gathered so ominously. At the same time, it is to impress upon us the stark consequences of challenging the sovereign's laws, reversion to the natural condition. In a society bound by law, there can be no place for the word "tyranny." Hobbes was by no means alone in being preoccupied with the linguistic entailments of notions of legal and civil hierarchy (Lawson, chap. 15, sec. 7–8). And when pressed on the issue of altering the succession of an absolute sovereign (see chapter 4, "Between Conventionality and Revolution"), the only room to maneuver Hobbes allowed was to say that when the monarch was dying, the commonwealth itself was perhaps dissolved and all its members returned to a state of nature. Implicitly, such a condition allows a new state and new rules of succession to be determined. The definitional, even tautological, austerity of Hobbes's theory expresses a world in which there is only law determining meanings or a meaningless and violent state of chaos. The choice between them was always meant to be simple.

Rights and the Office of the Ruler

Civil law's agreement with natural law does not foreclose on differences of interpretation from one city or polity to another. Natural law was for Hobbes rational. We have the God-given faculty of reason, but we reason differently. Thus, almost as a rabbit from a hat, the sovereign becomes through legislation the mediator of natural law and hence is invested with a shadow of divinity. He made the same sort of move specifically with respect to divine law (*De cive,* 15.1), arguing that we must obey civil law unless it countermands divine law and then proceeded to show the impossibility of this because God has commanded that we live in peace. But to repeat, Hobbes went further. Commands needed to be declared to those who are governed by them (*De cive,* 15. 3) and can be declared only by the mediating sovereign. There is, as he remarked in *The Elements of Law,* some small scope for seeing divine law as distinct from civil within society: almsgiving, or freely helping others, is commanded by divine law but not by civil. But nothing can be done by divine right that is not also done by civil right (*Elements,* 2.10.5). To put the matter a little differently, earlier in the *Three Discourses* Hobbes had placed divine, natural, and municipal laws on a continuum of strictness where "strictness" seemed to mean only specificity. In *De cive* he would have us believe that there is a similar continuum of strictness from natural to civil law, but this is more than specificity; it is also a matter of civil laws being, as it were, more strictly laws as they must involve the two aspects of the legislator's office—authoritative command and enforcement—that together mediate the general rationality morally required by God or nature.

It is only from these complementary aspects of office that rights can come. Rights themselves must never be confused with law, although the names "are often confounded" (*Elements,* 2.10.5.186). A right is only a liberty left by the law; it is as different as liberty from restraint (*Elements,* 2.10.5). Natural and divine law are not unequivocally or reliably enforced unless there is a more immediate legislator than God. The plausibility of this point is enhanced by Hobbes's predominantly contractual notion of the content of law. What he put forward, then, was a multifaceted concept of law, but as in many contexts, he simply wrote of law. It is not always clear which features are pertinent to the sense of the term at the time.

This amounts to something more than a simple legal positivism, partly because of Hobbes's willingness to discount divine and natural law when they could not be co-opted to a cause, yet make use of them when they could. In *Leviathan,* Hobbes would give voice again to the position of *The Elements of Law* by referring to types of law rather than to the aspects of the office of the lawgiver, but broadly this remained at one with the argument of *De cive,* for the types of law were still claimed to come from the same authoritative source. Hobbes was also determined to distinguish law from counsel. In one clear sense the difference would seem to follow uncontentiously from his understanding of law as command. Counsel, by contrast, has no authority and may be asked for and dispensed with as the counsellee requires. It was an activity of a satellite office to the sovereign (*Elements,* 2.10.4; *Leviathan,* 25). Again, the distinction is immediately relevant to the controversies of his day. Parliament was an institutionalized council and a court of law. This ambiguous status made it easy for some to hold that the monarch was obliged to take its considered advice. For one like Hobbes, such a view was a threat to the legal integrity of the office of the sovereign, and the legitimate though clearly subordinate office of a counselor could be abused and become a euphemism for bullying and usurpation of legal right. Thus the distinction between law and counsel was integral to the attempt to combat the heady rhetorics of tyranny and arbitrary rule and the claims of common law that would destroy or limit the author of civil law.

Given Hobbes's sensitivity to such matters, we can expect him to claim for the sovereign the right to interpret all laws analogous to the right to interpret scripture and always to be indisputably above those laws. The sovereign's interpretative authority carrying with it the knowledge of a maker was designed to destroy any possibility of judicial independence, of judges declaring as they did in the "Ship Money" case (1637) what the law meant in opposition to the king. The more qualified notion, which had sometimes been voiced by James I, that normally he lived under his laws messily suggested some division of sovereignty between the law and the monarch's abnormal (prerogative) rights of action in disregard of it. Such a potentially accommodating vagueness could only encourage great entanglements of conflicting opinions.

Hobbes sought to cut the Gordian knot: the sovereign is above the law and an arbiter of its meaning. The consequence was to reduce the legal profession to the same position as the clergy; he would make them parallel executionary ranks of the sovereign's declared law—a view, it seems, that had been shared by Lord Chancellor Bacon (Martin, 72–104). In this legal sense, therefore, the Hobbesian sovereign is legally absolute; no office can licitly interfere with the sovereign's responsibilities, which entails the sovereign being unbound by what it creates. The extremity of Hobbes's European or civilian logic did much to isolate him, for despite the familiar story of an ideology of absolutism in conflict with something more liberal, there were very few consistent or persistent absolutists in England like Hobbes, their rhetoric being mainly directed against the claims of the pope.[4] The mounting conflicts in the years before the civil wars were around rather more complex fault lines.

Civil Law versus the Rule of Lawyers

Hobbes's distrust of lawyers was not as persistently expressed as his hostility to priests, but as a class he did think that they had done great damage. This did not stop him from having specific common lawyers among his close friends, such as John Selden, who was a Parliamentarian as well; but he seems to have believed with William Cavendish that priests and lawyers were two casts of men vying for supremacy in the commonwealth. This is supported first by Hobbes's claim that misunderstandings of the role of Parliament helped bring about the civil wars (*Behemoth,* 2.68–82), and second by his *Dialogue,* in which it is gradually made clear that the whole, self-aggrandizing hocus-pocus of Cokian common law theory was inimical to sovereignty and thus ultimately to peace. It was instead well suited to the development of lawyers. As the legally cynical John Warr argued many years before, the rule of law is the rule of lawyers.[5]

Hobbes, the voice of the "philosopher" in the *Dialogue,* accepts the centrality of reason to the law and that common law is reason. Formally this is what common lawyers claimed, but his point is to subvert the meaning of legal rationality. For Hobbes argued that law is rational insofar as it conforms to the law of nature expressed in statute form, which thus becomes the only way in which natural law is clearly available to us. "It is not wisdom but authority that makes the law" (*Dialogue,* 5). So too with custom: in statements that show how far he had come since the early "Discourse of Laws," he asserted that no custom has the nature of law. Only the voice of a present sovereign can make custom law, no matter how old the custom is. Moreover, laws yet to be declared or discovered, dredged up from old maxims and obscure ancient cases floating in a perpetual present of the legal mind, leave us living effectively in ignorance of our own legal standing. Paradoxically, then, the common law can undermine the very sense of protection justifying law in the first place. Added to this, of course, is what Hobbes took to be the weakness of common law conceptions of law well suited to the advancement of the legal profession. Law is a mystery involving a special language and arcane meanings and insofar as it claims to be authoritative, it must therefore challenge sovereignty. Thus he would not allow the legitimacy of distinction drawn by the lawyer in the *Dialogue* between common law and statute law. They are both but law (*Dialogue,* 5).

In the context of seventeenth-century argument, Hobbes was on strong ground here. Lawyers had accepted a role in law for legislation, but once something became law they claimed with increasing confidence uniquely to understand its legal meaning, even the intentions of the legislator if they were legal intentions. Partly we come back again to the centrality of the right to interpret texts. Thus on the question of felony, the philosopher in the *Dialogue* remarks that no "private man should presume to determine, whether such or such a fact done be within the words of a statute or not . . . [For] this is to give a leading judgment to the jury, who ought not to consider any private lawyer's institutes, but the statutes themselves pleaded before them for directions" (*Dialogue*, 95). But there are also wider issues involved. As Glenn Burgess has pointed out, what is at issue is control over the great kudos attached to the words "reason" and "rationality." At least implicit in common law thought as developed by men such as Coke (1552–1634) was the claim that only lawyers could understand the rationality of the law and it was this rationality that ultimately gave it authority, or at the least provided a hedge against interference with individuals from on high (Burgess 1996, 171). The philosopher will have none of this: law may well be an art, but the very notion of "legal reason" is obscure. There is only human reason (*Dialogue*, 5).

In the *Dialogue* the lawyer gradually gives ground, but beyond the page, the common law view remained firm. Codification and exposure to nonlegal minds could only make a mess of the law and might compromise its independence. Hobbes and his philosopher in the *Dialogue* could never accept the civic implications of bowing to the authority of a private legal language. In the interests of supporting sovereign legislation as the essence of law, thus denying the special claims of legal rationality, Hobbes was forced to adhere to a highly static and abstract sense of law and reason, an unqualified notion of reasoning not clearly in agreement with his views of the sciences and their differing definitional sign systems (see chapter 2, "Definition, Resolution, and Composition"). He also clung to a naive notion of interpretation. Common lawyers were not slow to see the problems in this, not least Sir Matthew Hale (1609–1676), whose rebuttal makes it clear that Hobbes's *Dialogue* was part of an on-going debate in England on the relative merits of common and civil law, sovereignty theory and legal autonomy. Each side could construe the other as interfering in its legitimate domain.[6]

As others have suggested, Hobbes's *Dialogue* may have been based on Christopher St. German's much reprinted *Dialogues betwixt a Doctour of Divinitie and a Student of the Lawes of England*.[7] If so, common lawyers were well prepared for Hobbes's "philosopher." Reformulating the voice of the lawyer in Hobbes's *Dialogue*, Hale pointed out that principles have to be applied and application entails interpretation. On this other interpretations must then build; otherwise, the principle provides no sure guidance from one case to the next and it is always in the end with individual cases that the law is concerned. Much of the law's complexity lies in trying to work out which general principles might apply and how.[8] Effectively, in this process of interpretation and the metarules of reading principles, the law must get some autonomy from the statute. Systems of Roman law, like common law, have traditions of interpretation. Hale's reading has been taken as a proto-Burkean defense of cumulative reason (Goldsmith, 294). It was, however, more directly a legal use of common principles of casuistic argument, which in religion, law, and private morality sought to qualify the impact of universal principle by looking at the context of specific cases and by developing metarules to control the potential arbitrariness of interpretation. As Hobbes himself was accused of being a casuist, there is a sense, presumably not lost on Sir Matthew, of hoisting Hobbes on his own petard.

Hobbes thought deeply about law, and the *Dialogue* shows him to have been cognizant of English common law, statutes, cases, and ad hoc defenses that thread through the urbane and courteous discussion between lawyer and philosopher, just as his more formal and polished theories draw on a considerable knowledge of the principles of civil law and its Greek and, above all, Roman origins. From around 1640, his arguments about the nature of law were broadly consistent, but just as important as his emphasis on origin and command was his concern with the semantics of law. Words seeming naturally to occur in the ambit of law—justice, equity, right, punishment, tyranny, counsel, judgment, reason, command—seem always to be subjected to the same question as to whether their use can be made to support the integrity of the office of the sovereign. Those words and expressions that could not be co-opted to the Hobbesian defense of sovereignty must have their salience destroyed. Such was the impulse behind Hobbes's discussion of tyranny. Those that could be marshaled, such as divine law, natural law, reason, and right, are duly pressed into service. Indeed, the notion of eternal or divine law was characteristically described by Hobbes through metaphors of sovereign office that could only have the effect of elevating the significance of that office. From his relatively youthful complaisance about law, custom, and justice, Hobbes came to recognize and participate in the crisis of law, religion, and polity. He saw clear parallels between the claims of legal and clerical independence and did his best to bolster the case of legal sovereignty against them. Although his views remained minority ones, it would be an uneasy and unresolved mix of common law and the sort of civil law Hobbes advocated that was to characterize later conceptions of the English, then British, state.

In this light, it seems odd that law has so often been a marginal topic in Hobbesian scholarship; but Hobbes's theory of law is a statement of sovereignty theory and most of what he says about politics can be subsumed under his discussion of law. His political theory is largely a modern academic reconfiguration of a theory of law in all its diverse resonances. This may in turn tell us something about sovereignty as a word either much misunderstood or so divorced from its early modern formulations that one can hardly criticize modern sovereignty theory by routinely attacking Hobbes and his like. Sovereignty in seventeenth-century Europe was not a theory of global or total independence of states or nations, but an abstraction from legal discourse, a lawyer's manner of looking at distinct units of human association that in other ways might be variously mixed together or be held mutually dependent. A sovereign state or commonwealth, a city as Hobbes symbolically expressed it in *De cive,* was something identified in terms of three legally recognizable variables, a source of law, for a given finite population in a given space. It was what he took to be the logic of this, in the face of what he also deemed dangerous, interested, or willful ignorance, that his political theories sought to explore.

Chapter Six
Rhetoric, History, and Poetry

The Darker Side of Language

The centrality of language to our humanity entailed, for Hobbes, dangers comprising philosophical confusion, deceit, and self-delusion. Language could be a bottle of buzzing philosophic flies or Pandora's box of social evils, unhinged. It was at the root of most evil (*De homine,* 10.3). Much of Hobbes's exultantly pessimistic sense of the wayward power of language is captured in his hostility to rhetoric or eloquence; it is displayed in his historical writings and refracted in his theories of poetry. These discrete topics are drawn together by fear of deviant word-use. The black magic of discourse had for him enormous explanatory and ad hominem power. If there could be no society without language, stable society without a stable language, then without rhetoric there could be no political conflict.

With few exceptions, older studies on Hobbes singularly overlooked this dimension to his work, subjecting it to modernly established priorities and commending his linguistic sensitivity only for anticipating the protocols of contemporary philosophical analysis. The balance, however, has been more than rectified in recent scholarship. Rhetoric has been somewhat triumphantly rediscovered and seized upon by some as so central as to be the key to explaining just about everything in Hobbes's work. This too has generated a mythic image of Hobbes as the arch rhetorician, to displace the mechanic philosopher.[1] But it does add credence to Hobbes's belief that our language can trap us like birds: the more we struggle the more we are belimed in words. For now, as in the seventeenth century, rhetoric remains a flighty beast uncertainly related to all sorts of terms from which it seems to be distinct, most crucially from philosophy, science, teaching, history, and poetry. Nothing illustrates the difficulties of making sense of rhetoric in such a semantic context than the writings of Thomas Hobbes.

Rhetoric, Eloquence, and Philosophy

A shadowy battle of the books between philosophy and rhetoric has long been projected with writers such as Cicero, Quintilian, and, closer to Hobbes's own day, Lorenzo Valla (1407–1457) extolling the primacy of rhetoric, with Plato and, it would seem, Hobbes and Locke, standing firmly by philosophy. But things have never been quite what they might seem. We need initially to distinguish two senses of rhetoric both carried along in Hobbes's train of thought; rhetoric as eloquent technique, from rhetoric as the persuasive dimension of language use as a whole. For clarity I will reserve Hobbes's preferred term "eloquence" for the first specific sense, and "rhetoric" for the more general persuasive function of language.[2]

Traditionally eloquence was regarded as a teachable art essential for public life and was conventionally seen as comprised of three genera: forensic or legal, demonstrative or epideictic (the speech-making of ritualistic public occasions such as funerals and weddings), and deliberative, the discourse of the political assembly. There was common ground to all three justifying the broad classification of rhetoric. Each drew on patterns of assumptions shared by an audience, and each involved some sort of combined appeal to what was thought to be honorable, right, or useful. Each was predicated on probability and a degree of uncertainty, that the world might be other than it appears and that people might respond to it in different ways; and each was aimed at generating a certain sort of reaction from the targeted audience, a verdict, a sense of edification or delight, a decision to act. Each did so by describing or depicting the world and its possibilities in ways appropriate to the desired ends of discourse.

The differences, however, were held to be equally considerable. Each genus could be seen, as Hobbes rendered Aristotle, as having its own proper time: "To the *Demonstrative* , the *Present*. To the *Judiciall,* the Past, and to the *Deliberative,* the *time to come*".[3] Forensic and deliberative eloquence were also associated with different institutional settings, the law court and assembly respectively, and each appealed to audiences in different capacities. Each had a different sense of decorum, and developed different constitutive rules and strategies for success within them. According to Aristotle, each also had a different end. Forensic eloquence concerned guilt or innocence, deliberative eloquence had its end in action. Epideictic eloquence did not fit very easily in this pattern, but generally it had come to be associated with inventive display, ceremony, celebration, and delight. The general awkwardness involved in the generic distinctions is not the point here. Rather, what the genera reinforced was the notion that there could be different sorts of eloquence, identifiable in part through differing rules of argument, conventions, and techniques. There were, then, distinct teachable skills or arts for eloquence in public life. Thus as a specification of rhetoric as persuasion we find the learnable rules suitable for the law court or assembly: Hobbes's eloquence.

The association of rhetoric or eloquence with teaching was also traditionally very close: eloquence could be taught and as a means of conveying information about the world, it could be seen as a medium of teaching. Concomitantly, the association with public participation was marked. The arts of eloquence are only needed where people participate, have choices, where knowledge is probable and action important. The point common to all forms of rhetoric, the end of eloquence, was to achieve some victory over the contingent responses of people, usually a victory over an alternative view. There was a continuing sense that in the arts of eloquence lay the civic equivalents of the teachable and portable skills of warfare.

When Hobbes wrote of eloquence it was usually this fairly specific image and this sort of claim that he seems to have had in mind. Eloquence sought to shape opinion and move men to action. That is, with the exception of his *Dialogue between a philosopher and a lawyer,* his concern was with deliberative eloquence, for this was about projecting an image of "the time to come" with potential action *"Exhortation* and *Dehortation."* (*Briefe,* 41) It was heady, wayward, and destabilizing. It was rightly associated most with democracies, which, as he remarked in *The Elements of Law,* are little more than aristocracies of orators punctuated with the "temporary monarchy of one orator" (*Elements,* 2.2.5.120). He usually made allusion to specific groups of people, opinion-makers or the victims of opinion-making, priests, sectaries, lawyers, and "democratical gentlemen" much enamored with ancient rhetorical theories of participation and liberty (*Behemoth,* 1.39).

Above all, Hobbes usually claimed, eloquence was not philosophy. One was a constellation of tricks and turns effecting opinion and seeking power through controlling actions. It relied on tropes and figures appropriate to the passions of the audience, and it was noted for exploiting equivocal terms and using language metaphorically. The other sought truth through the right ordering of clearly defined propositions and properly used language. Philosophy was rational, certain, and universal; eloquence was passionate, doubtful, and particular. Eloquence involved persuasion; philosophy was communicated by teaching or demonstration. There was, he held, a mighty difference between teaching and persuading, the principal sign of which was controversy (*Elements*, 1.13 3).

Yet, as technique, eloquence was a moveable feast; it could be used for good if made a subsidiary of demonstration. Hobbes's contrasts were very much aimed at undermining or restricting eloquence's credibility. And although this went against the grand claims of classical and Renaissance rhetorical theory, it was in keeping with the drift of the educational reforms associated with near-contemporaries such as Peter Ramus (1515–1572). The gist of these may be captured in the diminished scope of the notion of ornamentation. Traditionally, eloquence had been about ornamentation in the double sense of ornamenting an argument and verbally arming a speaker. *Ornatus* meant properly equipped.[4] The associations were very strongly of warfare: arguments were won, opposition was vanquished. The rhetorician, as Lorenzo Valla had put it, was a general deploying discursive forces. Such metaphors remain with us and Hobbes certainly employed them, sometimes in order to contrast victory with truth and to implicate eloquence in violence. He did this, for example, in *Of Libertie and Necessitie* (*Libertie*, 241), where he took delight in reworking Bishop Bramhall's military metaphors to suggest that the arguments gathered against *Leviathan* were forces looking one way, marching another and fighting amongst themselves. During his day, however, eloquence was assuming its now familiar place, restricted to the business of ornamenting in the sense of coloring something that was independently expressible. In sum, a dual sense of ornamentation could give an unexamined impression that eloquence was socially destabilizing and intellectually derivative.

The serious invention of argument was done by philosophy. Geometry appealed as a paradigm of philosophy for Hobbes because it obliged inexorably.[5] Accept the rules and with their proper application conclusions necessarily followed. There was, therefore, no need for persuasion, ornamentation, any appeal to the passions, or recourse to verbal manipulation; understanding and following the rules was enough. This tightly textured discourse could thus easily be transmitted socially and lead to cumulative certain knowledge. It was the finest example of the potential stability and clarity of language. For just these reasons, it was in a sense supremely undemocratic. Opinions were not of equal value; the teacher had a proper authority by virtue of being a master of what could be taught. Hobbes's vision was idealized and extreme. Most recognizable forms of discourse in Hobbes's day, arguably including much of mathematics, exhibited a need for eloquence, and so some rhetorical dimension can be seen as intrinsic to them. This has a consequence for understanding Hobbes despite his privileging the image of geometry.

Aristotle's *Rhetoric* and the Ambiguous Legacy of Adaptation

Two of Hobbes's early works illustrate different aspects of his attitude toward eloquence—his stupendous translation of Thucydides's *Peloponnesian Wars,* a work born of deep and unqualified admiration that will be discussed below, and his translation of Aristotle's *Rhetoric,* a work he regarded as exceptional in a double sense, exceptionally fine and thus an exception to the Aristotelian norm. His *Briefe of the Art of Rhetoric* is, however, very different from his translation of Thucydides, which Hobbes determined to make as accurate as possible.[6] It is much more of a creative paraphrase and appropriation, a sufficient act of conceptual translation to render it a Hobbesian imprimatur on antiquity.

Un-Hobbesed, Aristotle's *Rhetoric* remains perhaps the most fertile and important study of rhetoric, and although, like all his surviving works, only in note form, it was clearly and implicitly an attempt to restore the balance upset by Plato's hostility to eloquence, to which Hobbes was altogether more sympathetic. Aristotle's was an attempt to give a dispassionate survey of the functions of rhetoric, its presuppositions and limitations, its principal types and the skills proper to them. He explored both the techniques of eloquence and rhetoric, the persuasive dimension of language, itself necessary because it traded in probabilities and the contingencies of audience reaction.

There are two main features of Hobbes's *Briefe.* First is the deletion of detail. He omitted points irrelevant to English and subtle variations on themes, but secondly he ignored Aristotle's discussion of the differences between the more logically certain dialectic and rhetoric, constrained as it is by the probable.[7] He was then able to massage, as it were, Aristotle's necessarily creative and contingent art into something closer to a teachable adjunct to philosophical demonstration. Insofar as eloquence was legitimate it had to be made to look more like philosophy and so come under its authority. In one sense, Hobbes's Aristotle is Platonized, made to conform to Plato's project of philosophical control. In another, it is made consistent with the diminished status of rhetoric in Hobbes's own day. Hobbes's Aristotle is a caged bird.

His treatment of Aristotle's central rhetorical concept of the enthymeme captures the transformation. Aristotle had argued that the enthymeme in rhetoric is analogous to the syllogism in philosophy. Each was a tripartite argumentative structure, a building block of discourse. Whereas, however, the syllogism provided a certain conclusion from its major and minor premises and might not have anything to do with genuine experience, the enthymeme was only a probable conclusion, often in the form of an injunction, derived from shared assumptions from experience. Having omitted Aristotle's preliminary discussion of the differences between dialectic and rhetoric, Hobbes could proceed to regard the enthymeme as ultimately demonstrable. It was only "a short Syllogisme; out of which are left as superfluous, that which is supposed to be necessarily understood by the hearer; to avoid prolixity, and not to consume the time of publique businesse needlessly" (*Briefe*, 40). Thus theoretically a syllogism should be able to substitute for an enthymeme, which might be pithy but imperfect. Similarly, an "example" in rhetoric is a short (logical) induction.[8] In effect, Aristotle's *Rhetoric* came close to being good, that is philosophically compatible, eloquence. In the last analysis, "a *Logician* . . . would make the best *Rhetorician*" (*Briefe*, 39).

The uncertain status of rhetoric is captured in the definition Hobbes gives: "*Rhetorique*, is that faculty, by which wee understand what will serve our turne, concerning any subject, to winne beleefe in the hearer. Of those things that beget beleefe: some require not the helpe of Art; such as *Witnesses*, . . . and the like, which wee invent not, but make use of; and some require Art, and are invented by us" (*Briefe*, 40). Such a definition is not unduly problematic in the context of Aristotle's *Rhetoric*, as it was but a preliminary to a discussion that embraced rhetoric and the specific rules of eloquence. For Hobbes and many of his generation, however, the more intellectually creative and general aspects of rhetoric had been reassigned to philosophy. So, Hobbes's definition exemplifies early modern attempts to circumscribe rhetoric to ornamentation and to see it as a portable subordinate skill, but it does not do so securely. Its identification as a faculty about our capacity to make others believe us on any subject, see things as we do, spoke more of rhetoric than eloquence and opened the door to what Hobbes would formally exclude—the use of witnesses—and what he did not discuss—the process of describing the world, picturing a situation that is itself persuasive or prepares the ground for persuasion.

These had been central notions for Aristotle and important for his claim that discourse should appear to be natural. Sharing presuppositions with an audience is intrinsic to the persuasive process as a whole. Hobbes's rendition of Aristotle's concern with language was restricted to what graces a discourse (*Briefe,* 115). The choice between terms, the whole problem of rhetorical redescription, was reduced by him only to a matter of balance. The problem of rhetorical redescription, its potential for restructuring whole visions of the world, had been at the heart of the more inflated claims for the rhetorician's power and the deep suspicion that, as a corollary, was directed at eloquence. This was an issue that was to assume considerable significance for Hobbes. In the *Briefe,* however, the whole problem of redescription, or *paradiastole,* is reduced to a simple bland Polonian injunction: the chosen expression must be neither above nor below the thing signified (*Briefe,* 108). For such advice to be securely founded, there must be some access to the thing signified independent of discourse, a somewhat un-Hobbesian possibility. Hobbes sets down, for example, some of Aristotle's guidelines for effective metaphorical redescription but, as John Harwood notes, omits Aristotle's vital point that metaphor, in fact the most radical form of *paradiastole,* cannot be taught (*Briefe,* 109, 109 n).

The consequence of all this was to sustain in Hobbes's later philosophy and accounts of eloquence a degree of ambiguity that has also left its mark on modern scholarship. In a number of works he attempted to write philosophy without eloquence, but because the distinction between eloquence and rhetoric was unstable, his philosophy can still be seen as having a rhetorical dimension. In *Leviathan* he expressed his distaste for eloquence, yet formally places rhetoric next to logic with both under the auspices of philosophy (*Leviathan,* 9.61). This situation was exacerbated by Hobbes's doctrine that language could be seen as a form of action in the world, the fundamental means of processing impressions and getting others to act in concert with us (*Elements,* 1.13). As, in fact, he put it in the *Briefe,* without warrant from Aristotle's text, "the end of *Rhetorique* is victory; which consists in having gotten *beleefe*" (*Briefe,* 41, 41 n). His understanding, to use a modern linguistic term, was of language as pragmatics; he adhered to a rhetorical understanding of language and its power despite his hostility to eloquence.

This meant that how the world was presented in language assumed a far greater significance for Hobbes than it would have done to others who did believe that, for example, there was a direct access to truth against which language could be measured for deviance. Thus for

Hobbes, in a preconditional or inescapable sense we all operate in the world on opinions shaped by and expressed in language, we act on *"beleefe"*; but he also used "opinion" as a term referring to ill-founded, usually eloquence-induced belief. In *De cive,* for example, a discussion of the internal causes of the collapse of government is a catalog of opinions and beliefs he considered seditious and erroneous. The argument is also prefaced with a general statement about action rendering it consistent with the movement of natural bodies. There must be a disposition internal to the actor or object, an external agent, and the action itself (*De cive,* 12). Since men are internally disposed to wayward behavior, the propagation or teaching of specific opinions causes them to believe certain things on which they act to the dissolution of the commonwealth. This, at one level, as we will see, is a very Thucydidean view of causation, not least because Hobbes had in mind the manipulation and misplacement of fears. It is also consistent with Hobbes's seeing rhetoric as, in the broadest sense, a branch of philosophy (*Leviathan,* 9.61).

Nevertheless, in the context of Hobbes's epistemology and ontology his whole argument might equally be called opinion designed to induce a firmer belief in obedience and a just fear of the sovereign. Such terms, however, are characteristically reserved for the powers of deliberative eloquence. In the word "opinion" is captured the compound sense of rhetoric/eloquence. As Quentin Skinner has pointed out, Hobbes's whole state of nature can be seen as a condition of redescriptive anarchy, or radical *paradiastole* (Skinner 1996, 338–42). We all play Humpty-Dumpty because we think we are in charge of our own words, we describe anything as we wish, the paradox being—and it is an expression of Hobbes's paradox of freedom—that we can persuade no one. In effect, we project private languages, marks that are never properly systems of public signs. Leaving the state of nature is opting for a linguistic order, creating a sovereign as an arbiter of meanings, of *paradiastole* and its limits. It is, I think, not too fanciful an extrapolation of the figure of the natural condition to see it as an exposé of the Olympian claims for rhetoric's creative powers to which the sovereign is the only response as the font and arbiter of eloquence.[9]

Hobbes's equivocation with respect to rhetoric and eloquence is important in a number of ways. First, it made it easy for him to claim that eloquence and philosophy can be consistent with each other (*Leviathan,* "Review and Conclusion," 483–84), which presupposes that they are in fact separate and indeed potentially in conflict. This is also a clear impression given in *Leviathan,* in which the almost arithmetically pure image of philosophy implies an opposition to eloquence: it is rhetoric misliked, a demonized means of delineating science. Conversely, he had held in the *Briefe* that the logician is the best rhetorician, rhetoric a portable means to an end, its enthymemes fundamentally respectable syllogisms, its examples philosophical inductions. Consistently with this, he would in *Leviathan* formally classify rhetoric next to logic as a branch of philosophy. This is altogether stronger than saying that, if well handled, rhetoric and philosophy can be made consistent with one another.

Second, the consequence for modern scholars, especially noting the color and passion of his style, his urgent exhortations, his mastery of metaphor and the tropes of eloquence, has been to see rhetoric everywhere, explaining all. But it is rhetoric in, of, and opposed to philosophy depending on context and the sense that seems most evident. Hence it provides no single key or solid foundation for understanding what attention to Hobbes as a plain philosopher has also failed to establish.[10]

Rhetoric and History

The unstable ubiquity of rhetoric is further shown if we turn to its other semantic neighbors, history and poetry. Rhetoric, as Hobbes argued in the *Briefe,* is very much a matter of finding the right examples, his short inductions. "*Proofes,* are in *Rhetorique,* either *Examples,* or *Enthymemes"* (*Briefe,* 40). And from the time of Aristotle, history was effectively a branch of rhetoric because it provided the principal source of examples. It was, to use Johann Vosius's famous summary expression, "philosophy teaching by example." Hence the importance Hobbes attached to Thucydides's *History,* which he commended and defended as eloquence of the written word for the reader to meditate upon (*History,* xxiii). It exemplified the powers of rhetoric and the difficulties of deliberation in a democracy. To extrapolate with the aid of what Hobbes made of Aristotle: Thucydides did not need to lecture on the matter, because the examples were an immediate and powerful form of proof. Hobbes had not needed to provide a lecture on the matter, either, because in presenting the *History,* he was not engaging in what he would call the arts of eloquence, but offering what did not require "the helpe of Art." He was proffering "*Witnesses, Evidences,* and the like, which we invent not, but make use of" (*Briefe,* 40). Thucydides was then a sort of witness, but had, somewhat awkwardly for Hobbes, himself been a creative one.

Thucydides's *History* had drawn attention to the distinctive power of deliberative eloquence in the Athenian Assembly. He used set speeches to explain changes of opinion and courses of action. Such highly crafted exhibitions of eloquence did not purport to be literal accounts of what had actually been said on any given occasion; they were rather hypothetical and imaginative accounts of how the world and its possibilities would have needed to have been presented to an audience to explain its later conduct. This pivotal explanatory device was not lost on Hobbes. Thucydides, he remarked, puts us in the assembly by his own great skill so that we can understand the issues of deliberation. He had what, indeed, is a feature of Hobbes's own style: a capacity to create a sense of immediacy. Thucydides thus wrote history that could act as an extension of our own experience, allowing us to draw out lessons for ourselves "and be able to trace the drifts and counsels of the actors to their seat" (*History*, vi).[11] Indeed, as Gabriella Slomp has recently argued, there was much in Thucydides that Hobbes found convincing and that shines through in his translation. Most important is what Slomp calls the "controlled fear" seen as the cornerstone of peace. Obliterated or untrammeled fear proves equally disastrous, and eloquence exploits it. Hobbes would never depart from this assessment.[12] That the whole war ended in disaster for Athens, that her conduct had been wayward, at times foolish, at others unjust, was explicable in terms of eloquence; and this is not anything that required a separate lecture, either from Thucydides or his translator. The facts and the chief witness, he would persuade us, speak for themselves.

Yet this is more problematic than it might seem. Hobbes's own translation sought to be powerful and immediate; the use of modern political terms such as "state" for polis brought Thucydides into the present, and Hobbes introduced his main witness with an eloquently structured essay on his life and authoritative status (Skinner 1996, 244). This could hardly have been coincidental. It is clear that by putting the translation on the market after it "had lay long by me" (*History*, vii), Hobbes was attempting to help extend the experience of his countrymen, not least with respect to the potentialities of eloquence. He was fighting fire with Greek fire. The year of publication was singularly appropriate. In 1629 Charles's relationships with his Parliament were disintegrating in acrimony, distrust, and above all mutual fear; eloquent opposition presented as counsel would push him in directions he did not like and it was certainly possible for the prejudiced eye to see the Parliament as some sort of hostile and unruly democratic assembly.[13]

Much later in *Leviathan* Hobbes would express a view seemingly consistent with his earlier but compromised theory of history by remarking that in "good History, the Judgment must be eminent; because the goodnesse consisteth, in the Method, in the Truth, and in the Choyse of the actions that are most profitable to be known. Fancy has no place but only in adorning the stile" (*Leviathan*, 8.51). I will return to this comment in the context of Hobbes's understanding of poetry, but meanwhile it is evident that the notion of rhetoric is made very difficult by its ambivalent relationship to history that can be included in rhetoric (a profitable choice of actions and exemplary proofs) and excluded from any art of eloquence (it is not invented and fancy finds no place). But as we will see, the evocation of a concept of fancy will not in the end help matters.

Given the slippage between rhetoric, philosophy, and eloquence, one cannot expect the relationship between history and philosophy to be as simple as first meets the eye. In its most beguilingly obvious formulation, history was seen by Hobbes and many others as a register of facts from which we might learn. These might be facts about nature or humanity. History itself was not philosophy, neither in certainty nor scope, though it might provide a reservoir of examples the philosopher might use. At the same time, history had been seen as a branch of rhetoric, or more precisely a resource for different forms of eloquence. A historian like Thucydides was a rhetorician, so the status of history as a form of discourse was uncertainly located between philosophy and rhetoric. In many ways, Hobbes's views on history were conventional and express a widespread double ambivalence much explored in the sixteenth and seventeenth centuries and still with us. On the one hand, history is by turns claimed to be autonomous and subordinate to other moral ends. On the other, history is either the events of the past, Hobbes's register of fact, or it is what historians have done with this register by selecting, describing, accounting for, and analyzing the evidence they have. It is in this latter process that any mere register of facts is transformed into something that might be construed as philosophy, rhetoric, or both.

Not surprisingly Hobbes's own forays into history have a variable status within the unstable modality of his own intellectual world. If one rejects Hobbes's claim that there can be artless evidence, just the presentation of fact, it is easy to see a rhetorical dimension to history, but even if one accepts the literal Hobbesian doctrine of history as a register of fact, history may still easily be construed as rhetoric as Hobbes understood it. This accounts, for example, for Hobbes's highly ambivalent attitude to the inheritance of antiquity. Much as he loved its poetry and delighted in its languages, knowledge of it had been dearly bought. Its rhetorical potential for destabilization was unparalleled; antique authors had been given great authority and the recorded events of Greece and Rome were at once of the past and dangerously in the present as exempla of misunderstood liberty. So, we may say, for Hobbes, Thucydides had been among the few to glean the right rhetorical proof from history. Although Hobbes did not regard his own historical writings as eloquence, they were all examples and so rhetorical proofs. The *Historia ecclesiastica* was a proof of clerical corruption and an example of what can happen to any church and any religion when it is forsaken by its priests. The *Historical Narration Concerning Heresy* was a proof of the dangers of ancient philosophy contaminating early Christianity and an example of how a word becomes a political weapon. And that word is an example also of Hobbes's attempts to purge the resources of eloquence. In the end we are entitled to suspect something altogether more specific behind the formal subordination of history to philosophy. Histories, to put the matter a trifle unfairly, were apt to disagree with Hobbes's philosophical conclusions; one suspects that had they all been Thucydides, his image of Clio would have been considerably more elevated.

History, Rhetoric, and Philosophy in *Behemoth*

Behemoth, however, can be taken as perhaps the most instructive case of the problems in disengaging rhetoric, history, and philosophy from each other. Literally, Hobbes did not call it a history nor give it its familiar title. A single narrative history did not suit Hobbes's purposes, but a pirated edition was published as a history of the civil wars just after his death. It comprises four dialogues between *A* and *B*. Throughout, it is the function of *B* to ask questions and accept the answers of *A*. The first two dialogues deal with the development of the civil war; the final dialogues, "drawn out of Mr. Heath's Chronicle" (*Behemoth,* dedication to Lord Arlington), comprise an epitome of the war but are at one with the rest of the work. As a whole, *Behemoth* was a cautionary tale of civil disintegration and of the power of opinion, of the combustible nature of error conjoined with ambition and fear; as such, it exhibits conventional and long-standing beliefs that history should be relevant and instructive.

If "The Discourse on the Beginning of Tacitus" *(Three Discourses)* was by Hobbes, it had a generally similar point: to commend the relevance of Tacitus's analysis of the development of Augustan Rome from the

dregs of the Republic. But the salutatory lessons had been more dis-
persed and urbanely presented by the young Thomas than those found
in the histories of the old Hobbes. It is curious that in the aftermath of
civil war, a Tacitean image of politics with its characteristic *topoi* of interest, fear, and corruption is not more evident than it is in *Behemoth*. A
brief reference to Augustus (*Behemoth,* 3.115) might suggest a rough
parallel with Cromwell, but Hobbes makes nothing of it. Perhaps
Hobbes had ingested too well his own doctrines on the dangers of
ancient models. It is more likely that such a pattern of extraneous allusion might, to use Hobbesian imagery from a different context, call up
spirits difficult to control in the interests of the present fragile regime
(see "The Poet and the Rhetor" in this chapter). Be this as it may,
because of his close attention to social insecurity and causation, *Behemoth*
is like Hobbes's translation of the work of Thucydides, "the most poli-
tick historiographer that ever wrote." And Hobbes clearly wanted *Behemoth* printed for much the same reason as he made his translation public.
Each work was significant evidence of the language-induced precarious-
ness of civilization. To recall, Hobbes had particularly commended
Thucydides for his capacity to make the past immediate, a sort of extension of our own experience, thus rendering exhortatory lectures about it
supererogatory. And, similarly suggesting that history is a sort of register of communal memory, he wrote in the preface to *Behemoth,* "There
can be nothing more instructive towards loyalty and justice than will be
the memory, while it lasts, of that war" (*Behemoth,* dedication to Lord
Arlington).

   The style of *Behemoth* is unelaborate, appropriate to the presentation
of the rhetorical proofs of evidences and witnesses (*Briefe,* 40). Hobbes
resiliently resists the imaginative possibilities the device of a dialogue
put at his disposal. *A* and *B* are more austerely scholastic; they are
author functions used simply to get the issues clear and the evidence
down. Despite this, *Behemoth* is nevertheless not a bare register of facts
and if an exercise in history, it is not history as Hobbes's conception of
history would seem to require it to be. It is partially in narrative form,
but it narrates different themes according to the questions that *B* asks
A. In *Leviathan* Hobbes had claimed that history requires the predomi-
nance of judgment, by which he meant discrimination and discretion.
Although this may be a feature of *Behemoth,* the work is conspicuously
marked by judgment in the different sense of bringing down moral ver-
dicts upon the actors. These occur sometimes without any show of evidence, as when *B* remarks "I have seldom heard the word *justice* occur in

their sermons" (*Behemoth*, 2.63). More often they arise plausibly in the narrative, not principally because the facts have been selected but because of Hobbes's own preparatory choice of descriptive language concerning those involved.

Consider the following on the suspicions generated by Charles I's queen Henrietta-Maria: "*B*. Strange injustice! The Queen was a catholic by profession, and therefore could not but endeavour to do the Catholics all the good she could: she had not else been truly that which she professed to be. But it seems they [unspecified enemies of the king] meant to force her to hypocrisy, being hypocrites themselves. Can any man think it a crime in a devout lady, of what sect soever, to seek the favour and benediction of that Church whereof she is a member?" (*Behemoth*, 2.61). Hobbes is here pleading a case before the "bar of history," a metaphorical slide into forensic eloquence. Again, in more detail, the very character of Thomas Wentworth, earl of Strafford, as described by Hobbes makes the charges against him questionable and in need of explanation (*Behemoth*, 2.65). Such a man was surely innocent. Similarly, in the third and fourth dialogues, the chronicle materials are redescribed to reinforce the instructive themes: "*B*. What silly things are the common sort of people, to be cozened as they were so grossly! *A*. What sort of people, as to this matter, are not of the common sort? The craftiest knaves of all the Rump [Parliament] were no wiser than the rest. . . . For the most of them did believe that the same things which they imposed upon the generality, were just and reasonable." We are back with the etiological centrality of belief and opinion (*Behemoth*, 4.158; compare *Leviathan*, 30.233). This delusion was especially marked, *A* continues, in those who had learning whose negative ideas on monarchy had been taken from "Cicero . . . and other politicians of Rome, and Aristotle of Athens, who seldom speak of kings but as of wolves" (*Behemoth*, 4.158). The counterpoint between *A* and *B* is more than a means of rehearsing Hobbes's hostility to Aristotle and Cicero. It becomes a mechanism for presenting a typically provoking paradox about who really are the common people, who are guilty. In short, if we look for an example of what Hobbes calls history, it comes within the ambit of what he had understood rhetoric to be and for this it does not need to be more than occasionally eloquent.

More than this, however, what has attracted scholars to *Behemoth* as history is its strong sense of causation, which in Hobbesian terms makes the history as much philosophical exemplification as it is rhetorical eloquence. And the causative structure is much as it had been set down in

De cive: inherent disposition in conjunction with external force causes a specific reaction or form of behavior. The narrative sections provide accounts of the behavior described in such a way as to make plausible the inferences of dispositions and external pressures upon them. This is Hobbes moving from known effects to hypothesized causes in a way that makes the whole work philosophy, the whole civil war a fit subject for a resoluto-compositive method. Most of this mass of hypothesized causation, we should hardly be surprised, is more specifically a matter of dubious motivation and opinion or belief leading to disaster and injustice. This is illustrated simply enough from the passage just quoted on the Rump Parliament. *B*'s innocent prejudice about the common people becomes an explanation; paradoxically we are all potentially common people in this way, especially the uncommonly well educated from the universities. Damage to the monarchy and confusion about what really is justice had been brought about by exposure to dangerous beliefs inherited from antiquity. It was not, concludes *A,* lack of wit that made people "silly things." You will not persuade "a subtle lawyer," an "eloquent orator," or a "ravishing poet,—all three types sat in the Parliament—that he has no wit.[14] What such men lacked "was the knowledge of the causes and grounds upon which one person has a right to govern, and the rest an obligation to obey." There was a "want of the science of justice" (*Behemoth,* 4.159–60).

Behemoth can be seen, then, as a set of philosophical dialogues about the power of eloquence working on ambitions and fears and at the same time as a persuasive work to teach the modern, Hobbesian science of justice. Even without eloquence, philosophy and rhetoric are two dimensions of the same historical discourse. Here, incidentally, emerges another parallel with Hobbes's translation of Thucydides. Just as the translation put before English readers is an image of Athens as a horrible warning, so in occasional outbursts that had marked Hobbes's more formal political theories, the authority of antiquity is seen as a cause of philosophical and civic confusion. In this way, albeit sporadically, *Behemoth* sided very clearly in the rhetorical battle between ancients and moderns. Despite, then, Hobbes's assertive modal demarcations, *Behemoth*'s appearance of being driven by causal analysis does not stop its also being rhetoric and history. The problem with Hobbes's rhetoric, eloquence, and history lies less with his practice than with the incoherence of his delineations of the intellectual world, which his practice could only exhibit.

Rhetoric to the Rescue of Public Philosophy?

Excepting the translation of Thucydides, Hobbes's essays on human history are all late works and so seem to confound the old view of a simple linear development away from Renaissance humanism toward modern science. They also give some support to the notion that Hobbes, having rejected rhetoric for science in his relative youth, returned to it. This apparent trajectory has been explained in different ways in important studies by David Johnston and Quentin Skinner. Johnston has emphasized the austerity of *The Elements of Law,* which was intended for manuscript circulation among a small, scientifically literate audience, and how by contrast *Leviathan* is dramatically rhetorical, a work designed for a public that could not live by science alone.[15] Johnston is apt to use rhetoric in a very general sense, focusing on the end of persuasion rather than on the specifics covered by eloquence. Skinner has explored in detail Hobbes's understanding of eloquence and his considered use of its tropes and figures, especially in *Leviathan.* His conclusion is that Hobbes came to believe that it was not possible to convince men by science alone; eloquence was a necessary evil of packaging. The optimism coming with the discovery of science was worn away to be replaced by a pessimism that took Hobbes back to a reliance on the Renaissance and ancient art of eloquence.[16]

There can be no doubt that Hobbes could think he had failed to get his science across to those who needed it. In *Behemoth* the question is asked why men cannot be taught "the science of *just* and *unjust* as divers other sciences have been taught from true principles and evident demonstration; and much more easily than any of those preachers and democratical gentlemen could teach rebellion and treason" (*Behemoth,* 1.39). To which it is bleakly replied, "But who can teach what none have learned? Or, if any man have been so singular, as to have studied the science of justice and equity; how can he teach it safely, when it is against the interest of those that are in possession of the power to hurt him?" (*Behemoth,* 1.39). From what I have argued, it should be clear that Johnston and Skinner focus on complementary and overlapping aspects of the rhetoric/eloquence problem in Hobbes, and so come to differing conclusions. But rhetorical proofs, historical examples, are found even in *The Elements of Law* and *De cive,* his most scientific works on politics. And *The Elements of Law* is additionally noteworthy for a sustained metaphor. In the form of a 25-line catechism, Hobbes likened the passions to an imagined race in which there is no other goal than "being foremost" (*Elements*, 1.9.21). It ends with the lines, "Continually to be outdone is misery. Continually to out-go the next before, is felicity. And to forsake the course, is to die."

The notions of rhetoric and eloquence, especially in their relationships to history as well as philosophy, may be too slippery to allow any neat movement through Hobbes's stages of development. The quotation from *Behemoth*, however, might superficially allow a further possibility, that the use of eloquence is tied to an increasing sense of persecution. Such a neo-Straussian hypothesis may run thus: Hobbes tried to teach science (*Elements* and *De cive*), feared persecution, so dressed his lessons in a coating of eloquence to make them acceptable (*Leviathan*). Uneloquent *Behemoth* was itself publicly unacceptable, at least so Charles II feared, and Hobbes dutifully did not publish it. Such a theory, however, begs the question of whether there is any clear-cut change. If in the past *Leviathan* has been rendered too scientific, there is danger now in paying the same compliment to *The Elements of Law* in order to illustrate how rhetorical *Leviathan* really is! A persecution hypothesis seems doubly implausible in a way that neither the Johnston nor Skinner theses is. The sense, and it was real enough, of persecution comes after and largely in response to the most eloquent of Hobbes's political works, *Leviathan,* which then had some of its tricks of eloquence removed when Hobbes translated it into Latin. As I have sought to indicate, *Behemoth* may not be marked by a high and obvious eloquent stylistic adornment but it certainly has a rhetorical dimension and pretty much as Hobbes's *Briefe* would have understood it: it is a use of evidences for a clearly persuasive end, to achieve a victory for the king and for peace in "having gotten beleefe" about immediate history (*Briefe,* 41).

We are left, I think, with the following incomplete and untidy picture: Hobbes did alter his style, his art, depending on his sense of audience, be it a semiprivate manuscript-reading one, a broad and unknown public one, an English- or a Latin-reading one. He did also claim to have lost faith in the possibility of teaching justice and equity by science alone. But he also carried with him ambivalences and confusions in his understanding of rhetoric to make any clear pattern of linear change for any single reason difficult and unnecessary to sustain. It may be better to see his works marked more by shifting emphases between inadequately distinguished dimensions of discourse than to see such dimensions as separate and assignable to periods of development. On this score it might also be noted that when Hobbes wrote *Leviathan,* he had hardly written anything, excepting translations intended to be published in English, so secure points of comparison for shifts in an English public style are difficult to find.

The Problem of Poetry

Hobbes also carried with him to the end a love of Homer to match his affection for Thucydides, and his appreciation of poetry adds the final complicating dimension to his understanding of rhetoric. As I have suggested, Hobbes lived in a world in which the intellectual respectability of rhetoric was under question and in which it was increasingly reduced to a moveable art of elaboration (see "Rhetoric, Eloquence, and Philosophy" in this chapter). In this way, it might seem that effectively the last refuge for rhetoric was within poetry. A great deal has been written on the self-conscious adaptation of rhetoric to poetry, especially among metaphysical poets whose works were often self-contained exercises in argumentative eloquence and metaphorical ingenuity. Marvell's exquisite "To His Coy Mistress" is in this sense an elaborate enthymeme. But the poet's function, philologically related to that of the rhetor, was both an intellectually and religiously august one. In sixteenth- and seventeenth-century terms there was nothing unduly pretentious in claiming that the rhetor or the poet might vie with the philosopher or the historian as an arbiter of truth. Sir Philip Sidney had made the case at length.[17] As we might expect, given the insecure distinctions within Hobbes's intellectual conspectus of the world, his work is something of a microcosm of the fluid status of poetry, at once distinct but not separate from its surroundings. An obvious identity, it is almost impossible to contain it within the contours of a map. Poetry was more than a form to which other intellectual pursuits such as religious devotion, husbandry, or philosophy might shape themselves, but less than an autonomous intellectual perspective on the world like theology or law or geometry; the sense of the aesthetic was always alchemically mixed with the moral.

When Hobbes provided his *Briefe* of Aristotle's *Rhetoric,* he transposed some material from the *Poetics,* and because so much of the *Rhetoric* is concerned with style, meter, ornamentation, and metaphor and is illustrated from poets such as Homer (e.g., *Briefe,* 115–16), the dividing line between poetry and rhetoric can be most uncertain. Hobbes's early Latin poem *De mirabilibus pecci* (c. 1636) is extraordinarily rich and metaphorically resonant. It is at once a symbolic country house poem, most famously exemplified by Marvell's "Upon Appleton House," and an elaborate epideictic celebration of the Cavendish heartland of the Peak district of Derbyshire. Full of allusion to classical poets, it assimilated Derbyshire to the ancient Mediterranean, and by implication bestowed a mythic heroic significance on the Cavendish family, not without wit and exploitation of the scatalogical potential suggested by the Peak district. In addition, it carried a dark undercurrent of concern about the transience of life and fame and the corruption of achievement and purity. It has proven largely resistant to effective translation, but seems to have been much appreciated during the seventeenth century, though not, it seems, by Hobbes. Much later, his *Historia ecclesiastica,* which has an undeniably direct and typical anticlerical deliberative force, also took verse form, even though Hobbes called it history. Late in life he translated Homer, which involved a poetic creativity as much as poetic replication. Shortly before Hobbes died he wrote a three-stanza love poem that John Aubrey quotes in full in his "Life." It begins:

> Tho' I am now past ninety, and too old
> T' expect preferment in the Court of Cupid

and ends

> Thinke not the man a Fool tho he be old
> Who loves in Body fair, a fairer mind.
>   (Aubrey, 237)

Throughout his life poetry was by no means incidental to Hobbes, but, being Hobbes, it was important to theorize about what he loved. His ideas on the nature of poetry have commonly been held to be part of the shift toward an ordered Augustan sensibility and so in their own terms are important. They are set down most clearly in *The Answer to the Preface before Gondibert.* In this we see the relationships between rhetoric and philosophy are further complicated by Hobbes's understanding of the poetic imagination.

The *Answer* is formally a thanks and address to Hobbes's friend Sir William Davenant (1606–1668) and a compliment to his epic poem *Gondibert,* which would be left unfinished because its author apparently got bored with the enterprise. This might seem to make Hobbes's flattering tribute fall flat on its face, especially as Davenant's own judgment to stop rather than Hobbes's encouragement to finish has been the one commended ever since. While Davenant would turn more suc-

cessfully to opera, Hobbes would be tetchily embarrassed by his effu-
sive praise of what contemporaries considered execrable verse.[18]
Hobbes's *Answer* is an urbane, polished piece, marked by the disingenuous modesty characteristic of works written with one eye on the
addressee and the other on the public world. It was effectively a letter
unlike Hobbes's more genuinely private correspondence. It was written
around the same time that Hobbes was writing *Leviathan,* and
deployed, though somewhat differently, some of the same conceptual
distinctions. Care, however, is needed in making direct comparisons,
for as Miriam Reik has remarked, the *Answer* had no pretensions to
being a piece of formal philosophy.[19]

The *Answer* begins by the author's disclaiming any pretension to
poetic capacity, and then through the medium of a flattering address
specifies the roles and qualities of poetry for the wider public. "I never
yet saw poem," Hobbes exclaims, "that had so much shape of art, health
of morality, and vigour and beauty of expression, as this of yours." The
only thing stopping it becoming as renowned as the *Iliad* or *Aeneid* is
that these were written in immutable languages, a fate unlikely for any
modern tongue (*Answer,* 456). His hyperbolic assessment, and the mirth
it would generate among Restoration wits, is not the point. Rather, the
question is what for Hobbes constituted poetry, good poetry, and how
well this fits with his adjacent ideas of rhetoric, philosophy, and history.[20]

Initially we find a firm distinction between philosophy and poetry,
the former concerned with natural causes, the latter with human manners (*Answer,* 445). This is at one with what was being developed in
Leviathan, neither poetry nor history is found in the table of sciences
(*Leviathan,* 9). It is, however, rather unlike Hobbes to make such distinction in terms of subject matter. Poetry is then obscurely delineated
from prose. There are three main types of poetry (heroic, scommatic,
pastoral) and three structural forms (narrative, dramatic, comic). Not
everything in verse form is poetry, sonnets and epigrams being but parts
of a poem (*Answer,* 444). *Leviathan,* which after all has bigger fish to
catch, is altogether more brisk, referring only to epic, sonnets, and epigrams exemplifying poetry. In neither work was Hobbes much interested in poetic taxonomy. In the *Answer* his focus was more on establishing the qualities and responsibilities of the office of the poet, especially
the epic poet, through reference to the status of the ancient poet; and it
is this that allowed him to develop a subtheme on the misuse of language in the present. We are back with the problem of eloquence very
much more to the fore in *Leviathan.*

The Poet and the Rhetor

The result is to obscure the initially posited relationships between poetry, philosophy, and rhetoric. Poetry must exhibit decorum, treat its subject matter appropriately. There is no sense of untrammeled imaginative license. Singularity mars a work, though variety and novelty of imagery are to be commended (*Answer,* 453). Under such constraints, this is hardly the sense of originality we have now, but there is certainly some scope for creative figuration. Unnecessary ingenuity, however, to overcome purely self-inflicted "unprofitable difficulties, is great imprudence," as when poets make their lines conform to a physical shape (*Answer,* 446–47). Here there is a clear dismissal of the pattern poem, and probably George Herbert's development of it, one of the more baroque fancies of metaphysical poetry. Hence Hobbes's admiration for *Gondibert* being written relentlessly in lines of 10 syllables. Such criteria of excellence as decorum, invention, and rhythm deriving from the purpose of poetry are supremely illustrated by Davenant's work. The aim, specifically of the epic, is to celebrate, delight, and teach or adorn virtue by the presentation of exemplary figures. Such an understanding would lead Hobbes to sum up the virtues of epic in one word, discretion, consisting in the good order of all parts to the poet's design.[21] In such commendation of sober restraint we can see that there has been some sense in placing Hobbes with one foot on the road to Augustan theory, and, moreover, even some warrant for making him a figure of mechanical reductionism. More to the immediate point, however, the Hobbesian understanding of good poetry makes it little different from demonstrative eloquence, the celebratory display for the delight or edification of an audience and always appropriate to the subject matter; the funeral oration restrained by regret, the wedding speech or epithamalion exuberant with anticipation.

The coincidence of poetry and some forms of eloquence is reinforced by Hobbes's deliberate evocations of the role of the poet in ancient Greece. Poets were effectively teachers, men of divine and spiritual authority (*Answer,* 448). It was from the authority of the poet that the claims of the rhetor were derived, becoming self-proclaimed teachers of virtue and magicians of language. Hobbes does not make explicit the historical connection between the spiritual authority of the poet and the magic of the rhetor, but he does draw on the familiar association of magic and rhetoric that had been with him for a long time. In *The Elements of Law* he had referred to rhetoric without judgment as similar to

"the witchcraft of Medea, to cut the commonwealth in pieces" (*Elements,*
2.9.15.178).[22] In the *Answer* he evokes the ancient similitude once more
and turns it in a typically Hobbesian way against the dangerous eloquence of the present. In what appears to be an allusion either to Regi-
nald Scot's *The Discovery of Witchcraft* (1584) or Shakespeare's 1 *Henry IV,*
Hobbes comments on the danger sometimes to be feared from lack of
verbal skill. Incompetent conjurers "mistaking the rites and ceremo-
neous points of their art, call up such spirits, as they cannot at their
pleasure allay again; by whom storms are raised, that overthrow buildings, and are the cause of miserable wrecks at sea. Unskillful divines do
oftentimes the like; for when they call unreasonably for *zeal,* there
appears a spirit of *cruelty* . . . instead of *reformation, tumult* . . . Whereas in
the heathen poets . . . there are none of those indiscretions to be found,
that tended to the subversion, or disturbance of the commonwealth"
(*Answer,* 448). *Leviathan* too would unfavorably compare the spiritual
authority of the Christian priest with the heathen; the topos of magic
would be used extensively as means of satirizing the Catholic Church
and its abuse of priestly office (*Leviathan,* 47). In the *Answer,* however,
Hobbes returns immediately to what it is appropriate for a Christian
poet to use as ornamentation, rather than trying to speak through pure
inspiration "like a bagpipe" (*Answer,* 448).

Philosophy and the Poetic Imagination

Poetry, as it represents the human world, must be grounded in experience and this we have through memory. "For memory is the world,
though not really, yet so as in a looking-glass, in which the judgment,
. . . busieth herself in a grave and rigid examination of all the parts
of nature . . . registering . . . causes, uses, differences, resemblances"
(*Answer,* 449). Two things are important about this. First, Hobbes
accepted that a sense of poetic plausibility is culturally variant and so he
was far less rigid in his understanding of decorum than one might initially think (Reik, 140: Prokhovnik, 94). Newcastle would put the point
simply and powerfully: even a word like "white" will conjure up different patterns of association and so provoke different reactions depending
on education, experience, and disposition. It will not mean quite the
same thing to a gallant who will think of a lady and a pious man who
will imagine a surplice and soon be about his prayers with "holly Eiacu-
lations" (Cavendish, 82; compare *Elements,* 1.5.2).

Secondly, however, this is clearly to suggest that judgment embraces philosophy. As Reik correctly insists, the vocabulary of fancy, imagination, and wit was unstable during the seventeenth century and varied according to context in Hobbes's own arguments (Reik, 136–38). Hobbes postulated relationships between memory and fancy (imagination) in chapter 2 of *Leviathan*. Imagination, which the Greeks called fancy, is decaying sense; memory is effectively the same thing. In the "Review and Conclusion," however, fancy and judgment are taken as complementary, being used "but by turns" (*Leviathan*, review and conclusion, 483). The *Answer*, however, suggests a sort of continuum, of memory, the looking glass of reality, judgment, and *then* fancy. Given the serious responsibilities of poetry, it must be grounded in judgment, "whereby the fancy, when any work of art is to be performed, finds her materials to hand and prepared for use" (*Answer*, 449).

Art can be taken in two senses here—as specifically referring only to the arts, such as poetry and painting, which one would expect from the immediate context; or, as artifice, to any form of human activity, thus covering poetry and philosophy, architecture, mapmaking, and engine-building. If art is taken specifically, there is an incipient contradiction with the initial contrast between poetry and philosophy; for, to repeat, poetry must build on judgment and that can be philosophical. If taken more generally, fancy is not being used as a defining quality of poetry at all, but in the preconditional sense given early in *Leviathan*. Yet Hobbes writes immediately in the *Answer* of the celerity of fancy, a phrase also cropping up in *Leviathan* (*Leviathan*, "Review and Conclusion," 483), consisting largely of "copious imagery discreetly ordered . . . which most men under the name of philosophy have a glimpse of." The emphasis on imagery associates fancy strongly with poetry, while men's seeing fancy under the heading or name of philosophy indicates something more general and far more primordial, the very images that make the mind. This broader meaning of fancy is exploited immediately in a passage that is strongly reminiscent of chapter 13 of *Leviathan*. It is the fancy of man "that has traced the ways of philosophy, so far it hath produced very marvellous effects to the benefit of mankind" (*Answer*, 449). Hobbes proceeds to list engines, buildings, "the account of time, from walking on the seas," and whatever has distinguished the civilization of Europe from the barbarity of the American Indians. Fancy has done all this guided by true philosophy. Commenting on this, Raia Prokhovnik remarks not only on the similarity with Sidney but concludes that in joint operation poetry and philosophy create "the achievements of civility" (Prokhovnik, 95). Where precepts (presumably philosophical ones) fail, as hitherto they have in "the doctrine of moral virtue," then fancy must take on the philosophic role (*Answer,* 450).

Hobbes concludes the passage on fancy by saying that the epic poet whose fancy must be so well developed must be a philosopher, "to furnish and square the matter" (*Answer,* 450). Perhaps, one might think, to square the circle. For Hobbes seems here to be confounding not just what he began by saying in the *Answer* about philosophy as very different from poetry, but he is also contradicting his usual accounts of it in which precision of language and the exclusion of metaphor ("copious imagery discreetly ordered") seem to be fundamental. This is a matter that needs discussion in its own right (see chapter 8, "The Matter of Metaphor").

What is happening is that on the one hand Hobbes's notion of metaphor is potentially unstable; it was normally used as a marker of nonphilosophical discourse, yet occasionally Hobbes allowed it some philosophical function (*De corpore,* 2.12). On the other hand, the notion of fancy has become an ambiguous mechanism whereby poetry, rhetoric, and philosophy are becoming entangled. Hobbes draws no distinction between fancy as a principal characteristic of poetry as opposed to, or building on, judgment and/or philosophy, and fancy as the imaginative capacity to order sense impressions in which sense it must have a prior status to judgment and so ipso facto be a feature of all organized human ratiocination (see also *Elements,* 1.10.4). He does, however, distinguish simple from compound fancy, remembrance, and association. In chapter 2 of *Leviathan,* Hobbes introduces both words, imagination and fancy, but makes only a philological distinction—one is Greek, the other Latin— and then goes on to refine imagination into understanding and regulated trains of thought. Thus when Hobbes distinguishes between poetry and history in terms of differing balances of fancy and judgment (*Leviathan,* 8.51), it is not clear what this can amount to. For in one sense, as in the earlier passage of *Leviathan,* fancy must proceed and permeate judgment; but in another sense, present in the *Answer,* fancy is contingent on prior judgment by degrees. It is this sense that Hobbes seems to be introducing into chapter 8 of *Leviathan.* In the "Review and Conclusion," fancy has become a complement to judgment analogous to the strategic relationship between rhetoric and philosophy. Repairing to the *Answer* for clarification is not clinching, however, for there the vocabulary is even less discriminating and, as I have suggested, the terms memory, judgment, and fancy are related differently.

It is also apparent that the same unstable relationship between philosophy and rhetoric/eloquence holds for philosophy and poetry in virtue of the general and particular senses that fancy can carry. In one sense this is analogous to rhetoric, in another it is analogous to eloquence. Skinner's argument has been that by the time Hobbes came to write *Leviathan* he believed that philosophy could not succeed without the aid of eloquence. The *Answer* seems to suggest that where philosophy has failed as, according to Hobbes, it has in moral science, poetry has actually to take its place. Hobbes was not uniformly confident that political science had started properly with the publication of *De cive*. It also indicates that Hobbes's skepticism about philosophy was altogether more profound than attention to eloquence alone as an argumentative aid can make clear. It might also illustrate that Hobbes had not thought through the relationships between rhetoric and poetry and these muddy his sense of philosophy and what it can do in the world. Something more than or instead of philosophy was needed, but then everything he says erodes the distinction between a reified philosophy and that something else. The more general consequence is that the placement of Hobbes on the way to the ordered world of Augustan poetics, and the image of him as a spokesman for poetry so decorous and formulaic that it left no room for the imaginative inspiration, is itself grossly reductive. Still evident is a Jacobean classicism and a resonance of Renaissance poetics (Reik, 155, 157; Prokhovnik, 95). In the ambiguities of fancy lay the decaying sense of the metaphysicals and even some mental anticipation of the romantics.

The argument of the *Answer* shows that poetry can be perilously close to demonstrative rhetoric and claims that poetry itself must needs be philosophy. Usually Hobbes regarded philosophy as nothing more than the ordered activity of philosophizing, but in the *Answer* it is close to taking on an objectified identity independent of this, and this disembodiment creates the verbal illusion that the poet can be a philosopher without ceasing to be a poet. Even noting Hobbes's ambivalence about metaphor, the result is highly discrepant with his understanding of philosophy in terms of procedural method. And indeed in *De corpore* (*De corpore*, 1.3.4), he would point clearly enough to the philosophical error involved here, the creation of insignificant words by the mistaken projection of abstractions independent of their substantive characters. In modern parlance it is a form of reification or of category mistake. Hobbes's collapsing philosophy into poetry in the *Answer* is no flippant or thoughtless aside, for once it is possible for the poetic fancy to take the place of philosophy, the sort of objections that Hobbes would voice in *Leviathan* about bad philosophy become relevant to judging a poem. Just as he complained about the meaningless vocabulary of philosophy, he lamented the verbiage of so much of our language: so many words, "like the windy blisters of troubled waters, have no sense at all." As he had dismissed those philosophers who took their arguments from the authoritative books of the past, so he waved away those poets who rather than relying on "experience and knowledge of nature," take from books "the ordinary boxes of counterfeit complexion" (*Answer*, 453). Yet Hobbes himself seems now and then to allude to Shakespeare. As Davenant was allegedly Shakespeare's natural son, we may have here but an echoing conceit. When, however, he calls poets "painters" (*Answer*, 451) he is quoting the much quoted, a metaphor "defaced by time" "sullied with . . . long use" (*Answer*, 455).

A Return to First Reckonings

This may seem to have been an unduly convoluted chapter, but then its topics have been subject to some undue ironing out. After such complexities, however, the privilege of some oversimplification of my own by way of brief summary: in most isolated passages where Hobbes deals with rhetoric, history, or poetry, their relationships to each other and to philosophy, are probably clear and univocal enough. An overview of the broad range of his comments, however, reveals considerable shifts, and not always over significant periods of time and sometimes within a single work. The upshot appears to be something like this: In one sense rhetoric is a part of philosophy and in another is inimicable to it. In its turn, history is excluded from rhetoric; in another, it is a form of rhetorical proof. So history, in a way, can become philosophy, teaching by examples. Similarly, poetry is excluded from philosophy but in another the poet must be a philosopher. Eschewing problems of motivation in Hobbes, confusions and changes of mind, the mechanism for all these slippery relationships, is, ironically, an insufficiently discriminate conceptual vocabulary. It is this that has made it impossible to treat the topics of history, rhetoric, and poetry separately. The very terms rhetoric, history, and fancy carry differing patterns of meaning and association with respect to the relatively stable, because much more formally explored, concept of science or philosophy. Hobbes insisted that philosophy involved taking all words back to first reckonings, but what he taught or what he would persuade us and what he did were rather different things.

Beyond the immediate mechanism of his own conceptual vocabulary, one needs to recall what I have called Hobbes's official conspectus on the world (see chapter 2, "Sense Beyond Science"). This chapter has illustrated how his discussions of intellectual activities, their rules and relationships no less than juridical and religious practices, frequently shift into a concern with the offices of practitioners. Hobbes wrote as much of the poet or the rhetor as he did of poetry and rhetoric. In a world that delineated all social activity in terms of office, it was only to be expected that any one person was involved in complementary offices: a woman might simultaneously be parent, child, spouse, and trader. Naturally, this created problems but it carried with it a familiarity of multifaceted identity that might be taken into descriptions of the intellectual world as a tolerance of coalescent activities. Hobbes was always more than just one of those philosophers for whom he tried to legislate. He was no eclectic but perhaps in the end our more austere emphasis on philosophical coherence and the purity of intellectual demarcation, because we see him mainly as a philosopher, might, historically speaking, be excessive. This possibility needs to be borne in mind more than Reik's specific comment about the *Answer* that we should make allowances because it wasn't really philosophy (Reik, 146). The question becomes, what was Hobbes doing in *Leviathan*?

Chapter Seven
A View of *Leviathan*

Allegiance and Illegitimate Government

While Hobbes was peering out from Paris, *Leviathan* was printed in London by Andrew Crooke at the sign of the Green Dragon and it came like fire through the city smoke. After its initial appearance in 1651, *Leviathan* was reprinted twice during the century but with its original date of publication.[1] It has been something of a myth to see it as an unlooked-for and alien interjection into English debate. *Leviathan* descended in controversy and controversy has trailed it ever since. The elaborate presentation was a handsome costly folio. With its famous epitomizing artwork engraved by Abraham Bosse of Paris, probably from a drawing by Wensilaus Hollar,[2] it forewarned of the author's sense of occasion and self, a brisk old man with a substantial reputation, ready like Milton's Uriel to burn through the air, intellectually impatient, and in a hurry to be home.

Leviathan was written in what was probably a remarkably short time after the exiled Hobbes had fallen out of favor at the royalist court in France. Excepting two translations it was his first intended major work in his native tongue and was printed toward the end of the Engagement controversy with which it was henceforth uncomfortably associated. The political moment of its appearance is certainly of explanatory significance and in terms of the simplest gist of *Leviathan*'s cautionary exhortation to "keep a hold on nurse for fear of finding something worse," the Engagement controversy is the place to begin.

The controversy, however, was hardly unprecedented. Effectively, it was the second of a three-act public drama on the issues of oath-taking and allegiance that gave a certain rhythm to seventeenth-century upheaval. The first of these acts occurred in the early years of the century, when the issue of Catholic allegiance to the English Protestant throne had been crucial. An assassination plot (the infamous Gunpowder Plot of 1605) was followed in 1606 by the requirement for Catholics to take an oath of allegiance. This had to be sworn in the context of the Jesuit justification of equivocation in the interests of true reli-gion. An equivocation in this casuistic sense involved a clear statement, qualified or contradicted by a silent clause spoken only to God. No could mean Yes. Some theorists of equivocation excluded oath-taking, but how equivocal was the qualification? Indeed, the opponents of the Jesuits' theory (including many Catholics) regarded this doctrine as merely a euphemism for lying and thus not only as a cloak for disloyalty but also as a rationalization for the destruction of public language and so the trust that bound a society together.

Act two was played out between 1649 and 1651. Between 1648 and 1650 the House of Commons was purged of all members not support-ing Oliver Cromwell's army; Charles I was executed; the House of Lords was abolished. All vestiges of traditional government were replaced by a military junta with the support of a rump Parliament. Therein it was debated whether clerics, ministers of state, and others should be obliged to swear an oath of allegiance to the new commonwealth, or republic, to engage publicly with it by rejecting all previous allegiances. Demanding an engagement was intended to flush out traitors just as the earlier oath had been enforced to expose disaffected Catholics. Although the strat-egy was adopted, it was argued that such a requirement would be quite counterproductive. Malcontents would lie or equivocate when con-fronted with an oath, and others would be forced to a moral decision that otherwise could be avoided. The two-year Engagement controversy, 1649–1651, proved the skeptics had a point.[3]

On one side, some argued that might did not make right; oaths were sacred and the new regime could not be rendered legitimate by forcing ink on parchment; its power was usurped and tyrannically acquired, although there might be nothing that could be done about it. Con-versely, it was claimed that even conquest had a divine cause, that we were enjoined by the Bible to obey the higher powers (Romans 13), that the functions of government were to provide peace and security. If it did so obedience was due; it was not the prerogative of subjects to judge effective rulers. Usurpation had to be distinguished from tyranny in office, and so a new government must be given a chance; few regimes had not originated in some morally disquieting fashion; all oaths were contingent on circumstances. Those arguing in such terms, most notably Francis Rous, Anthony Ascham, and Marchmont Needham, were deemed de facto theorists, or Engagers. They were a mixed bag, by no means all of them personally committed to the new regime, and they drew on a rich if motley inheritance of argument. By stressing the contingencies that qualified oath-taking they were drawing on Jesuit and Protestant casuistry; by appealing to a sense of right, self-interest, and the functionality of office, they were giving further casuistic and quasi-Machiavellian advice to ordinary people when faced with the phenomenon of a new, illegitimate prince—what could such people be expected to do with a clear conscience? Complicating the debate was the question of who had the authority to guide consciences, the clerics or the laity (Sampson, 734). To the decidedly casuistic pamphlets put out by the laity may be added Andrew Marvell's "Horatian Ode on Cromwell's Return from Ireland," which told of Charles not calling for vindication of his "helpless right" and thus on the scaffold giving way before Cromwell who had come "burning through the air."[4]

Leviathan stands ambivalently with this group.[5] Hobbes was certainly seen as providing arguments at one with the Engagers. It is probable that the pirated edition of *The Elements of Law* and the anonymous translation of *De cive* were printed for the occasion. As they had been written in full awareness of the earlier allegiance controversy, their immediate relevance is hardly surprising; that they had been written by a known royalist may well have added piquancy to their appearance. The "Review and Conclusion" to *Leviathan* addresses the Engagement crisis by directly referring to the recent literature and it certainly gives support to the de facto case. While Hobbes would have it as an additional law of nature that a man should endeavor to support the authority that has protected him in peace, once conquered he is obliged to submit to another, and the point of obligation occurs when he has liberty to consent expressly or tacitly. When a legitimate ruler can no longer effectively protect, his office of rule is ended and the "Enemy" may assume the position of protector. Conquest is the acquisition of a right (*Leviathan,* review and conclusion, 484–85) through the consent of the vanquished. Here Hobbes's general doctrine of motivational indifference has a specific legitimizing force: the motivations, such as fear or ambition, that might explain our actions in consenting do not compromise the liberty of choice in consenting.

In this way, Hobbes's arguments undercut any later rationalized disloyalty by claiming consent under duress. His argument about conquest may well have been formulated as a defense of Charles I against the assertion that the monarchy was based on the conquest of 1066, but in 1651 its reaffirmation had a very different force. As had been the case in *De cive,* Hobbes was also unmoved by accusations of tyranny whether in the acquisition or exercise of power. There are almost no states in the world "whose beginnings can in conscience be justified," (*Leviathan,* review and conclusion, 486) and the name tyranny is nothing more than a term for sovereignty (*Leviathan,* "Review and Conclusion," 486). One of the problems he held, quite simply, has been that new regimes try to rely on needless justifications, derived from what they see as their own special virtues and thus bequeath rhetorics of justification suited to future rebellion when those qualities are lacking. All that is necessary is a regime's capacity to secure peace and then maintain protection for its subjects (*Leviathan,* review and conclusion, 486). As Marvell concluded his Horatian Ode, "The same arts that did gain / A power, must it maintain" (Marvell, ll. 119–20).

It is likely that the "Review and Conclusion" was added or amended to address the issues of the Engagement, but it is nevertheless generally at one with the exhortatory dimension of much of the work preceding it. That itself is consistent with Hobbes's earlier political writings that were now eddying in the controversy. Hobbes's persistence in maintaining that sovereign power may take many forms provided the general auspices under which the new regime might settle itself. This would have been aided by his predominantly functional emphasis in analyzing the office of rule and by his longstanding view that oaths added little to commitments exhibited through consent.

At the same time, certain typical de facto arguments are absent from *Leviathan* and others are expressed so generally that their point must be seen as altogether more universal in scope. The de facto literature, quite a bit issuing from clergymen whose livings were at stake, proffered providential arguments: conquest was ultimately the work or punishment of God. "'Tis madness to resist or blame / The force of angry heaven's flame" (Marvell, ll. 25–26) This was an escatological pathway Hobbes was reluctant to tread. The whole force of his arguments in *Leviathan* was to undermine the clergy as an independent source of advice on public issues. Yet where, for example, Anthony Ascham emphasized the practical difficulties in the way of ordinary people judging their rulers, because of their lack of access to the motivations for seeking power,[6] Hobbes argued in the main body of *Leviathan* that on principle there should be no such judgment; insofar as rulers manage to rule, their subjects have actually authorized their actions—a point that applied to ordinary and extraordinary people alike. It is, in fact, the latter whom Hobbes regarded as the most dangerous to authority (*Leviathan,* 30.233; see also chapter 6, "History, Rhetoric, and Philosophy in *Behemoth*" in this volume). Such a line of argument was to condemn the initial rising against the king far more than it was to accept the fait accompli of Cromwell's embryonic regime. Implicitly, it was also to criticize all those who had given only qualified support to Charles. It was a doctrine that was bound to leave very few feeling happy. There is also the occasional note of ambivalence: Hobbes could insist that a sovereign's right does continue to exist even when in Marvell's terms it was "helpless," but that under such circumstances, the erstwhile subjects are entitled to seek protection from another. Such a sense of lingering legitimacy does not fit well with Hobbes's predominant functionalism and suggests a reluctant and almost euphemistically expressed support of the Commonwealth. His actually presenting Charles II with a copy of *Leviathan* just after the young monarch's ignominious defeat at Worcester adds a further complication to any neat ideological positioning.

After the Restoration of Charles II in 1660, Hobbes would vehemently deny having been any sort of supporter of the de facto regime of Cromwell. This has created further confusion as to *Leviathan*'s political meaning in 1651. But there is a sense in which Hobbes's denials were quite understandably disingenuous. Certainly, as he always asserted, he was by conviction a supporter of the Stuart monarchy. The emblem of fitting loyalty and proper civic virtue was Sidney Godolphin, Hobbes's dear friend killed in a early skirmish of the Civil War by "an undiscerned and undiscerning hand" (*Leviathan*, "Review and Conclusion," 484) and to whose memory *Leviathan* was dedicated. If all had been as loyal as Godolphin there could have been no war and no need for *Leviathan*. It seems most plausible also to suggest that one reason for Hobbes putting forward a form of de facto argument in *Leviathan* was, as he later maintained, to encourage his aristocratic (and now impoverished) friends, such as the Cavendish family, that having fought for the king loyally they could now submit to the victors with honor and to expedite settlement. If this was the force of Hobbes's plea, however, it was only applied awkwardly to his closest surviving royalist friends. Newcastle, in particular, one of Charles I's generals, had walked out in a huff long before the king's cause was lost. This was a gesture hardly consistent with what Hobbes would have as a law of nature—for every man to support an embattled sovereign in war *"as much as in him lieth"* (*Leviathan*, "Review and Conclusion," 484). Hobbes had actually made this point (*Leviathan*, 14), but not with the italicizing insistence of calling it a law of nature. So for the sake of honor and appearance, it might have seemed that by 1651 Newcastle had to show himself irrationally loyal to the defunct monarchy—the costs of which would have been horrendous.

Thus at one level, the work may have been something of a palliative against an overreactive emotional adherence to a "helpless right." If so, the presentation copy to Charles may have carried the casuistic recommendation that the king accommodate himself to his father's executioners. But then again, Hobbes's diminution of the significance of formal oaths undermined the oath of Engagement—those swearing it could well submit to a future king. Be this as it may, the entailment of Hobbes's irenicism was exactly what he would later wriggle away from: the acceptance of the new regime because it was indisputably the de facto power (Burgess 1990, 676–78).

On a less personal level, the force of Hobbes's definitionally functional expressions of sovereignty theory, his apparently casual attitude to conquest, his attempts to purge the political vocabulary of tyranny, all left him a hostage to fortune. If a language without injustice, arbitrary rule, and tyranny was bound to support the sovereign status of Charles I, the absence of such an accusative repertoire of terms would hardly disadvantage his conquering successors. Thus once the old regime had been newly restored in 1660, anything smacking of fellow-travelling with the Cromwellian commonwealth could look like disloyalty. Hobbes's enemies were not slow to exploit this and underline the paradoxical weakness of de facto theory in general, classifying it as casuistry and reveling in the anticasuist's casuistry; he was, Bishop Bramhall sneered, "an Excellent Casuist" (Sampson, 773).

Hobbes had been acutely perceptive in suggesting that elaborate rationalizations for the illegitimate acquisition of power become sites of rhetorical vulnerability. But his minimalist alternative appeared brittle in an insecure world. As soon as a regime was perceived as running into difficulties, there was some color of reason for changing sides and so weakening a rule that with less rational support might survive. Hobbes had tried to counter such perceptions with his insistence that every man support the sovereign as long as humanly possible, but he himself had been one of the first to run away as Charles I's political crisis deepened in 1640. The later satiric image of "the vicar of Bray" is testimony enough to the deep-seated suspicion of de facto allegiance, which could be seen as loyalty all the time it wasn't needed. Hence during the Restoration, Hobbes had to waste his energies on denying Cromwellian sympathies or rewriting the political force of *Leviathan* and maintaining his loyalty.

Within 10 years of his death the third repetitive act of allegiance and oath-taking was played out following James II's flight from England

and the assumption of power by a William and Mary backed by an invading Dutch army. This crisis of allegiance saw the reprinting of earlier Engagement controversy literature and the metaphorical birth of the Vicar of Bray. Had he lived, Hobbes would have been caught up in it all over again, as was his reputation and the image of *Leviathan*. His final fragment on sovereignty, which I have suggested provided a little-noticed escape clause for inconvenient loyalty in the case of the dissolution of the monarch, indicates that his enemies were not entirely wide of the mark (see chapter 4, "Between Conventionality and Revolution"). In the last analysis, and *Leviathan* is the most telling instance of this, Hobbes's own emotional and personal loyalty to the Stuarts did come second to an intellectual allegiance to the concept of sovereignty. In this way, the argument of *Leviathan* went well beyond and could only partially be bent to the needs of any competing political faction or governmental form. It is a point that holds for applications and critiques of *Leviathan* held in the academic courts of quasi-history. The work was less about the specifics of legitimacy than the generalities of explanation. The law of nature requiring us to seek peace in conjunction with our own interests in doing so provided for Hobbes an overriding injunctive force; expressed in 1651 it had of necessity a Cromwellian implication. What for Hobbes was an unpleasant corollary was misleadingly reduced by his point-scoring enemies to the totality of his teaching.

The Philosophic Thread

Leviathan did not feed merely on a doctrine of obedience. It is also something of a manifesto and a qualified application of Hobbes's developing scientific theories. The work, especially in part 1, interlaces an explicit emphasis on all the features of Hobbes's conception of philosophy with a scientific account of the generation of political society from a causal analysis of human nature. The argument nevertheless does not consistently follow a singular method. It is not as austere as *The Elements of Law*, definition is ad hoc, and opinion is now divided as to how far Hobbes actually applies resoluto-compositive methods he advocated as so central to genuine science. *Leviathan* is formally divided into four parts, excluding the review and conclusion: "Of Man," "Of Commonwealth," "Of A Christian Common-wealth," and "Of The Kingdome of Darknesse." Although an analytic-synthetic method is not uniformly manifest through parts 3 and 4, it can be seen as explaining the conceptual structure of the whole through which the chapters are numbered consecutively. Resoluto-compositive methods generally started with a complex problematic identity, then analyzed its constituent parts and synthesized them imaginatively in a way that explained the nature of the whole. And, especially for Hobbes, the process could be presented from cause to effect, or vice versa.

Expressed in these general terms, *Leviathan* does fit well enough, once we recognize that the problematic identity is neither human nature nor the state, but any corrupt or potentially unstable Christian commonwealth described in part 4. Hobbes's world was made up of such societies, all of them priest-ridden; so the problematic beginning, that which needs explaining, may be seen as actually outlined as an effect in part 4. The final four chapters focus on what Hobbes took to be the principal destabilizing aspects of Christianity in their most robust and virulent forms. To be sure, the attention is to Catholicism; but this was the ascendant form of Christianity, certainly a danger to Protestantism as Hobbes had long believed. The dangers, however, were implicit in all organized forms of Christianity. So reading backwards, part 3 is an attempt to specify the legitimate features of a Christian Commonwealth, to think away excrecenses, and is thus an analysis of Christianity's component parts once the corruption has been discarded from the terms of reference. Part 2 is an analysis of the Commonwealth once religion has been put to one side. Part 1 is an analysis of the components of a Commonwealth, including the human drive to religious belief, and it begins with an account of the hypothesized patterns of endeavor that move men to form it, drives and passions that implicitly are just as relevant to explaining the kingdom of darkness with which the work ends.

The general structure of *Leviathan* offers, then, a sort of symbolic Galilean trajectory, a description of causative movement. Or, as he would summarize matters in *De corpore* 4. 25.1, one proper method of philosophy is to proceed "from effects or appearances to some possible generation of the same." Greater symbolic resonance is provided by Harvey's Paduan proof of the circulation of the blood and the function of the heart, with all its capacity to draw on and reshape the figurative associations of the human for the political body (see chapter 2, "Definition, Resolution, and Composition"). Hobbes explicitly synthesizes the mechanical and organic in the introduction. Wheels and tissues, springs and nerves are all matter in motion and so equally subject to definition and the causative analysis of their movements.

As I have suggested, methods of causative resolution and composition are contingent upon rigorous definition (see "Definition, Resolution, and Composition"). *Leviathan* espouses this doctrine with extremity. Words must be taken back to first reckonings. Science is knowledge of the consequences of words (*Leviathan*, 7.48). "But if the first ground of such Discourse, be not Definitions; or if the Definitions be not rightly joyned together into Syllogismes, then the End or Conclusion is . . . OPINION" (*Leviathan*, 7.48). All of this fits firmly enough with Hobbes's more detailed accounts of science, but acts more as a guiding aspiration for *Leviathan* than a persistent practice. It is noteworthy, for example, that although Hobbes does not depart from the view that geometry is paradigmatic of philosophical reasoning, the imagery and exemplification of the reasoning process is from the most elementary mathematics with which any reader could be expected to be familiar. Reasoning is computation, casting accounts, adding and subtracting. Right reasoning as easy as $1 + 1 = 2$ is a claim that implicitly ridicules the word-mongers of bogus inherited philosophy. Yet the example is also philosophically apposite. What definitional practice we have is similarly nominal. Definition is the arbitrary imposition of stability on orders of interrelated words; it is for this reason that so many definitions are set down in clusters at the outset and on inspection create a distinct air of circularity.

With these comments in mind, one can appreciate why the work starts where it does with a set of hypothesized causes for known effects. It begins not with the full malfunctioning edifice of a body politic but with the microscopic matter that explains both how and why a commonwealth is formed and how it always carries the seeds of its destruction. Hobbes commences with the moving matter of individual human beings, with the concepts of sense and imagination in the individual, putting forward his doctrines that we understand not by directly grasping realities but by processing impressions. We order these internally into trains of imagination (*Leviathan*, 3). Speech, our greatest invention, allows us to communicate these trains of imagination and thus create shared patterns of anticipation. At its highest, and most rigorously organized, speech culminates in science.

This central point of composition from the resolution of society into people and people into passions is superbly captured in the frontispiece.[7] In fact, this pictorial epitome might also be seen in Hobbesian terms as a demonstration of his case, for it is a visual putting forth of the argument (see chapter 2, "Definition, Resolution, and Composition"). *Leviathan* is an artificial man whose body is composed of a chain mail of human bodies. It is thus not merely evocative of Harvey's scientific anatomy but also stands as a symbol of Hobbes's nominalism and his claims to sound method. Its strength is caused by those linking with each other to form its body; it is the effect of their conjoining. Without them, it is literally a heavenly disembodied head. The picture also displays the Commonwealth as a protective agency, a functional creation, and the only barrier between the individuals that comprise it and the war of a natural condition. As a barrier it looms over a peaceful landscape, analogous to the famous Lorenzetti topographical image of good government in the Pallazzo Publico in Siena. Beneath the landscape are two sets of parallel lozenges, one with a motif of straight lines, the other of circles. These deal respectively with the military and ecclesiological entailments of the sovereign's authority; the command of the word and the sword, of law within the commonwealth and war beyond it. It follows from this, of course, that for Hobbes, if the state does not protect its subjects according to the pattern of nominal definition on which he relies, it does not exist or oblige as a state.

Overall, as science or philosophy, what Hobbes would persuade us he has done is to have demonstrated the necessity of a principle of sovereignty, by definition and through something close to biconditional analysis. His philosophically central notion of demonstration carries the potentially ambiguous meanings of teaching and showing, of discovering and proving (see chapter 2, "Definition, Resolution, and Composition"). Hence the notion of demonstration plays a part in maintaining the fuzzy line between the certainties of philosophy and the mere probabilities of rhetoric. To minimize uncertainties in the process of demonstration, Hobbes also made an explicit appeal to introspection through a manifestly intertextual injunction: "Nosce tiepsum"—"read thy self" (*Leviathan*, introduction, 10). Thus he drew not just on a model of reasoning to overcome skepticism, best evidenced in geometry, but on the belief in the philosophically privileged status of the maker's knowledge. We make and trade in our own conceptions of ourselves as we make definitions and so can know them with a degree of confidence. In this way, drawing on long-held scholastic beliefs in the importance of reflexivity to human identity (Brett, 16, 97), he appeals to our sense of ourselves to assess his claims. It may even be that this is partially the force of his emphasis on the artificiality of the sovereign. Social relationships are made by us and the sovereign is a synthesis of individuals as subjects, so we should be able to have certain knowledge of our duties to the sovereign because we made it for our needs.

The Creation of the Sovereign

There is a dual function in Hobbes's notion of man; he is both a legitimate point of reference in a scientific inquiry and a causative subject matter. Human beings as sentient creatures are matter in motion; while they move, they live. They process the world through sense impressions, while they order and store through memory and are thus able to anticipate possibilities and exercise some control over the world.

Then, drawing on his distinction between voluntary and involuntary motions (see chapter 3, "Endeavor"), Hobbes turns to the beginnings of voluntary motion in the passions and the language through which they are expressed (*Leviathan*, 5). It is these passions and their expression that are subjected to a detailed controlling set of definitions, clearing the ground for the argument that men are driven principally by passion that at best reason can but channel. The passions are defined in terms of directional movement, to or from what is desired or feared, arbitrarily named good or evil, respectively. Although there is no one substantial good to which we all aim, there is one generally feared evil—unnatural death—of which all other fears are shadows. In the manipulation of this greatest of fears will lie our hope of civilization. In the meantime, there is nothing on the surface to stop language being quite meaningless, but as Hobbesian men are roughly equal and sufficiently similar to desire and fear much the same things, there exists or, more importantly, is anticipated to exist among them a state of competition. This seems also to mean that their language can acquire a sort of public stability. While there are no constraints on individuals with respect to how they may seek felicity, there is consequentially no security in what they may enjoy. That is, they have perfect liberty to try to do what they will but, paradoxically, unrestrained action is effectively meaningless because it is so uncertain.[8] Concomitantly, there is nothing to stop them using language as they wish to further any desired end. The natural condition is at the very least a world of Jesuitical equivocation, or more generally, a condition of what Quentin Skinner has called radical *paradiastole*—a situation in which anything may be redescribed as individuals think fit.[9]

This is the condition in which there can be no arts, no cumulative knowledge, no civilization; a war of all against all consequent upon the tensions of ambition and fear and their unlimited expression. The result is a hypothetical model of what human life would be like without the artificial constraints of a governmental system. Hobbes's point is not just explanatory, it is also strongly exhortatory; and the more bleakly the natural condition is described, the more any state or commonwealth seems preferable. At the same time, the more difficult it is to render plausible the transition to a commonwealth through such human beings agreeing among each other to leave themselves defenseless that they might be protected by creatures just like them.

It is partly, perhaps, to overcome the difficulties of self-inflicted explanatory paradoxes that Hobbes explicitly invokes the laws of nature. As I have suggested, in the seventeenth century rights were overwhelmingly seen as the obverse of and contingent upon duties (see chapter 3, "Images of the Natural Condition"). Thus when Hobbes wrote of the right of nature called *jus naturale,* being the liberty of each to use all his powers as he sees fit for his own preservation (*Leviathan,* 14), the intimations of a duty to seek peace were not as strained as they might seem now; and certainly, he did evoke a sense of natural or even divine law as requiring us to seek peace. For Hobbes this entailed a series of supporting specifications (*Leviathan,* 14, 15) that words should be spoken according to their significations (no Jesuitical equivocations); and that contracts and faith should be kept, all of which he summed up in the maxim that we should not do what we should not want done to us (*Leviathan,* 15). This was to reinforce an appeal to self-interest, in rhetorical terms *utilitas* with an injunction to do what is right, *honestas.* There would have been little point to this if Hobbes saw people only as self-interested. Thus there were for Hobbes two discernible, if inseparable, imperatives, from intrinsic character and divine requirement urging us to peace, and, ipso facto, providing us with a simple criterion for virtuous behavior (Skinner 1996, 342).[10] This is not to say he gave them equal force but he did deal himself two cards to play. He was able to say that by a law of nature "we are obliged to transferre to another such Rights, as being retained, hinder the peace of Mankind" (*Leviathan,* 15.100), conjoining a sense of self-interest, divine warrant, and logical entailment.

Given their minimal rationality, people are then able to contract with each other to create a supervening artificial protective agency for them all—the Commonwealth, state, or sovereign. This was put forward, however, in the context of a set of definitions about what it is to give or transfer. Hobbes was insistent that with respect to the *origins* of the office of the sovereign, what is involved is a transference of rights and so the creation of obligations, not a revocable delegation or trust. Again this drew on the conventional belief that rights and duties were correlatives. Rights can be transferred because they inhere in the body with the duty to protect. He briefly confronted the issue of what limits are entailed by the transference of the rights that might hinder peace, limits crucial to understanding the *functions* of the office; and when he wrote of the office of the sovereign he did write of a trust (*Leviathan,* 30.231). Hobbes's argument may not be satisfactory but it cannot be said that he had two distinct positions, a failed absolutist position that gave rights to a sovereign and a more satisfactory one that only entrusts the sovereign.[11] But whatever rights the sovereign has, its subjects cannot be taken to abandon a right to self-preservation, entailing that they are never obliged to condemn or accuse themselves (*Leviathan,* 14). Rather, in the version of the contract elaborated in *Leviathan,* people authorize a person or a group to act for their protection. Thus as a sovereign personates, or impersonates, its subjects, it represents them in as irrevocable a sense as possible. A sovereign's protective actions are the subjects' own. In a compound sense the state is an artificial person; it is both human artifice *and* a person.

It is here that there emerges a tension between two features of Hobbes's argument. The state is a consequence of individuality, authorized to act for those it protects, and consequent upon that duty flows a whole constellation of rights and powers. Yet although Hobbes claimed that natural rights are transferred for security, epistemologically, he always held that human beings remain locked in their own world of impressions; fear remains an internal passion (see chapter 3, "Images of the Natural Condition"). And, as he insisted, fear is a pattern of expectation, just as bad weather is more than an occasional shower (*Leviathan,* 13); and thus the right of self-defense includes some preemptive action (such as running away to France before it is too late). Hobbesian people operate in the world only by imagining the future in terms of an ordered sense of the past (*Leviathan,* 3). As he had always been brave enough to insist, a right to some end entails a right to all necessary means (*De cive,* 1.8). Just how much can consistently be given up for security is a moot point. Hobbes simply appealed to peace as a uniformly recognizable fact. But, according to his conception of human nature (see "Images of the Natural Condition"), security is not literally given by any set of external conditions; it is a matter of internal anticipations consequent upon the sovereign's actions. In this way, the persuasive force of the doctrine sits ill with its epistemological postulates. Consistency would have required Hobbes to insist that the commonwealth can only hope to convey what transforms itself as a sense and memory of felicity within the fearful mind. The fragility of the state, the way in which the sovereign is itself paradoxically a creature of controlled fear it tries to generate, was not lost on Hobbes, although it was not a point to stress. It does, however, clarify why it was so important for him that the Leviathan provide not just "bare preservation," which, after all, may be both objective and unrecognized, but "all other Contentments of life" consistent with its "trust" to procure the good of the people (*Leviathan,* 30.231). This also helps explain why he was so keen to strip the political vocabulary of tyranny and its cognate terms; there can be no passage or median ground between natural enmity and civic obedience. Tyranny, as *Leviathan* sharply puts it, is monarchy, and anarchy is democracy misliked.

There is an air of definitional conjuring in Hobbes's argument: If Leviathan exists, it protects and we own its protective actions, so it cannot be tyrannous or anarchic; if it does not protect, it does not exist as a sovereign for the would-be protected. There is only an enemy at the door. It is for this reason that Hobbes allows the condemned criminal to exercise a right of self-defense regardless of guilt. A man standing on the scaffold is returned to the natural condition. Hobbes did not allow that such a man, in anticipating execution, could get others to band with him for better protection, for this would be to put them in a state of danger and rebellion against the sovereign. But Hobbes's argument was drawn up in an arbitrary fashion in order to insure against there being any effective casuistry of disobedience. Again to be consistent, in Hobbesian terms it is certainly wrong for those protected by the state to band with one effectively in the natural condition; but on Hobbes's description of that condition, it cannot therefore be wrong for the natural creature to seek support when it has an explicit right to any means to the end of survival.

The creation of the sovereign redefines all individuals under its protection as subjects. Part 2 of *Leviathan* is taken up with what Hobbes took as the entailments of these mutually defining offices, not losing sight of the fact that subjects may take on subordinate offices within the commonwealth and that they remain the people of passion who created the sovereign in the first place. Hence the subjects remain a potential cause of the sovereign's dissolution. While it is the office of the virtuous subject to obey, to recognize the rightness and benefit of obedience and so willingly support the sovereign, it is the duty of the sovereign to control all it thinks necessary. This, as has been pictorially announced in the frontispiece, is explicitly a matter of physical protection and the control of public language. This control is not just over debate but extends to the very meanings of words, like justice; it is a matter of the promulgation of law, the containment of religion, and presumably involves constant policies of reassurance. As Sheldon Wolin has argued, the Leviathan is strikingly analogous to the philosopher; the one defines and controls in the interests of peace, the other in the interests of truth. Both in differing senses educate.[12] Characteristically each exists only in its defining activity. If the sovereign is answerable to any other human agency in this regard it ceases to be a sovereign, that agency being disclosed as the real sovereign power. Sovereignty, then, wherever it is found, is in a legalistic sense absolute by definition.

It is, however, answerable to God (*Leviathan*, 30), which regardless of how seriously this might be taken or how consoling it might have been (not very), was Hobbes's quite conventional way of stressing that sovereignty too is an office, having rights *only* because of its duties (see chapter 3, "Images of the Natural Condition"). Thus the sovereign is not absolute in the sense of being purely for its own sake and unspecified by limiting purpose. That is, the sovereign might properly do much as it pleases, *if* the informing criterion of action is its sense of the public good. If it may do as it will, it must justify and explain only as the language of its office allows. If the sovereign does not so act, there is nothing that can properly or effectively be done; but from everything Hobbes says, the consequence of a sovereign neglecting or acting beyond the confines of office will be to increase insecurity, which will tend to the dissolution of the state. This is not, of course, a consequence Hobbes had any interest in exploring, and it is not a justification for rebellion. His focus was much more on the duties of the subject than on prudential advice that would encourage rulers to remain good ones. Again, while the argument may be seen as roughly conforming to Hobbes's notion of science in its broad contours, the point is as much persuasive as it is explanatory: the continuing rumbustiousness of subjects was underlined and the onerous and benign responsibilities of sovereignty conveyed by the terms of Hobbes's description of its office.

From Kingdom to "Kingdom of Darknesse"

Almost as an interlude, in part 1 Hobbes introduced a long chapter on religion and it encapsulates many of the general principles that would inform the more elaborate discussions in parts 3 and 4. The chapter is a microcosm of the interplay between philosophy, polemic, and satire. It begins by explaining religion as a known effect from hypothesized causes in human nature, curiosity, and fear and implicitly and demeaningly distinguishes religion from philosophy, a superior manifestation of curiosity and one totally conducive to peace. Formally Hobbes had earlier defined religion as *"Feare* of power invisible, feigned by the mind or imagined from tales publiquely allowed" (*Leviathan*, 6.42). Such fears "not allowed" are superstition. True religion, he had maintained, arose when the power "is truly such as we imagine" (*Leviathan*, 6.42). Fear of the unknown, a desire to placate or control it, and curiosity explain why men have worshipped the mysteries of nature: "Opinion of Ghosts, Ignorance of second causes, Devotion towards what men fear, and Taking of things Casuall for Prognostiques" comprise the "Naturall seed of *Religion"* (*Leviathan*, 12.79). Religion, like government, has a universal social function if not an edifying origin. It is the casual detail that imperceptibly facilitates the shift toward the sardonic and derisory tone that comes to dominate the chapter and prefigures the concentration of satiric venom in part 4. In a world imperfectly understood, we are told, there is almost nothing that has not been worshipped, from unformed matter to a "leeke" (*Leviathan*, 12.79). This hardly suggests a sense of confidence in priests who encourage the worship of sundry objects. And, Hobbes argues, this itself may explain the changes within and between religions. As he had already suggested, the line between religion and superstition may be arbitrarily drawn. The human drive to worship remains constant, but is disappointed by the institutionalized forms it takes and the ways in which priests desert their callings. New religions are a response to the failures of the old (*Leviathan*, 12.85). But more than this, as religious belief is and should be conducive to the peace of the commonwealth (*Leviathan*, 12.82), there is an irony in its so often being a cause of civil disruption. Paradoxically, the true religion proves in its misuse a greater enemy to peace than some pagan religions have been. As we might expect, the theme of "unpleasing priests" (*Leviathan*, 12.86) will loom larger in pages to come.

Analogous to *Leviathan's* arbitrary appeals to self-interest and what is right, Hobbes evokes a bifold notion of God, in one sense consistent with his sense of philosophy, in the other with the impulse to bend religion to his needs. In the first context, Hobbes's God is incomprehensible because infinite (*Leviathan*, 3) and omnipotent. We do not genuinely conceive of God but cast up images of honor (*Leviathan*, 3.34). This *apophatic* notion of God (see chapter 4, "The Mystery of God") provides a limit to philosophy and may be seen philosophically as a first cause, recognized "by the name of God" (*Leviathan*, 12.77). As a corollary, Hobbes believed it easy to show what logical messes theologians get into when trying to convert honorific expressions into philosophical propositions about God and infinity (*Leviathan*, 46.466–67).

Having said all this unequivocally did not deter him from presenting God as an actor in history, with special interests and relationships with his chosen people, and who through his word commands obedience to sovereigns and those to whom they are accountable. God is the author of scripture (*Leviathan*, 33.267); the understanding of which is to know his mind. This, Hobbes recognizes, is a tricky point. It is easy to claim that God speaks directly to us, but demonstrating it is another matter (*Leviathan*, 32.256). On such grounds he had dismissed the authority of arguments from conscience (*Leviathan*, 7.48; 30.244). To avoid arbitrary invocations of conscience or of God's voice and their social consequences, Hobbes briskly concludes that God requires obedience (the first law of nature is to seek peace) and in order to be obedient to God, we can but rely on the sovereign as the arbiter of God's commandments (*Leviathan*, 26.199). The sovereign is thus a representative of God as well as of the subjects. God exists in Christ and Hobbes's confident assertions about the office of the Savior are characterizations of God. Christ is redeemer, pastor, and king, though not of his world, and is subordinate to God (*Leviathan*, 41.332–38). This identifies an escatology threading through parts 3 and 4 of *Leviathan:* there is a divine history explicitly teaching obedience and standing in ominous contrast to disobedience and the usurpation of legitimate civil authority.[13] Thus from the Bible's beginning, the message of Eden and the fall is obedience, the message of the myth of Babel is obedience (Moloney, 255–59). The message of Christ and the apostles is obedience. For Hobbes, escatology reinforces the point that the civil sovereign has the right to arbitrate over hermeneutic disputes in the interests of peace; otherwise, disputes will arise, for Hobbes an incontrovertible proposition of hermeneutics. It remains open to question, however, how far the escatological dimension of *Leviathan* was designed to subvert all escatological patterning that did not issue from the sovereign, such is the satiric tone of so much of the latter part of the work.

Irrespective of this, the God who can be no part of philosophical discourse is the center of Hobbes's biblical exposition. If we read *Leviathan* as a purely philosophical work the contradiction between his God on the cusp of reason and God in faith is stark enough, and several commentators have referred independently to the two gods of *Leviathan*.[14] There may indeed be strong tensions here, but each God is found predominantly in the context of different kinds of argument, first by reason (parts 1 and 2) and then by faith. Hobbes had interlaced appeal to reason and faith in *De cive,* though with less obvious structural consequences. This is not to say that he loses all sight of his philosophy when discussing religion. He maintains, for example, that the Bible is consistent with his philosophy with respect to spirits and demons. There is no warrant for their incorporeality. In this way, he tries to undermine their mystery as a means of alleviating the false fears that priests may raise and that may be used to counteract the proper fear the sovereign seeks to engender. Similarly, he shows a willingness to press philosophy into the service of religious controversy, although parts 3 and 4 increasingly presuppose a religious faith that parts 1 and 2 only sporadically require or rely upon. Argument from reason and from faith might properly allow differing uses of the word God, but everything converges on the same nexus of propositions in support of sovereign authority.

Most of the other themes characteristic of Hobbes's various discussions of religion are intensified in *Leviathan.* The social functions of religion to allay fear and to promote civil obedience are explicitly itemized in chapter 12. The Erastianism of his unremitting belief that the priesthood is a subordinate civic office serving the needs of the church members is pervasive. He relentlessly advocates absolute poverty, the priestly ideal adhered to by the medieval spiritual Franciscans, seizing upon the obvious political consequences of a theological doctrine. His sense of what is necessary to believe for salvation remains egregiously minimal, so shrinking the ground on which dangerous controversies might flourish. His anticlericalism is concomitantly found throughout his discussion of religious matters. His mode of expression is largely satiric where the targets are mainly Catholic priests. Ostensibly, he might seem to be standing on shared ground with his coreligionists. But it is not difficult to see why he caused offense. The image of a legitimate priesthood—humble, genuinely poor officers of state—was implicitly critical of many Protestant churches including the Church of England, the beneficiary of taxation through tithes that had given independence to its priests as a whole, and considerable wealth to many of them. Hobbes's jibes were sufficiently general to embrace the Protestant clergy.

Hobbes's notion of a church remains true to the philological derivation found in *De cive.* It is a community of believers. In *Leviathan,* of course, Hobbes no longer writes of the city as the political unit; and in a commonwealth the number of churches allowed becomes purely a matter for the sovereign. The necessity for one national church, one *civitas*, one *ecclesia* seems a negotiable matter for the sovereign's sense of prudence. This was another possibility to worry many in the Church of England, but one to encourage those who felt oppressed by it. Only one theme was to develop significantly after *Leviathan*—Hobbes's interest in heresy; but what he was later to write was consistent with his recognition that heresy was a means of control and hence had to be defined by the sovereign. In all, *Leviathan* presents a very Roman image of the relationships between religious expression, cultus, and the sovereign; any religious belief might be allowable if subordinate to and not threatening civic order. Hobbes's audacity lay in arguing, in the face of early Christian and contemporary intolerance, that this is simply a pure Christian doctrine.

"Artificial Chains"

Hobbes's abiding interests in law are also widely manifested in *Leviathan*. It is this which most obviously signals the work as an English example of the capacious genre of "politica" literature. As Robert von Friedeburg has noted, most German universities produced examples of this during the early seventeenth century. In a letter referring to the nearly completed *Leviathan*, Hobbes called it a work of "Politique" and when he translated it into Latin, he effectively domesticated it to that juristic tradition of speculation.[15] With this in mind, what we may reasonably see as the political concept of the sovereign would probably have been understood by Hobbes juristically: it arises to make good divine or natural laws requiring peace, and it is judged in terms of its legal efficacy. For Hobbes law was always necessarily a protection as well as a restriction, so his sovereign as the ultimate protective agency is an expression of Hobbes's conception of public law and theory of sovereignty. Because its function is to provide security, Hobbes also construes law as giving liberty in the only socially meaningful sense of that term.

Liberty looms particularly large in *Leviathan*, where all its principal meanings come together but where the emphasis shifts from a preconditional liberty to liberty as socially contingent rights allowed by law (see chapter 3, "Freedom, Necessity, and Language"). Hobbes's discussions provide an ideal example of his skills in subverting and then co-opting the salient vocabulary.

A whole constellation of issues came together in appeals to liberty during Hobbes's lifetime. To reiterate briefly (see "Freedom, Necessity, and Language"), liberty was valued because it was seen as easily eroded or surrounded by a pressing sphere of the unfree, threatening servitude, tyranny, or enslavement; it was often associated more with some governmental forms better able to protect it than others, and so republics were sometimes called free states. Claims to liberty and rights were ubiquitously heard as expressions of higher obligations or duties. The result was to sustain the word as one of the most salient and emotional in the English political lexicon, frequently relied upon in arguments against governmental, especially monarchical, authority.

Whatever specific problems there are with Hobbes's use of the word, the general force of his argument is clear enough; it is to subvert the pragmatics of liberty and its antonyms tyranny and slavery and respecify the word as a correlative to absolute legal sovereignty. From *The Elements of Law* onwards, Hobbes had held to a doctrine of motivational irrelevance with respect to free action and in particular the belief that a promise of obedience undertaken out of fear is still agreed to freely. What Hobbes called natural liberty was our condition with respect to any given state of affairs before we actually will it or endeavor to alter it. This view of natural liberty was elaborated earlier in *Anti-White* and reiterated in *Leviathan* as the "proper signification" of liberty. This was merely the absence of external impediment to endeavor. Thus the banks of a river constrain its liberty: applied to humans, liberty is the absence of barriers or bonds to our willed actions—any internal impediment is a lack of power.

A man is not free when chained in prison, although he does remain free to try to escape his bonds, however fruitless his endeavors might be. Most of our actions are therefore irradicably free and simultaneously caused. When people say they are not free it is usually a euphemism for not liking the sort of choice before them. Thus far from being a precious because fragile condition opposed to tyranny and slavery, and a value to be cherished and defended, liberty is almost inescapable. Hobbes's argument is clearly one that would diminish the significance of liberty as it was normally understood. Indeed, it is only the application of a more general principle of Hobbesian argument, the belief that for any image to have meaning there must be points of relationship and contrast with other images. This was implicit in the discussion of the state of nature (see chapter 3, "Images of the Natural Condition"); men having equal right to everything and being free to take what they wanted meant that none of them were free in any meaningful sense. The ground prepared conceptually by natural liberty and the discussion of liberty in its proper signification placed Hobbes in a position to renegotiate most explicitly civil or legal liberty. When we live under law, liberty is at once restricted and meaningful. Civil liberty is the silence of the laws, the rights allowed by law, and liberty's enjoyment presupposes a supreme authority to make the law. Absolute sovereignty and liberty so far from being inimical to each other are therefore related as cause to effect.

The general force of this is underscored by Hobbes's insistence that liberty and obligation are opposed or mutually restricted. As I have suggested, it was typical of appeals to liberty in making rights claims to see them as derivative of and necessary for fulfillment of some higher obligation. For the most part Hobbes would have none of this.[16] And he was also able to dismiss the common notion that some governments were free and others not. His doctrine here is quite consistent with his treatment of the concept of tyranny. All sovereigns are free with respect to each other, but all subjects of any government are ruled by them. In all governments rights and freedoms begin where obligations end. Thus from a narrowly understood juristic notion of civil liberty in conjunction with a metaphysical theory of free agency, Hobbes was able to recast the significance of liberty in political argument—to make it either politically meaningless because preconditional or reduce it to the gift of the sovereign, a typically Hobbesian choice. But from this followed another general point underpinning so much of *Leviathan*. It is that as civil liberty is artificial and not natural, its restraints, the laws, are only artificial chains. We are free to break laws if we choose and many do. Playing on the multivalence of artificiality, he was able to promote the crucial importance of obeying the liberty-giving sovereign because it is sovereignty, not liberty, that is fragile.

Law is the command of the sovereign, who is both the origin and the arbiter of it. The sovereign's realm is understood in terms of the extent of the law's operation; it is both a geographic and a demographic domain. Thus liberty exists not just in the silent interstices of the law but in its effectiveness. In *Leviathan* Hobbes insists on the derivative nature of justice. It is consequent upon the law, defined by the sovereign, a notion that in fact goes back to archaic Greece and the postulated symbolic relationship between the mother goddess Themis and her daughter Dike (justice). In *Leviathan* a number of things follow most explicitly from this: that judges, like priests, have no interpretative leeway over the law; and that laws should be clear, prospective, codified, and available, to reassure and minimize the subject's fear of behaving illegally. Without such features, ignorance of the law may be an excuse

(*Leviathan*, 27). Uncertainty is the beginning of fear and in fear lies insecurity, the weakening of the protective relationship between subject and sovereign. For the same reason laws should not be retrospective (*Leviathan*, 27). Punishment in the proper sense of the term can only come from the public lawmaking authority who deems an act a transgression of the law (*Leviathan*, 28). Similarly, where there is no law, there can be no crime (*Leviathan*, 27).

Given Hobbes's emphasis on codification and command, the relationship between civil law and natural law is awkward. On the one hand, Hobbes co-opted the language of natural law, giving an authority to the civil, which is seen by him as always an application of natural law. On the other, he denied natural law any effective independence. The relationship between the forms of law is, in fact, parallel to Hobbes's understanding of perception and external reality. Perception and the sovereign alike mediate what exists but which is not otherwise available. With respect to law the existential ambivalence means that it is both law and not law, properly speaking, until blessed by the sovereign's mediation. The uncertain status of natural law is heightened in the natural condition where there is no commanding sovereign. Yet as I have suggested (see "Images of the Natural Condition"), even in this most atomistic expression of the natural condition, there is the occasional invocation of God's requirements of his creatures through the laws of nature. Hobbes needed the vestige of some subordinate relationship with God to assist the passage from the natural condition to political society. Thus the laws of nature forbid, which they could hardly do were he writing on them consistently only as prudential maxims.

Rhetoric Enlisted

Although it was necessary to discuss rhetoric in the context of Hobbes's understandings of history and poetry, these latter conceptions have little explicit function in *Leviathan*. Hobbes makes cursory use of history as a register of facts, allusions to English history in particular surfacing only to buttress or make more immediate what has been argued independently. His use of the Old Testament certainly treats it as a history of the Jews, but given what he took to be their special relationship with God his comments are perhaps better seen in terms of escatology. Hints of medieval ecclesiastical history would later be fleshed out as the story of papal usurpation; and in fact, there is one sense in which in *Leviathan* Hobbes regarded history as a burden. He argued that what should be regarded as a register of facts has been given authority and so presses onerously on the present; above all, this applied to the erroneous views of liberty held by philosophers of antiquity and displayed in the mayhem of ancient popular politics (see chapter 6, "Rhetoric and History"). There are even fewer references to poetry and poetic fancy in *Leviathan,* although the almost poetic qualities of its style will be taken up in the concluding chapter.

It is rather the theory and practice of rhetoric that is central and problematic. Despite Hobbes's austere image of philosophy, his notion of demonstration is sufficiently flexible to entangle it with rhetoric and with eloquence. If we continue to reserve the term "rhetoric" for the general persuasive dimension of language, *Leviathan* can certainly be called a piece of rhetoric as much as it is a work of philosophy. As it is advice to the subjects of a commonwealth as to how they should behave, it is a sort of deliberative rhetoric or eloquence—and Hobbes was not one to see rhetoric as only appropriate to the spoken word. In this context, as I have indicated, Hobbes appealed to the traditional criteria of persuasion. The notions of *utilitas* and *honestas* persistently inform his injunctions to peace. It is not only self-interest *(utilitas)* that impels peace; it is also a matter of *honestas,* obeying a right injunction, which in a state of nature comes only from God; thus the maxims or laws of peace are at once prudential and moral in their force. The whole persuasive momentum of the work arises from a relentless orchestration of a large range of the contentious resources of his society. By turns *Leviathan* exhibits argument from reason, specifically with respect to the claims and aspirations of the new science, and from faith, most notably through the co-option of the Bible. All is interspersed with appeals to shared values, prejudices, and conventional wisdom. To return briefly to the frontispiece, one lozenge depicts the weapons of argument, syllogism, dilemma, and indirection, as rightly within the domain of sovereign control; but insofar as the sovereign and philosopher are analogous, this depiction prefigures exactly what we find in the body of the text, the use of argumentative dexterity to the single-minded ends of the promotion of peace and philosophy. Hobbes's own table of sciences finds a place for rhetoric next to logic.

If this were all we would have a simpler text than we have, for Hobbes delineates and promotes science in a way that sits uncomfortably with the rhetorical dimension of *Leviathan.* In the *Answer* to *Gondibert,* Hobbes so reified science/philosophy as to sever it from its constitutive methods and this allowed the proposition that the poet can become a true philosopher (see chapter 6, "Philosophy and the Poetic Imagination"). To repeat, this is inimical to Hobbes's general notions of science and these, dominant in *Leviathan,* thus entail methods excluding much that might have been rhetorically permissible. A further problem arises because of Hobbes's strong separation of persuasion from teaching, the latter being associated with science. But it is difficult to see *Leviathan* as really fulfilling such a didactic aspiration. It is, however, certainly demonstrative as it displays a doctrine and this sense of demonstration is quite consistent with rhetoric. Hobbes confronts some of the difficulties of his argument in the review and conclusion by referring to the relationships between philosophy and eloquence as potentially complementary. Had he been thinking of rhetoric as it had earlier been classified in chapter 9 as a branch of philosophy, and as he had treated it in his *Briefe* as a form of logic, the argument at the end of *Leviathan* would not have needed to be made. The review and conclusion only addresses optional ornamentation, eloquence. It is thus a means to a persuasive end. What he does not do, and what the presentation of his philosophy in *Leviathan* does not provide, is a philosophy that excludes a rhetorical dimension.

The accepted need to co-opt and use eloquence, the specific tropes and figures appropriate to various forms of discourse, is of course an example of Hobbes's employing whatever resources he could; and it was particularly important for him to do so, for in *Leviathan,* true to his earlier thought, he regarded the manipulation of language to shape opinion or belief essential to explaining society. Opinion, as he had put it in *The Elements of Law* (*Elements,* 1.12.6.), drives the world. We are as his science held, preconditionally all creatures of opinion, locked in our own notions; hence the capacity to use sign systems to shape opinion and thus direct action is not just an inescapable (rhetorical) fact of life; it makes the eloquent powerful. As eloquence is typically misused, it is essential that it be enlisted for truth. This provides, then, a defense of what is implicitly accepted as nonphilosophical in *Leviathan.* At the same time, it should forewarn us that to treat the work solely as philosophy is to lose a great deal of what is entangled with that philosophy. Chapter 25, on counsel, encapsulates many of the difficulties of disengaging rhetoric from philosophy, as well as bringing to a head Hobbes's fears of the power of eloquence and oratory to misdirect or overwhelm sovereign right. Recognizing the importance and danger of the tools of oratory, its redescriptive powers through metaphor and simile, he draws out what he takes to be the philosophical entailments of the office of counseling and vehemently urges the control of counsel, painting a dark picture of its abuses. The chapter is at once a philosophy and an eloquent antirhetoric.

The coherence of the work, then, lies not in a propositional structure or the building of a system or in any rigidity of discursive form, nor even in a single permeating idea, but in bringing an extraordinary array of intellectual resources to bear on the problem of peace in society, and to do so in a highly combative way in order to preempt or subvert alternative uses of them. That the coherence achieved was relative is not the point here; it is simply to suggest that if we need to make sense of any specific point Hobbes is making, a reasonable start is to ask how it might fit into the context of a persuasive argument for peace. As Hobbes himself insisted, it is not single ideas that matter but trains of thought, and in reading we need pay attention not to individual texts, that is individual statements, but the overall scope and end of an argument.

The Defender of Peace

Hitherto I have attempted a general overview of *Leviathan* as an example of Hobbes's sustained interests. In the context of his intellectual energies it did not come like a bolt from the blue, but because of the significance it has assumed, there has been a tendency to isolate it and to see it as rather grandly distinct from other works. If it is then compared with the wrong sort of text, such as Machiavelli's *Prince,* which has stood at times almost as a ritual counterpoint, it is bound to loom large and different on the landscape. As recent commentary is clearly establishing, however, in some respects *Leviathan* was very much at one with Continental public law and sovereignty theory, most of which had fallen into obscurity and which in England was a minori interest. In other ways it did tie in with vibrant debates in England. Despite Hobbes's own dismissive remarks about philosophers and schoolmen, it drew on and adapted central themes from medieval and Reformation scholastic philosophy. Without wanting to suggest too homologous or exclusive a relationship, I want to illustrate this embeddedness in a rich and widespread environment by pointing specifically to a striking pattern of similarities with Marsilius of Padua's *Defensor pacis.* The early exposure of Hobbes to the works of Paolo Sarpi, and probably to other antipapal Italian writing, may have included Marsilius's still seminal and controversial text. Irrespective of this, there is a striking degree of consanguinity between the works. It was alluded to without any detail by Michael Oakeshott, and more recently Johann Sommerville and Patricia Spingborg have fleshed out Oakeshott's passing comment.[17] More significantly, perhaps, an assumption of sympathetic familiarity was first made soon after *Leviathan* appeared.[18] I want simply to list the most significant nonexclusive points of agreement, since they come close to providing a summary overview of Hobbes's work.

Like *Leviathan*, Marsilius's *Defensor pacis* (*The Defender of Peace*) of 1324 appeared amid great controversy, encouraging the author to flee Paris for exile at the court of Ludwig of Bavaria, appropriately enough since Ludwig was the avowed foe of Pope John XXII and *Defensor* presented an extreme and systematic antipapal argument. By the time Hobbes wrote, it was readily available and had even been translated into English as an aid to Henry VIII's embryonic Reformation in 1535. It has even been held as a sort of ideological guide for the English reformation process; much of what makes *Leviathan* look like an English Erastian polemic sounds like echoes of *Defensor pacis*.[19]

The similarities between it and *Leviathan* are in focus, structure, and specific doctrine. The shared focus is upon the fragility of peace, its necessity, and causes of its disruption. The principal cause of *intranquilitas,* as Marsilius called it, is the papacy, which stands in a position of extraordinary self-aggrandizing power after centuries of the usurpation of secular authority: exactly Hobbes's position.[20] Marsilius argued his case in a way structurally similar to the organization of *Leviathan.* This can be seen in two complementary ways. First, there is a good sense of Paduan method in discourse 1. The problem of *intranquilitas* is stated and then the component functional parts of society are specified and analyzed. The problem is restated in the conclusion to the discourse as a way into the detailed analysis of the major cause of disruption, the corrupt edifice of the Roman Church.

Second, the work is divided into three discourses. In discourse 1, analogous to *Leviathan* parts 1 and 2, Marsilius argues from reason. In discourse 2, analogous to parts 3 and 4, he argues from faith. The third discourse is a short review and conclusion. Bramhall's attacks on Hobbes were organized as arguments from reason and faith, which Hobbes then turned back upon the bishop. One obvious difference between Hobbes and Marsilius with respect to the arguments from reason is that where Hobbes eschews authority and explicitly rejects what he associates with Aristotle and Cicero, Marsilius embraces both. Despite this appearance, Marsilius's treatment was creative and highly adaptive, just as Hobbes's translation of the *Rhetoric* was as much Hobbes as Aristotle. And indeed, as Alan Gewirth notes, Marsilius's reading of Aristotle is particularly materialist; the focus is upon efficient causation, causation as Hobbes understood it; and the work is replete with the sort of organic and physical imagery appropriate to what is believed to have been a medical education in Padua (Gewirth, 34, 20–21). The argument from faith was more obviously similar to Hobbes. Both men attempted to bend the Bible and the history of the Christian church to their cause, each restricting its authority to the New Testament and each insisting on the differences between the mature Catholic Church and its ancient origins, and to this end they relied on a very similar pattern of biblical *topoi.* The use of discernibly different forms of argument and appeals to different standards of proof give each work an air of the "averroistic" theory of two truths that Marsilius erratically embraced.

Within the confines of discourse 1 stood a chapter on religion and its functions that is analogous to Hobbes's discussion of religion in chapter 12 of part 1 (Marsilius, 1.vi). Here we begin to see some doctrinal similarities: both men stressed the social functions of religion to aid in the maintenance of public order and peace; and implicitly for each there is an unfavorable contrast between the social functioning of pagan religion and corrupt Christianity, despite its being the true religion. Thus the importance of controlling priests for each is prefigured. It had been the practice of the Catholic Church to equate the church with the priesthood. Both men defined a church from *ecclesia* as a community of believers, whom priests can only guide and advise toward salvation. Thus for each priests are all equal; bishops a purely human invention derived from the organizational needs of a successful church. All should be meek and embrace the ideals of Christ's poverty; and no priests have rights of excommunication. This power resided for Marsilius with the church or its representative. Like Hobbes he too saw church and as we would say, state as parallel orders of authority concerned with the external behavior of the people. Hobbes's distinction between conduct and conscience that we first find elaborated in *The Elements of Law* is the same as Marisilius's distinction between transient and intransient acts (Marsilius, 1.iv.4–5).

Marsilius's notion of representation both in its secular and ecclesiological manifestations was also like Hobbes's. It was irrevocable. As Marsilius insisted, he took the *valentior pars,* the weightier part of the whole people, to be the same thing as the whole people (Marsilius,

1.12).[21] Here there emerges a strong difference of preference rather than theory. Marsilius's notion of the governing part of the polity *(pars princi-pans)* is an agent accountable to the *valentior pars,* not itself a sovereign. What comes remarkably close to a principle of sovereignty is invested with the people or its representative. But it should also be said that, especially in the second discourse, such a sovereign status seems to be more closely associated with the ruling part. The adaptations of the English translation effectively made the *pars principans* the uncontrolled (monarchical) representative of the people. Nevertheless, if we put aside Hobbes's strong pragmatic preference for a monarch, his locus of sover-eignty is much like Marsilius's representative *valentior pars,* a more or less democratic or aristocratic artificial multitude acting for and being the same thing as the people. There is no natural condition in *Defensor pacis,* although Marsilius does present a similarly pessimistic view of humanity to Hobbes. He also has a similarly ambivalent doctrine about the status of natural law. He underlined the significance of the absence in this world of a command dimension to what is called natural or divine law. Thus, as Hobbes would argue, it is not properly or fully law until the sovereign interprets its specific content and promulgates it. The principal difference is that where Marsilius formally accepted a dualistic notion of law, composed of authoritative command and justice, putting more emphasis on command, Hobbes would simply declare justice to be derivative of law. There is little practical difference between the two doctrines and, for a good while, Marsilius was read as if he were a legal positivist like Hobbes.

Overall, then, there is a significant range of salient similarities show-ing the resilience of medieval forms of discourse even in the processes of adaptive transmission, and they give considerable textual warrant for Hobbes's Erastianism, representation, and law. They return us to some of the dangers noted at the outset of this study—those of drawing a neat line between medieval and even early modern thought, especially as a prelude to placing Hobbes on the nearer side.

Chapter Eight

Intellectual Style and Brief Afterlife

A Plain and Evident Style

Those who now study Hobbes sit crowned upon a grave of towering philosophical ambition. At every turn it is possible to see how Hobbes, who sought a system of plain and evident truth, was thwarted by his own self-critical energies and the intractable nature of his subject matter: matter, movement, method, and mankind.

He put great faith in scientific method and definitional rigor, but only sporadically practiced what he preached. All visions of what exactly his method was require some qualification. Although in any one work his position may reasonably be captured, specific ideas and other works render him resistant to those procrustean dichotomies and chronological divisions we would impress upon him. Thus only some aspects of Hobbes's work render him in any way modern: in some ways he was a Renaissance man, in others a late scholastic. A precursor of the Enlightenment perhaps, yet hardly so in his relentless skepticism; an empiricist perhaps, who wasn't quite that; an Englishman, yet in salient ways intellectually something of a Frenchman or an Italian. He was a modern driven by a passion both for and against the ancients. He strove for universal understandings with a vehemence that kept him buffeted by the controversies of his day. Here again, simple questions asked and commitments expected can be frustrated by the nuanced paradoxes in his answers. He was a philosopher who to a remarkable degree explored the complex functionings of language but seems almost to have taken a perverse delight in exhibiting them. He twisted, subverted, exploited, and exposed much that his contemporaries wanted to take for granted, giving new emphasis to some notions while trying to consign other central terms to obsolescence. Nothing illustrates this better than his treatment of natural law and liberty. And as a consummate antirhetorician he was frequently determined to surprise through unpalatable reasoning or

143

unexpected conclusions. It is little wonder he has been subject to mythic simplifications; yet where the basic ideas are easy to grasp, such as the principle injunctions to peace in *De cive, The Elements of Law,* and *Leviathan,* these are the least interesting things about him. Finally, a man of science, Hobbes was as much a poet and visionary of mathematics' potential. So it is how he failed that has in many ways stimulated others. Although he resists a definitive summary, we may get a final perspective by turning to the nexus of his written style and formal doctrines.

In a eulogistic poem, Abraham Cowley called Hobbes's style a *"Wardrobe* of rich *Eloquence"* and "A *Shield that gives delight* / Even to the *enemies* sight."[1] The praise was not without foundation. Clarendon, for example, remarked on the beguiling presentation of otherwise dubious argument.[2] Hobbes has since been anthologized as a fine writer of seventeenth-century English and instructive attention has been paid to his style.[3] It is on this I wish to comment. Connections between style and substantive doctrine should not surprise us, given Hobbes's preoccupation with language and his love of poetry. His self-consciously plain style expressed a concern with avoiding the easy pitfalls of obscurity. A claim to plainness additionally suggests an unpretentious honesty about the author and may further intimate a degree of incapacity in those who have disagreed with him.

Plainness, however, is a matter of degree. Hobbes had learned his language in Elizabethan England and so although plain enough by comparison with many contemporaries, he carried something of a Jacobean oratundity into the increasingly plain tongue era of Commonwealth and Restoration writing. His style can be seen as part of an anti-Ciceronian movement toward less ornate expression appropriate to his distaste for Cicero.[4] Yet, as a master of the difficult new Latin and a lover of the rough-hewn Greek of Thucydides, something of their sinuous robustness is taken into his English. So to a modern ear brought up on parsimonious punctuation and regular phrasal structure, his language might seem anything but plain. When he lived people were still apt to read aloud to themselves and so the rhythm of his work is most easily appreciated when the requirements of breathing complement the phrasing. This practice can reestablish a sense that silent reading can dull.

Discussions of style can suffer a terminal imprecision; but if it is fair to comment on Andrew Marvell's studied evasiveness, we can say that Hobbes is very much the antithesis. He is direct, personal, insistent, given to dramatic changes of pace and striking figuration, presenting arguments in the form of provoking paradox as if to guard against any lapse in attention or any wandering from the trains of thought he would impress in the reader's mind. He strove constantly for perspicacity, anticipating potential doubts and then changing his angle of attack to insure the reader understood and accepted what he had to say. As I have suggested (see chapter 6), Hobbes's deployment of the weapons of argument could be strikingly dexterous, exuding a confidence of control if thereby relinquishing a formal consistency. It is, I think, the imposition of this authorial voice on the reader that underpins more specific characteristics of his prose.

One consequence of this relentless voice is the presentation of a strong sense of personality. Hobbes comes off the page as a man of great intellectual energy and passion, a man of wit, humor, and, despite his protestations to cowardice, intellectual courage. Yet there is also an impression of scornful arrogance and reluctance to spend time on distractions. The proposition is the thing, not the authority. Most of those mentioned by name in his works are targets of attack, which is often dogmatic, sometimes unfair and impatient. There is no sense of self-effacement, no false modesty, and only occasionally a willingness to give ground when in combat with others whom he characterized as knaves or fools, willfully distorting or unable to grasp his evident truths. An awareness of the potential distance between author as agent of words, text as printed artifact, and reader as agent interpreting that artifact had been much sharpened by Montaigne's legacy of skepticism and that was as much an issue for philosophical inquiry as it was a stylistic opportunity. In a word, where Marvell exploited the suggestive distance between author and readers, where the text stood ambiguously as medium of and barrier to communication, Hobbes did all in his power to overcome it so that the propositions of his text might be forced home, patterned upon the mind. The authorial voice, in short, is a controlling feature of the text.

This is an aspect even of Hobbes's translations. He is one of the great English translators, but from his pioneering rendition of Thucydides, where he sought to maximize accuracy, to his late work (one does not have to make the point about the translation of Aristotle's *Rhetoric*), it is very much a matter of creation through mediation. At close to 90 he translated Homer, sacrificing polish and avoiding what would be the sometimes stilted elegance of Pope. He was still an energetic old man in a hurry, the race was yet to be quit.

Let now our men's activity be tried,
That when the stranger is where he doth dwell,
He to his friends and countrymen may tell
How much we do all other men excel
At wrestling, buffets, leaping, running well.
Odysseys, bk. 8, ll. 92–95, 373

His handling of dialogue form may be seen in a similar vein. There is no sense that the philosophical dialogue is an opportunity for dramatic effect, a means of presenting an enticing balance of views, inviting the reader's creative engagement. For Hobbes, dialogue is a mechanism for the orderly procedure of establishing his points and anticipating any doubts as pithily as possible. It is closer to the medieval *quaestio* than to the Renaissance ideal or David Hume's practice of it. So too with paradox. This had often functioned dialogically with the reader being required to negotiate creatively between possibilities, or as John Donne put it, to resist them. Hobbes was a lover of paradox in two senses but not to open-ended conclusions. He was more than happy to be critical of common opinion. In the more narrow meaning he presented arguments in a contradictory fashion, drawing the unexpected inference; thus, above all, the paradox at the heart of his contract theory: the antisocial propensities in human nature explain society. Again, in *Behemoth,* the predictable notion that the common people, ignorant as they are, will not understand their civic obligations is presented by *B* only to be dismissed roundly by *A*. It is education and privilege that obscures right judgment (see chapter 6, "History, Rhetoric, and Philosophy in *Behemoth*"). Provoking and disjunctive he may be, but we are never left in suspension—Hobbes is there to stimulate attention that he may teach.

The Problem of Philosophic Conviction

For Hobbes, then, although language may certainly delight for its own sake, style was best in the service of sound doctrine; and it is usually the logic of a complex proposition that controls the order and extent of a Hobbesian period (Reik, 158). As he held language to be the best means of ameliorating the isolation and uncertainty of existence, there was a heavy responsibility to use it in the interests of truth. Yet his skepticism about communication left him with only two potential areas of certainty. One was made of the general definitional truth of public propositions, best illustrated by mathematics; the other was the particular knowledge given by introspection (e.g., *Elements,* 1.5.14).

Hobbes made much play with definitional forms even when he was not formally defining, for not everything with the copula "is" constitutes a definition: Eloquence is power (*Elements*, 2.8.14). He also did his best to associate his propositions with mathematical certainty, suggesting a simple model of arithmetical conviction to which, he would persuade us, his own reasoning conformed. The errors of his opponents became the childish blunders of calculation. Hobbes's emphasis on introspection set the tone for his appeals to individual experience, his intertextual invitations to read ourselves against his general propositions, and his penchant for succinct and surprising examples. Thus in the famous chapter 13 of *Leviathan* he juxtaposed his hypothetical account of the state of nature, calculated on the basis of definitions and pseudodefinitions, with a direct appeal to self-understanding, a change of stylistic attack to implicate our common experience and individual behavior in his doctrine to gain certain belief. When a man locks his chests, Hobbes asked directly, "Does he not there as much accuse mankind by his actions , as I do by my words?" (*Leviathan*, 13.89).

There is, then, in Hobbes's work, a constant interplay between the general and particular. Science always seeks the general explanation; its cogency and demonstrability depend on tying it back to particulars, from which, good nominalist as he was, it must be derived. Yet experience itself "concludeth nothing universally" (*Elements*, 1.4.10). But if this sort of stylistic variation expressed a philosophical doctrine about the philosopher's business in theorizing about particularity, it also gave rise to characteristic difficulties in Hobbes's work. The precise relationships between general and particular are not always stable. It remains uncertain how far his descriptions of the natural condition were encoded metaphorical accounts of localized civil wars and how far a universal model of individual motivation and social formation. Less remarked upon is a characteristic slippage in his definitional procedures. On a number of occasions he used terms central to his arguments in a general sense only to slide into a discordant particularity. Words such as endeavor, opinion and belief, imagination and fancy, rhetoric, liberty, and obligation are all given senses that make them ubiquitous features of the human condition, but each also functions in a specific and contrasting way to other concepts. Imagination is preconditional for understanding the world, thus rendering all internal images matters of belief; but in a particular sense, imagination is a feature of poetry in contrast to history and philosophy. Belief and opinion are also used in a very general sense effectively embracing philosophy. Yet sometimes they are used as contrary to philosophy. Opinion can be other people's views misliked. To clarify Hobbes's understanding of rhetoric it was necessary to reserve the term for his sense of the persuasive dimension of language in general, retaining eloquence for the particular tropes of persuasion of which he was often so critical. What has been called Hobbes's "confusing clarity" is particularly apposite for his shifts between liberty in its metaphysical senses and specific legal manifestations.[5] Finally, Hobbes's critics exploited the potential slippage between the general and the particular by reading a global theory of sovereignty as a specific apology for a new regime.

Simile, Satire, and Wit

In the seventeenth century Thomas Sprat shrewdly commented on Hobbes's sparse but effective use of simile and Miriam Reik has endorsed the insight. An apt simile keeps or reinvigorates the attention, but without loss of clarity or philosophical direction (Reik, 158). One salient feature of simile is that its marking terms—such as "like"—help insure that all words are used in established contexts, and such ordered juxtaposition is distinct from metaphor.[6] Hobbes was aware of this and so his use of simile is quite consistent with his philosophical procedure and the insistence on the need to avoid equivocation. Simile, then, for Hobbes was a vital stylistic handmaid to philosophy. It aided clarity and provided a sense of discrimination between phenomena without which we cannot make a distinct sense of anything. Thus in dealing with the incoherence of our dreams he wrote: "whereby it cometh to pass, that our thoughts appear like the stars between the flying clouds . . ." (*Elements,* 1.3.3.10). In this way, the recourse to simile is also an appeal to experience, for its effectiveness depends on shared sets of semantic association that a proper philosophical doctrine can make coherent and universal. Moreover, unlike metaphor, it can dramatize an argument by marginal delay. When Hobbes referred to poets trying to write beyond the limits of decorum, the point was made devastatingly vivid by the typically simple rhythmic phrase that ends and contrasts with the elaborate preceding period. It is like a man wanting to be thought to speak by inspiration, "like a bagpipe" (*Answer,* 446).

The image also indicates how easily Hobbes shifted into characteristically Lucianic satire, often by means of trivializing example or deflationary simile, an expression of scorn by *tapinosis* (Skinner 1996, 422–25). Indeed, as Skinner has noted, part of his odious reputation was brought

about by the perception that he was given more to scoffing than argument (Skinner 1996, 425). This is always a danger for an aggressive
satirist, but by the standards of his day Hobbes's style was by no means
as philosophically indecorous as it might now seem. Some satire from
Lucian onward had explored philosophical issues and more immediately,
Hobbes may be seen as exhibiting a specifically Baconian belief in the
value of satiric philosophy. The ready shift into satire is also illustrated
by Hobbes's occasional resorting to incongruous catalogs to illustrate an
argument hitherto free of satiric edge. The claim about the diversity of
human religion gradually slides into satire by an enumeration of what
has been worshipped, from chaos to "a Bird, a Crocodile, a Calf, a
Dogge . . . a Leeke, deified" (*Leviathan,* 12.79); again we see the concluding short phrasing rhythms. Similarly, to convey a sense of arbitrary
poetic self-indulgence he reels off a decontextualized list of items into
whose shapes poems had been forced, "an organ, a hatchet, an altar, and
a pair of wings" (*Answer,* 446). This arbitrariness is a feature of the list
more than the poems whose shapes were frequently a visual expression
of their themes—not a little like a frontispiece.

Hobbes is a witty writer occasionally given to a delicious pun, as
when he writes (*Dialogue*) that where there are no laws, clubs are
trumps. He did go out of his way to make people laugh. On his own
much-rehearsed theories of laughter, themselves an inheritance from
antiquity, the provocation of mirth had a place in his armory of persuasion. It was to join the laughing reader with the author in an attempt to
ridicule an enemy. As Hobbes's contemporary Samuel Butler appositely
remarked, no man laughs fully without baring his teeth.[7] In this way,
Hobbes's attempts to stimulate laughter, smirk or sneer at the expense
of Catholicism, was a means of persuading Protestants of the importance of sovereign power by demonizing Catholics as a principal enemy
(*Leviathan,* 44–47). Not keeping the targets of his wit within such a
denominational demarcation was a major cause of his later troubles.

This section of *Leviathan* also exhibits a rare occasion on which
Hobbes artfully plays at relaxing his authorial control. Despite his eloquent virtuosity, it is noticeable how rarely Hobbes resorts to *aposiopesis,*
the trope of leaving a statement unfinished, where the readers in com-
pleting it for themselves are creatively implicated in the claim. It was
to become a classic technique in vaudeville and music hall bawdy com-
edy, but was well enough known from antiquity. In chapter 47, however, Hobbes produces an elaborate example of just this.[8] As he had
made abundantly clear, Hobbes had no belief in ghosts, hobgoblins, or

fairies; but then assuming an intimate tone of gossip and rumormonger-
ing, comically appropriate to such gullibility, he embarks on an
extended simile between the kingdoms of priests and fairies. Everything
that is rumored of one, he says, is taken to be true of the other. "The
Ecclesiastiques are *Spirituall men,* and *Ghostly* Fathers. The Fairies are *Spirits,* and *Ghosts. Fairies* and *Ghosts* inhabit Darknesse, Solitudes and
Graves. The *Ecclesiastiques* walke in Obscurity of Doctrine, in Mon-
estries, Churches, and Church-yards" (*Leviathan,* 47.481). The tone having been set and ingeniously extended, a later point of comparison concerns the sexual habits of fairies. "The Fairies marry not; but there be
amongst them Incubi, that have copulation with flesh and bloud. The
Priests also marry not" (*Leviathan,* 47.481). He then proceeds to further
comparisons.

The plot is so well laid here that the implied conclusion is inescapable
and so the relaxation of authorial control is formal more than substantive. In the use of folklore about fairies he is additionally insinuating a
deep skepticism about priests in general. The point is rammed home in
the chapter's peroration: just as fairies have no existence except in the
fancies of the ignorant, derived from old wives' tales, so the spiritual
power of the pope rests on the fears of seduced people upon hearing false
tales and traditions. It then becomes easy for Hobbes to describe the
Reformation through the metaphor of exorcism. All this would be toned
down in the Latin translation, in which the splendid example of *aposiopesis* disappears.

The Matter of Metaphor

This whole passage also illustrates one of the most significant features of
Hobbes's style, the imaginative capacity to develop image and arguments, like a metaphysical poet. Often a single topos becomes a powerful model for understanding and on occasion suggests more than he
might have wished to maintain. This may take the form of sustained
satiric comparison and so be essentially a matter of simile. It can also be
developed purely as metaphor. Thus in *The Elements of Law* Hobbes
introduces the simile of a race for human existence, then lists the human
passions as if they described features of a race. Again in *Libertie and
Necessitie* he elaborates metaphors of warfare, a controlling image for
rhetoric he never escaped; and at the beginning of *De corpore* he sustains
a metaphor of plant growth and cultivation for intellectual development.

Hobbes's metaphorical sense immediately raises the specter of a radical incoherence between his style and his philosophical doctrines. As he has been famous for insisting, metaphor is inimical to philosophy. In *Anti-White* he used metaphor as a criterion for delineating philosophy from activities in which it is allowable, such as history, poetry, and rhetoric. Because metaphor is by nature equivocal it could have no role in a form of discourse concerned to extirpate all ambiguity (*Anti-White*, 106). Later, however (*De corpore*, 1.2.12), the tensions between theory and practice of metaphor are much eased. Hobbes reiterates that metaphor is inherently equivocal, but its value depends purely upon context. His understanding seems strikingly to prefigure Donald Davidson's influential theories.[9] Notwithstanding difficulties with such a view, Hobbes did not need any problematic distinction between metaphor and the literal, only a notion of the purposes and theoretical contexts of language use. If the use is consistent with the purpose of the discourse and the context is sufficiently stable and understood, metaphor can operate as decorously as simile to aid perspicacity. Such a theory helps accommodate his rigid procedural understanding of philosophy to his metaphorical imagination. Thus the race imagery found in *The Elements of Law* does occur in a context of argument sufficiently controlled for it to be little more than a grace note to what is independently clear. The sustained plant imagery that introduces *De corpore* is really a prefatory exhibition of eloquence and so its implications and associations are weeded out by the austerity of what follows. The martial imagery in *Libertie and Necessitie* is a little different inasmuch as it seems to function as a polemical distraction, but such metaphorical imagery was so highly standardized as to constitute a pattern of clichés, the metaphors clear by being, as Hobbes put it elsewhere (*Answer*, 455), "defaced with time, sullied with vulgar or long use."

Nevertheless, the problem of metaphor is acute in *Leviathan,* at once Hobbes's richest figurative work and the one exhibiting greatest hostility to metaphor, for it elaborates polemically on the a priori dogma of the *Anti-White*. *Leviathan*'s bold claim that metaphor is an abuse of language urged without any adequate clarification or qualification actually vulgarizes the earlier doctrine and the more subtle one to be put forward in *De corpore*. Interestingly, there is no linear development in Hobbes's theories of metaphor, for the Latin translation of *Leviathan* repeats the extremity of the English. Now given that *Leviathan* is much more than a work of philosophy, it might be suspected that in practice metaphor functions principally in its nonphilosophical dimensions—where we find

the pope sitting crowned upon the grave of the Roman Empire, ecclesiastical Latin, a mere ghost of "the old *Romane Language*" (*Leviathan*,
47.480–81). Alternatively, we can reasonably expect that metaphors
are introduced into the constraining context of philosophically rigorous
definition and so do not unduly disrupt the argument. But neither is
always the case.

Hobbes directly prepares the ground for his metaphorical dexterity in
the introduction, where he collapses the difference between the organic
and the mechanical, thereafter using the terms of one domain for the
other. Some of his philosophical propositions are expressed only through
metaphor or rely on metaphor more than any other independent argument to carry force. Imagination as the decaying sense of impressions on
the mind, the image of reading ourselves, seems most immediately to be
derived from optics and the physically tactile. When Hobbes claimed
that reasoning is a matter of calculation, it remains unclear whether he
is himself arguing *pars pro toto* or extrapolating from an arithmetical
metaphor (see chapter 2, "Definition, Resolution, and Composition").
Most importantly, there is a strong ineradicable metaphoric dimension
to his whole notion of a social contract and of representation that is
almost flaunted in the deeply symbolic frontispiece. The overall force,
according to Prokhovnik, is to create a virtual philosophical allegory
(Prokhovnik, 195–225). Ultimately, the stylistic imagination that
might aid Hobbes's argument can run exuberantly out of his control. As
Hobbes was well aware, any metaphor or symbol is hostage to interpretative fortune, subject to an imposed multivalence unless authorial controls are particularly firm. Yet the processes of establishing additional
safeguards are often in tension with the drive to intellectual economy.
This too was a feature of Hobbes's style; as Leibniz acknowledged,
Hobbes mewed up mighty thoughts in few words.[10] It is, of course,
from the words, their ellipses, their associations, and their symbolic
potentiality that the grand philosophy must be constructed and in this
lies a partial explanation of Hobbes's continuing fascination and a cause
of hermeneutic controversy.

Interpretative Afterlife

Thomas Hobbes is made modern by contemporary adaptation exemplifying the fact that cultural inheritances exist only in transmission and
transmission must be adaptive. He might have approved; only in movement is there life and those who idolize the past are its prisoners. As

Hobbes's *Briefe of the Art of Rhetorique* demonstrates, even lengths of Aristotle could be made bearable if cut to suit a Hobbesian cloth.

Although contemporary hostility to Hobbes has often been exaggerated, there has nevertheless been a change. He suffered, it now seems, an almost concerted effort to damage him by a holy alliance of Presbyterians, Church of England men, and the universities, yet now he has the presence in universities he craved, even if it is his texts and not his doctrines that are taught. This reversal of fortune raises problems. Why was he more admired on the Continent than in England? Did his contemporaries not understand him? Do we know him better than he could be known at the time, or do we just know him differently and in ways that more easily and safely facilitate appreciation? All I can do here is touch on some of the patterns of use and evocation to give an idea of the history of interpretation that is yet to be written.

Some sense of early use in England should already be clear. His enemies saw the following overlapping areas of deep concern: his materialism and determinism, his anticlericalism and Erastianism, his use of de facto argument, and his employment of juristic sovereignty theory. His mathematics also brought coals down upon his head; even discussions of his squaring the circle were brought back to the still center of these other issues. From these were teased out specific criticisms often expressed with wit and panache and often with real substance to them. It is a convenient myth to regard his adversaries as fools. Many were not.[11]

The problems of materialism and determinism were most extensively taken up by Hobbes's fellow exile in Paris, Bishop Bramhall (1594–1663), by Richard Cumberland (1631–1718), and by Sir Robert Boyle (1627–1691). These doctrines, they held, were logically flawed and inimical to Christianity. It was particularly the compatibilist view of free will and determinism that Bramhall found evasive and unconvincing. Cumberland, although accepting the importance of mathematics, considered the deductive nature of geometry of far less value than the mathematics of probability. Hobbes had wasted an opportunity. Boyle, concentrating on Hobbes's physics and his denial of the possibility of a vacuum, argued that a sense of the immaterial was not contrary to good, that is, mechanical, science, which in fact was compatible with and supported Christianity. The more ecclesiological and political issues arising from Hobbes's work were taken up, belatedly, by another exile and former friend, Edward Hyde, earl of Clarendon (1609–1674). He wrote in the most complimentary tones about Hobbes's character and personal integrity, but felt particularly embittered that Hobbes should accuse

Charles I's moderate supporters of disloyalty when he was among the first to desert the cause. Adapting the kind of argument used by anti-Engagers against de facto allegiance, he found it perplexing that Hobbes seemed to allow the subject's desertion at the very points at which a sovereign might need support. Beneath this was also a hostility to absolutism and to Continental public law, which required what Clarendon, a common lawyer, saw as a slavish allegiance. Government had to be limited and there must perforce be a standard of justice beyond statute law to which one could appeal—words like tyranny did have legitimate meaning. Hobbes's notions of human nature abstracted from deviance were ill-judged and offensive. Clarendon's late critique summarizes a good deal that had been said earlier and what critics have spent much time elaborating since. But it should not give the impression that hostility to Hobbes was quite as uniform as even Hobbes seemed to think. Lawson, as incensed at times as Clarendon would be, stressed the explanatory difficulties of Hobbes's position and his tendency to what he saw as a conceptual oversimplification of political relationships—the Hobbesian purging of political language. Yet he shared with Hobbes a de facto emphasis in matters of obedience and, as I have indicated, came closer to a Hobbesian position when he published his own independent theory of politics.[12]

This suggests that despite a certain shrillness, differences might only overshadow important similarities. Hobbes remained conspicuously excluded from the Royal Society, public hostility and personal animosity overriding significant areas of agreement.[13] At least once, however, admiration and criticism went hand in generous hand. James Harrington (1611–1677), dismissing the preoccupation with mathematics, considered Hobbes the greatest intellect of the age and quite a diverse cluster of admirers can now be listed. Hobbes's friend John Selden (1584–1654) was a Parliamentarian; Edward Bagshaw (1629–1671) and Henry Stubbe (1632–1676) were university men; apparently Cromwell's chaplain Dr. John Owen (1616–1683) expressed some degree of respect. The pietistic Muggletonians, who survived deep into this century, regarded Hobbes highly, but then they were Christian materialists. The centrality of religious issues is illustrated by this sort of approbation for Hobbes. Men such as Bagshaw had an interest in religious toleration, and found in Hobbes's Erastianism his extensive notion of the biblically indifferent and in his anticlericalism a theoretical encouragement that had been all too rare in an episcopal society.

Qualifications aside, it remains true that the bulk of Hobbes's articulate enemies were clerics, predominantly Presbyterians and members of the Church of England. This cannot be explained purely in doctrinal terms, for many of his views were expressed within the Church of England. Hobbes simply went out of his way to offend them. No Protestant cleric likes to be told he is but the thin end of a papal wedge. Satire was never certain of being grasped and might offend beyond its targets. So Clarendon thought Hobbes's mirth was misdirected at the Bible itself. Gilbert Burnet's self-serving but often extremely insightful *History of His Own Time* sums up much of the burden Hobbes's name was made to carry: under pretext of teaching mathematics, he corrupted Charles II; *Leviathan* was dangerously popular because of its novelty and its attractiveness to the corrupt. It was impious in teaching that fear and interest were the foundations of society and religion dependent on the will of the prince or the people. It was a work, Burnet adds, written first to promote absolute monarchy and then altered to gratify republicans. Hobbes "seemed to think that the universe was God, and that all souls were material." In all it was "a very wicked book."[14]

The epicenter of admiration for Hobbes in England was the court of Charles II. Given the court's reputation for libertinism and atheism, Hobbes's reputation might have been better off in the hands of his enemies. Yet while he was alive, his immediate fortune may have depended on friends at court and the king himself to buoy up his own flailing defenses against the circling ecclesiastical sharks (see *Mr. Hobbes Considered in his Loyalty* and *Considerations on . . . the Reputation of Thomas Hobbes . . .*). By the time of his death, his name was often severed from any substantial reference to what he had actually argued or how he had lived, and he became a surrogate for attacks on the court and an emblem of real or imagined sins of the age—a combination of arcane science, irreligion, and dangerous and foreign politics. Such a developing image was an unintended consequence of Charles II's aspiration to an absolutist rule and of the atmosphere in which he ruled. This was partly a matter of pervasive fear of renewed civil wars; but Charles was also quite open to criticism and even satire up to a point, thus knowing where and when to draw the line must have been difficult. "Hobbism" provided a convenient foil that, like many "-isms" before and since, began to take on an independent if amorphous identity and a bogus explanatory life of its own.

It has long been noticed that Mandeville used broadly Hobbesian dogma to satiric effect and that no doubt helped make him controversial. Less explored has been Hobbes's position as an *eminence manqué* behind the scriblerian satire created by Swift, Pope, and Arbuthnot; but he does so, to use John Pocock's phrase, as a "scientific atheist" (Pocock, 742). Lord Chesterfield (1694–1773), a friend of the satirists, remarked of Hobbesian philosophy that it created "logical completeness and spiritual contraction," resulting in a sort of reductive insanity where everything is at once covered and left out (Reik, 195). This sort of intellectual madness precisely characterizes the eponymous hero Martinus Scriblerus, a *reductio* of the fears that a formula could be found for everything and sold like snake oil. He is duly made to echo Hobbesian claims and language. The sort of rule that, according to Hobbes, should govern the creation of epic poetry (only lines of 10 syllables) is taken to extremes by Martinus. His understanding of poetry as something that can be mixed according to a recipe from a box of ingredients may even be a direct allusion to Hobbes's own dismissive image of poetry taken out of books, "the ordinary boxes of counterfeit complexion" (*Answer,* 452–53).[15] Various episodes in Gulliver's voyage to Laputa have a similar flavor, as does *The Art of Political Lying,* in which the anonymous "Author" makes Hobbesian claims about the cosmic importance of his own science and method, with the art of "pseudology" being codified only by his genius.[16]

In the context of such patterns of usage, Hobbes's almost displaced presence in Locke's political and philosophical works remains intriguing. From the same semantic materials Locke developed a very different vision of political society; but while he was writing the *Two Treatises,* (c. 1681), he was moving closer to the embrace of extensive religious toleration, and so some aspects of his work pushed him back into the shadow of *Leviathan.* It was left to later philosophers, further removed from the fears of civil war and living under a relatively tamed monarchy, to rehabilitate Hobbes. His works were partially republished in 1750, an indication of interest that does not always surface in print. What were taken to be his complete works in Latin and English were published by Sir William Molesworth between 1839 and 1845, and these have remained in use ever since. Hobbes was seriously studied in England by Samuel Taylor Coleridge, and later by T. H. Green and by the admiring jurist John Austin. He seems to lurk quite clearly behind Bentham's "felicific calculus," the centerpiece of early utilitarianism. I have already suggested that Hobbes's theories of causation are partially suggestive of Hume's momentous arguments, while the two philosophers shared a strong sense of moral sensibility being integral to human perception. Despite this, there was, during the eighteenth and nineteenth centuries, still the predominant sense of Hobbes's works as essentially unpalatable, brilliant but obviously wrong and wrong-headed.

Beyond Britain to the Modern World

Hobbes's reputation in England diverged from his status in France and especially the Low Countries, where a public law tradition flourished. He was openly admired and treated with critical gravamen by the major figures of his age, most notably the Dutch republicans, the de la Court brothers, Spinoza, and Leibniz.[17] Two critically perceptive but respectful letters written by Leibniz to Hobbes survive;[18] they never reached their destination but indicate the importance of Hobbes to Leibniz's own development. Latin and Dutch translations of *Leviathan* in 1667–1668 automatically enlarged Hobbes's contemporaneous audience. In the following century, Rousseau provided one of the most important critical treatments of Hobbes's contract theory. Hobbes's arguments about the compatibility of necessity and freedom provide a context for Kant's seminal distinction between the phenomenal (scientific) and noumenal (moral) realms of existence. Hegel gave Hobbes significant status in the history of philosophy and later idealist philosophers in the tradition of Kant and Hegel have confirmed the judgment. As has been noted earlier, Hobbes's anticlericalism had been less of a barrier in France than England and became even less so during the virulently anticlerical French Enlightenment even though his skepticism was out of tune in an age of moral optimism.

It is appropriate to Hobbes's Continental standing that it was in Weimar Germany that he was remade for the twentieth century if in no singular fashion. The Nazi sympathizer Karl Smidt saw Hobbes as pivotal to a world divided into natural friends and enemies, while for Leo Strauss, an exile from Hitler's regime, Hobbes assumed a symbolic status in the decline of western civilization. Similar use was made of Hobbes in England. R. G. Collingwood's *New Leviathan* took *Leviathan* as its starting point. Collingwood claimed only to be updating the greatest of all works of political philosophy. Over a far longer period of time Michael Oakeshott developed much of his own philosophy through interpretations of Hobbes.[19] In several other respects Hobbes has proved a stimulus to thought, or, more commonly, has been evoked to provide a sense of intellectual lineage. A simplified view of his psychology lies behind much game theory as well as rational choice theory, with his state of nature being taken as a classic formulation of the "prisoner's dilemma." More broadly, he has been seen as anticipatory of Freud in his sense of the explanatory power of hidden drives and even as the first great analyst of the market economy. Refashioning in the traditions of Smidt, Strauss, and Collingwood has continued since the Second World War, though to rather different ends. Hobbes has been imaginatively recomposed as a rigorous philosopher of liberalism by David Gauthier and Gregory Kavka and as a skeptical individualist by Richard Flathman.[20] Hobbes was partially rehabilitated in the realm of analytic philosophy once attention was turned to his philosophy of language, for he sounded, and still does, remarkably modern, by turns conjuring resemblances to Ludwig Wittgenstein (on language as action and expression), Donald Davidson (on metaphor), and Gilbert Ryle (on category mistakes and conceptual reification). More generally Hobbes's insistence on the philosophical task of unraveling linguistic muddle is one of the hallmarks of analytic philosophy.

The more formally historical interest in his work has risen to a high point. Less obviously carrying the burdens of pressing him into the service of relevance or arranging passages according to contemporary vogues, historical study remains a garden of many blooms. Agreement on Hobbes's significance is one thing, but the sense of his meanings and distinctiveness shifts in the winds of continual contextual reassessment, like a corpse creaking on a gibbet as a warning to us all who would be confident of our language and opinions. Paradoxically, in such a dance macabre is a sort of life: as Cowley concludes his poem, "And that which never is to die, for ever must be young" (Cowley, verse 6, ll. 16–17). Hobbes's texts live as they do, however, not as Cowley claimed, because "To Things Immortal Time can do no Wrong," but because of the failure to exhaust the resonance of words. It is their resistance to control that can but stimulate the celerity of later fancy; "Time" doing "Wrong" may be the immortality. Under such circumstances Hobbes would hardly complain about being incorporated into science fiction and fantasy: Lord Vetinari, the Patrician of Ankh-Morpork, has for a long time been writing a book presumably about rule. Investigating an attempted poisoning, his chief of the watch sees the manuscript on the Patrician's desk and comments, "To his surprise it wasn't writing . . . , but a careful drawing. It showed a striding figure . . . made up of thousands of smaller figures. The effect was like one of the wicker men built by some of the more outlandish tribes near the Hub, when they annually celebrated the great cycle of Nature and their reverence for life by piling as much of it as possible in a great heap and setting fire to it. The composite man was wearing a crown."[21]

Notes and References

Chapter One

1. John Aubrey, "Thomas Hobbes," in *Brief Lives,* 2d ed., ed. Oliver Lawson Dick (London: Secker and Warburg, 1949; Peregrine, 1962), 227; hereafter cited in text.

2. Thomas Hobbes, *The Life of Mr. Thomas Hobbes of Malmsbury. Written by Himself in a Latine Poem. And Now Translated into English* (1680), 2, lines 25–26; hereafter cited in text as *Vita.*

3. Noel Malcolm, "A Summary Biography of Hobbes," in *The Cambridge Companion to Hobbes,* ed. Tom Sorrell (Cambridge: Cambridge Univ. Press, 1996), 14–15; hereafter cited in text.

4. *The Correspondence of Thomas Hobbes,* ed. Noel Malcolm, 2 vols. (Oxford: Clarendon Press, 1994) 2:807–8; hereafter cited as *Correspondence.*

5. Hobbes to Sir Gervase Clinton, 19/29 April 1630, *Correspondence,* no. 4; and 10/20 May 1630, *Correspondence,* no. 5.

6. Hobbes to Christian Cavendish, 6/16 November 1628, *Correspondence,* no. 2.

7. *Correspondence,* 2:809.

8. For Hobbes's authorship see the extensive arguments of Karl Schuhmann, "Le 'Short Tract,' première oeuvre philosophique de Hobbes," *Hobbes Studies* 8 (1995): 3–36.

9. John Aubrey, "Lucius Cary," in *Brief Lives,* 2d ed., ed. Oliver Lawson Dick (Harmondsworth: Peregrine, 1962), 154; at greater length, Irene Coltman, *Private Men and Public Causes* (London: Faber, 1962), 54–60; see also J. A. R. Marriott, *The Life and Times of Lord Falkland* (London: Methuen, 1908), 73–122, for a more detailed—if hagiographical—account.

10. Coltman gives an interesting and moving account of these relationships.

11. Hobbes to William Cavendish, 16/26 October 1636, *Correspondence,* no. 21.

12. *Correspondence,* 2:809.

13. Glenn Burgess, *Absolute Monarchy and the Stuart Constitution* (New Haven: Yale Univ. Press, 1996), chap. 2; hereafter cited in text.

14. Thomas Hobbes, *Proefatio in Mersenni ballisticam* (1644) in *Thomas Hobbes Malmesburiensis opera philosophica quae latine scripsit omnia,* ed. Sir William Molesworth, 5 vols. (1845), 5:309–18.

15. Sir Leslie Stephen, *Hobbes* (Ann Arbor: Univ. of Michigan Press, 1961), 40–41; hereafter cited in text.

16. Hobbes to William Cavendish, May 1648, *Correspondence,* no. 58; Hobbes to Pierre Gassendi, September 1649, *Correspondence,* no. 62. See also Malcolm, 32.

17. *Correspondence,* 2:809.

18. François du Verdus to Hobbes, July 1654, *Correspondence,* no. 67.

19. See, for example, Hobbes to Samuel Sorbierre, June 1649, *Correspondence,* no. 61.

20. The "Advice" is Clarendon MS 109, Bodelian Library, Oxford, England; hereafter cited in text.

21. Thomas Hobbes, *Mr. Hobbes Considered in his Loyalty* (1662), in *The English Works of Thomas Hobbes of Malmesbury,* ed. Sir William Molesworth, 11 vols. (1839–1845), 4.

22. *Considerations on . . . the Reputation of Thomas Hobbes . . .* (1680), in *The English Works of Thomas Hobbes of Malmesbury,* ed. Sir William Molesworth, 11 vols. (1839–1845), 4.

23. Thomas Hobbes, *Historia ecclesiastica elegaico concinnata* (written c. 1659–1668; pub. 1688), in *Thomas Hobbes Malmesburiensis opera philosophica quae latine scripsit omnia,* ed. Sir William Molesworth, 5 vols. (1845), 5:349–408; hereafter cited in text as *Historia ecclesiastica* by line number and page number.

24. See also Miriam Reik, *The Golden Lands of Thomas Hobbes* (Detroit: Wayne State Univ. Press, 1977); hereafter cited in text.

25. Hobbes's knowledge of music was probably great. See the music listings in Arrigo Pacchi, "Una 'Biblioteca ideale' di Thomas Hobbes: Il MS E2 Dell'Archivo di Chatsworth," *Acme* (Milan) 21 (1968): 25–26.

26. Samuel Pepys, *Diary, 1660–69* (London: Bell, 1926). See entries for 26 April 1667, 390; and 18 March 1668, 473.

27. Noel Malcolm, introduction to *Correspondence,* xxiv–xxv; Aubrey, 238, provides a succinct description of the classic signs of a right-side stroke.

Chapter Two

1. Pacchi, 3–42, dates a reading list in Hobbes's hand, much of it on mathematics, to at least a decade before the "discovery" of Euclid.

2. See, at length, Richard Tuck, *Philosophy and Government, 1572–1651,* (Cambridge: Cambridge Univ. Press, 1993); hereafter cited in text.

3. Thomas Hobbes, *De homine* (1658), in *Thomas Hobbes Malmesburiensis opera philosophica quae latine scripsit omnia,* ed. Sir William Molesworth, 5 vols. (1845), 2:10.4–5; hereafter cited in text as *De homine* by chapter number, section number, and page number, as applicable.

4. Thomas Hobbes, *De corpore* (1655), in *Thomas Hobbes Malmesburiensis opera philosophica quae latine scripsit omnia,* ed. Sir William Molesworth, 5 vols. (1845), 1:1. 1, 7; hereafter cited in text as *De corpore* by part number, chapter number, and section number.

5. Charles B. Schmitt, "The Rise of the Philosophical Textbook," in *The Cambridge History of Renaissance Philosophy*, eds. Charles B. Schmitt and Quentin Skinner (Cambridge: Cambridge Univ. Press, 1988), 792–804, suggests that textbook production had something to do with the emerging distinction; empirical inquiry was too variable and unstable to be codified for teaching.

6. Yet here too there are exceptions. In *A Briefe of the Art of Rhetoric* he is more open to induction in some sense of the term.

7. Thomas Hobbes, *Dialogus physicus, sive de natura aeris* (1661), in *Thomas Hobbes Malmesburiensis opera philosophica quae latine scripsit omnia*, ed. Sir William Molesworth, 5 vols. (1845), 4: epistle dedicatory; hereafter cited in text as *Dialogus physicus*.

8. See, for example, Gary B. Herbert, *Thomas Hobbes: The Unity of Scientific and Moral Reasoning* (Vancouver: Univ. of British Columbia Press, 1989). Herbert has pointed to a range of similarities.

9. Thomas Hobbes, *De corpore* (1655), in *The English Works of Thomas Hobbes of Malmesbury*, ed. Sir William Molesworth, 11 vols. (1839–1845), 1:2.7.1; hereafter cited in text as *De corpore English* by part number, chapter number, and section number.

10. Thomas Hobbes, *The Elements of Law, Natural and Politic*, ed. Ferdinand Tonnies (London: Frank Cass, 1969), 1.2.9–10; hereafter cited in text as *Elements* by part number, chapter number, section number, and page number, as applicable.

11. Thomas Hobbes, *Decameron physiologicum* (1678), in *The English Works of Thomas Hobbes of Malmesbury*, ed. Sir William Molesworth, 11 vols. (1839–1845), 7: chap. 2; hereafter cited in text as *Decameron physiologicum*.

12. This has been published as Thomas Hobbes, *Critique du De mundo de Thomas White*, eds. Jacquot and H. W. Jones (Paris: Vrin-CNRS, 1973); hereafter cited in text as *Anti-White*.

13. Thomas Hobbes, *Leviathan* (1668), in *Thomas Hobbes Malmesburiensis opera philosophica quae latine scripsit omnia*, ed. Sir William Molesworth, 5 vols. (1845), 3: chap. 4; hereafter cited in text as *Leviathan Latin*.

14. Pat Moloney, "Leaving the Garden of Eden: Linguistic and Political Authority in Thomas Hobbes," *History of Political Thought* 18, no. 2 (1997): 257; hereafter cited in text.

15. Thomas Hobbes, *Six Lessons to the Professors of Mathematicks* (1656), in *The English Works of Thomas Hobbes of Malmesbury*, ed. Sir William Molesworth, 11 vols. (1839–1845), 7: epistle dedicatory; hereafter cited in text as *Six Lessons*.

16. See Hardy Grant, "Hobbes and Mathematics," in *The Cambridge Companion to Hobbes*, ed. Tom Sorrell (Cambridge: Cambridge Univ. Press, 1996), 112; hereafter cited in text.

17. D. W. Hanson, "The Meaning of 'Demonstration' in Hobbes's Science," *History of Political Thought*, 11, no. 4 (1990): 592, 606; hereafter cited in text.

18.   I am grateful for discussions with Dr. Andrew Fitzmaurice on these points.

19.   Douglas Jesseph, "Hobbes and the Method of Natural Science," in *The Cambridge Companion to Hobbes,* ed. Tom Sorrell (Cambridge: Cambridge Univ. Press, 1996), 94.

20.   William Harvey, *Exercitatio Anatomica de motu cordis et Sanguinis in Animalibus* (1616) (Frankfurt: 1628).

21.   Thomas Hobbes, *Markes of the Absurd Geometry, Rural Language, Scottish Church Politicks, and Barbarisms of John Wallis Professor of Geometry and Doctor of Divinity,* in *The English Works of Thomas Hobbes of Malmesbury,* ed. Sir William Molesworth, 11 vols. (1839–1845), 7:357–400.

22.   Tom Sorrell, "Hobbes's Scheme of the Sciences," in *The Cambridge Companion to Hobbes,* ed. Tom Sorrell (Cambridge: Cambridge Univ. Press, 1996), 53.

23.   Appendix 1 (439–40) is on the MS poem "De Motibus Solis." The text is from 441–47.

24.   Thomas Hobbes, *The Answer to the Preface before Gondibert* in *The English Works of Thomas Hobbes of Malmesbury,* ed. Sir William Molesworth, 11 vols. (1839–1845), 4; hereafter cited in text as *Answer.*

25.   Thomas Hobbes, *Leviathan, or the Matter, Forme and Power of a Commonwealth, Ecclesiasticall and Civill,* ed. Richard Tuck (Cambridge: Cambridge University Press, 1991), 9; hereafter cited in text as *Leviathan* by chapter number and page number. Thomas Hobbes, *Behemoth or The Long Parliament,* ed. Ferdinand Tönnies (London: Frank Cass, 1969), 1.39; hereafter cited in text as *Behemoth* by dialogue number and page number.

26.   Richard Tuck, "Hobbes's Moral Philosophy," in *The Cambridge Companion to Hobbes,* ed. Tom Sorrell (Cambridge: Cambridge Univ. Press, 1996), 175–77.

27.   See, for example, Richard Tuck, "Optics and Sceptics: the Philosophical Foundations of Hobbes's Political Thought, "in *Conscience and Casuistry in Early Modern Europe,* ed. Edmund Leites (Cambridge: Cambridge Univ. Press, 1969), 235–63.

28.   Jan Prins, "Hobbes on Light and Vision," in *The Cambridge Companion to Hobbes,* ed. Tom Sorrell (Cambridge: Cambridge Univ. Press, 1996), 129; hereafter cited in text.

29.   I draw at length on Prins here.

30.   Noel Malcolm, introduction to *Correspondence,* xxvi–xxvii.

31.   The reference to the *Tractatus opticus* is to F. Alessio, ed., Thomas Hobbes, *"Tractatus opticus:* Prima edizione integrale," *Revista critica di storia della filosofia* 18 (1963), 147.

32.   Hanson points out that this allowed Hobbes to see a union between geometry and physics.

Chapter Three

   1.   Alexander Pope, *An Essay on Man* (1732, 1735), epistle 2, lines 1–2.

   2.   Plato, *The Republic,* trans. Paul Shorey (Cambridge, Mass.: Loeb, Harvard Univ. Press, 1970), 514–17B.

   3.   For a useful discussion of this concept see Herbert, 40–43 and 56–59; and Bernard Gert, "Hobbes's Psychology," in *The Cambridge Companion to Hobbes,* ed. Tom Sorrell (Cambridge: Cambridge Univ. Press, 1996), 160–64; hereafter cited in text.

   4.   This emphasis on reflexivity was characteristic of late scholastic philosophy. See Annabel Brett, *Liberty, Right and Nature: Individual Rights in Later Scholastic Thought* (Cambridge: Cambridge Univ. Press, 1997), 16, 97; hereafter cited in text.

   5.   See also Thomas Hobbes, *De cive* (1642 and 1646), in *Thomas Hobbes Malmesburiensis opera philosophica quae latine scripsit omnia,* ed. Sir William Molesworth, 5 vols. (1845), 1.1; hereafter cited in text as *De cive* by chapter number, section number, and page number, as applicable.

   6.   Thomas Hobbes, *Of Libertie and Necessitie* (1654), in *The English Works of Thomas Hobbes of Malmesbury,* ed. Sir William Molesworth, 11 vols. (1839–1845), 4. 229 –; hereafter cited in text as *Libertie.*

   7.   Maurice M. Goldsmith, "Hobbes on Liberty," *Hobbes Studies* 2 (1989): 27, 37; Quentin Skinner, "Hobbes and the Proper Signification of Liberty," *Transactions of the Royal Historical Society* 40 (1990): 121–51; Roland J. Pennock, "Hobbes's Confusing Clarity—The Case of 'Liberty'," in *Hobbes Studies,* ed. K. C. Brown (Oxford: Blackwell, 1965), 104.

   8.   See, for example, Tuck 1996, 184.

   9.   See Tuck 1996, 185, for a lucid discussion.

   10.   John Milton, "Paradise Lost," in *Poems,* ed. Helen Darbishire (London: Oxford Univ. Press, 1960), 4:108–10.

   11.   Cicero, *De oratore,* ed. and trans. E. W. Sutton and H. Rackham (Cambridge, Mass.: Loeb, Harvard Univ. Press, 1942).

   12.   Francois Tricaud, "Hobbes's Conception of the State of Nature from 1640 to 1651: Evolution and Ambiguities," in *Perspectives on Thomas Hobbes,* eds. G. A. J. Rogers and Alan Ryan (Oxford: Clarendon Press, 1988), 107–23.

   13.   See, for example, David Gauthier, "Hobbes's Social Contract," in *Perspectives on Thomas Hobbes,* eds. G. A. J. Rogers and Alan Ryan (Oxford: Clarendon Press, 1988), 125–52; hereafter cited in text.

   14.   There is a very clear propositional reconstruction of the main argument in Stuart M. Brown Jr., "The Taylor Thesis: Some Objections," in *Hobbes Studies,* ed. K. C. Brown (Oxford: Blackwell, 1965), 66–68; one of the most seminal reconstructions is to be found in David Gauthier, *The Logic of Leviathan: The Moral and Political Theory of Thomas Hobbes* (Oxford: Clarendon Press, 1969).

15.　This claim is rather discrepant with the reciprocity normally implied by gift-giving and that was in Hobbes's day subject to elaborate convention, but then in the state of nature the conventions that give the word "gift" meaning were presumably absent.

16.　On the significance of authorization see, for example, Gauthier; for a recent critical discussion, A. P. Martinich, *The Two Gods of Leviathan: Thomas Hobbes on Religion and Politics* (Cambridge: Cambridge Univ. Press, 1992), 167–75; hereafter cited in text.

17.　See, at length, Jean Hampton, *Hobbes and the Social Contract Tradition* (Cambridge: Cambridge Univ. Press, 1986); hereafter cited in text. See also Gauthier, 125.

18.　Roger Coke, *Justice vindicated from the false Fucus put upon it* . . . (1660), cited in Brett, 206–7.

19.　George Lawson, *Politica sacra et civilis* (1660), ed. Conal Condren (Cambridge: Cambridge Univ. Press, 1992), for example, chap. 7.5; hereafter cited in text. John Lilbourne, William Walwyn, Thomas Prince, and Richard Overton, "The Agreement of the People" (1649), in *The Leveller Manifestoes of the Puritan Revolution,* ed. Don M. Wolfe (London: Frank Cass, 1976), 403.

20.　David Johnston, *The Rhetoric of "Leviathan": Thomas Hobbes and the Politics of Cultural Transformation* (Princeton: Princeton Univ. Press, 1986), at length.

21.　Edward Hyde (Earl of Clarendon), *A Brief View and Survey of the Dangerous and Pernicious Errors to Church and State in Mr. Hobbes's Book, Entitled "Leviathan,"* (1676), survey of chap. 14.

22.　Jean Peleau to Hobbes, January 1657, *Correspondence,* no. 110.

23.　See Margaret Sampson, " 'Will You Hear What a Casuist He Is?' Thomas Hobbes as Director of Conscience," in *History of Political Thought* 11, no. 4 (1990): 721, for a fine discussion; hereafter cited in text.

Chapter Four

1.　For a corrective to the indiscriminate "religion" see, for example, Martinich.

2.　For critical comment see Martinich, chap. 1. Guilt by association is something we need not spend much time on, but part of the problem has been that, among political theorists, Hobbes has been seen as a secret follower of Machiavelli. It is not clear why he should have been a secret follower when many others were quite safely public admirers of the Florentine and when Hobbes himself was outspoken to the point of political folly. Still, the fact that Hobbes never discusses Machiavelli may no doubt be taken to attest to the clandestine nature of the admiration.

3.　Martinich, chap. 1, discusses the accusation of atheism by implication.

4. Richard Cumberland, *De legibus naturae* (1672), trans. J. Maxwell (1727), 34.

5. Patricia Springborg, "Hobbes on Religion," in *The Cambridge Companion to Hobbes,* ed. Tom Sorrell (Cambridge: Cambridge Univ. Press, 1996), 347–48; hereafter cited in text. Springborg notes the misreading by modern commentators.

6. See, at length, Perez Zagorin, *Ways of Lying: Dissimulation, Persecution and Conformity in Early Modern Europe* (Cambridge, Mass: Harvard Univ. Press, 1990).

7. Noel Malcolm, introduction to *Correspondence,* xxxv.

8. Mark Goldie, "The Civil Religion of James Harrington," in *The Languages of Political Theory in Early-Modern Europe,* ed. Anthony Pagden (Cambridge: Cambridge Univ. Press, 1987), 212–22.

9. J. G. A. Pocock, "Thomas Hobbes: Atheist or Enthusiast? His Place in Restoration Debate," in *History of Political Thought* 11, no. 4 (1990): 742; hereafter cited in text.

10. Hobbes to William Cavendish, 26 January/5 February 1634, *Correspondence,* no. 10.

11. See the acute discussion by David Parnham, *Sir Harry Vane, Theologian* (London: Associated Univ. Press, 1997), chap. 3.

12. Arrigo Pacchi, "Hobbes and the Problem of God" in *Perspectives on Thomas Hobbes,* eds. G. A. J. Rogers and Alan Ryan (Oxford: Clarendon Press, 1988), 173; hereafter cited in text.

13. Thomas Hobbes, *Questions concerning Liberty, Necessity & Chance* (1656), in *The English Works of Thomas Hobbes of Malmesbury,* ed. Sir William Molesworth, 11 vols. (1839–1845), 5:442–43.

14. Thomas Hobbes, *Objectiones ad Cartesii meditationes,* in *Thomas Hobbes Malmesburiensis opera philosophica quae latine scripsit omnia,* ed. Sir William Molesworth, 5 vols. (1845), 5:260, objection V.

15. Alan Gewirth, *Marsilius of Padua: The Defender of Peace* (New York: Columbia Univ. Press, 1951; reprint, 1964), 83; hereafter cited in text.

16. Hobbes to William Cavendish, 1/12 May 1648, *Correspondence,* no. 58.

17. On the *spirituale* movement see Thomas F. Mayer, *Thomas Starkey and the Commonweal: Humanist Politics and Religion in the Reign of Henry VIII* (Cambridge: Cambridge Univ. Press, 1989), 169–99.

18. Marsilius of Padua, *Defensor pacis* (1324), in *The Defence of Peace,* trans. Alan Gewirth (New York: Columbia Univ. Press, 1956), 16–17.

19. Hobbes to Mr. Glen from Florence, April 1636, *Correspondence,* no. 17.

20. George Gillespie, *A dispute against the English-Popish ceremonies obtruded upon the Church of Scotland* (1637), 20, 47; pt. 3, chap. 1. In *Behemoth* (1.28), Hobbes had a very different perspective on these obtrusions.

21.   Edward Bagshaw, *The Great Question of Things Indifferent* (1660), in *John Locke, Two Tracts on Government,* ed. Philip Abrams (Cambridge: Cambridge Univ. Press, 1967).

22.   Hobbes to William Cavendish, 23 July/2 August 1641, *Correspondence,* no. 37.

23.   Henry Stubbe to Hobbes, 11/21 April 1657, *Correspondence,* no. 123.

24.   Quotation is from the English translation of Thomas Hobbes, *Philosophicall Rudiments Concerning Government and Society* (1651), 313; hereafter cited in text as *Rudiments.*

25.   Independently both Pacchi and Martinich have emphasized the two Gods in Hobbes's work.

26.   Thomas Hobbes, *Narrative Concerning Heresy* (1668/80), in *The English Works of Thomas Hobbes of Malmesbury,* ed. Sir William Molesworth, 11 vols. (1839–1845), 4:387–92.

27.   Thomas Hobbes, *Dialogue Between a Philosopher and a Student of the Common Laws* (1681), in *The English Works of Thomas Hobbes of Malmesbury,* ed. Sir William Molesworth, 11 vols. (1839–1845), 6:97, 100–2; hereafter cited in text as *Dialogue.*

28.   In what follows I am abstracting from Lawson's *Politica.*

29.   George Lawson, "Amica dissertatio," in The Baxter Treatises, Dr. Williams's Library (London: c. 1649), 1, fol. 99–130b, item 9.

30.   Quentin Skinner, "Hobbes on Sovereignty: an Unknown Discussion," *Political Studies* 13 (1965): 213–18; hereafter cited in text. The short article contains the whole text; quotations are from p. 218.

Chapter Five

1.   Julian Martin, *Francis Bacon: The State and the Reform of Natural Philosophy* (Cambridge: Cambridge Univ. Press, 1992), 104–6; hereafter cited in text.

2.   Thomas Hobbes, "A Discourse of Laws," in *Three Discourses: A Critical Modern Edition of Newly Identified Work of the Young Hobbes,* eds. Noel B. Reynolds and Arlene Saxonhouse (Chicago: Univ. of Chicago Press, 1995), 105; hereafter cited in text as *Discourses.*

3.   See, most forcibly, Martinich, chap. 4.

4.   Burgess provides a very careful analysis.

5.   John Warr, "The Corruption and Deficiency of the Laws of England" (1649), in *A Spark in the Ashes: The Collected Pamphlets of John Warr,* eds. Stephen Sedley and Lawrence Kaplan (London: Verso, 1992), 101–2, 104, 106–10.

6.   See, generally, Burgess, 136–41, for Hale's place in this debate.

7.   See Maurice M. Goldsmith, "Hobbes on Law," in *The Cambridge Companion to Hobbes,* ed. Tom Sorrell (Cambridge: Cambridge Univ. Press, 1996), 287–88 ; hereafter cited in text. Goldsmith succinctly outlines the main points listed here.

8.   Sir Matthew Hale, "Reflections by the Lord Chiefe Justice Hale Criticisms on Mr Hobbes His Dialogue of the Law," in Sir William Holdsworth, *A History of English Law,* vol. 5 (London: 1922–1952) 499–513.

Chapter Six

1.   For a critical survey see Conal Condren, "On the Rhetorical Foundations of *Leviathan,*" *History of Political Thought* 11, no. 4 (1990): 703–20.
2.   Brian Vickers, "Rhetoric and Poetics," in *The Cambridge History of Renaissance Philosophy,* eds. Charles B. Schmitt and Quentin Skinner (Cambridge: Cambridge Univ. Press, 1988), 715–45, for a valuable and succinct account that pays attention to the slipperiness of "rhetoric" and "eloquence."
3.   Thomas Hobbes, *A Briefe of the Art of Rhetorique* in *The Rhetorics of Thomas Hobbes and Bernard Lamy,* ed. John T. Harwood (Carbondale & Edwardsville: Southern Illinois Univ. Press, 1986), 1.3, p. 41; hereafter cited in text as *Briefe.*
4.   Quentin Skinner, *Reason and Rhetoric in the Philosophy of Hobbes,* (Cambridge: Cambridge Univ. Press, 1996), 48–51; hereafter cited in text.
5.   Victoria Silver, "Hobbes on Rhetoric," in *The Cambridge Companion to Hobbes,* ed. Tom Sorrell (Cambridge: Cambridge Univ. Press, 1996), 332.
6.   Thomas Hobbes, trans., *The History of the Grecian War Written by Thucydides. Translated by Thomas Hobbes of Malmsbury* (London: Whittaker, Parker and Bliss, 1823), vii; hereafter cited in text as *History.*
7.   John T. Harwood, ed., *The Rhetorics of Thomas Hobbes and Bernard Lamy* (Carbondale & Edwardsville: Southern Illinois Univ. Press, 1986), 39–40 n.
8.   Shirley Robin Letwin, "Hume: Inventor of a New Task for Philosophy," *Political Theory* 3 (1975): 144–47.
9.   These themes are well discussed in Skinner 1996, 338–42.
10.   For discussion and illustration, see Condren.
11.   For a short but valuable discussion see Jonathan Scott, "The Peace of Silence: Thucydides and the English Civil War," in *The Certainty of Doubt,* eds. Miles Fairburn and Bill Oliver (Wellington, N.Z.: Victoria Univ. Press, 1996), 96–102.
12.   Gabriella Slomp, "Hobbes, Thucydides and the Three Greatest Things," *History of Political Thought* 11, no. 4 (1990): 585; Leo Strauss, *The Political Philosophy of Hobbes,* trans. Elsa M. Sinclair (Oxford: Clarendon Press, 1936), placed much emphasis on the significance of Thucydides for Hobbes.
13.   For a detailed account see L. J. Reeve, *Charles I and the Road to Personal Rule* (Cambridge: Cambridge Univ. Press, 1989), chap. 3.
14.   Even in the context of poetry Hobbes did not consider wit an unquestionable virtue (Hobbes to the Honorable Edward Howard, 24 October/3 November 1668, *Correspondence,* no. 184).
15.   Johnston, at length.

16. See Skinner 1996, esp. the conclusion.

17. Sir Philip Sidney, *An Apologie for Poetrie* (1595).

18. Hon. Edward Howard, playwright and poet (1624–1698). See Hobbes to Howard, 24 October/3 November 1668, *Correspondence,* no. 184.

19. Reik, 145–46, gives a valuable account of this work.

20. One of the best general discussions is in Raia Prokhovnik, *Rhetoric and Philosophy in Hobbes's "Leviathan"* (New York: Garland, 1991), chap. 3; hereafter cited in text.

21. Thomas Hobbes, "To the Reader," *The Iliads and Odysses of Homer* (1676), in *The English Works of Thomas Hobbes of Malmesbury,* ed. Sir William Molesworth, 11 vols. (1839–1845), 10:iii.

22. The allusion is to the daughters of Pelias who, trying to restore their father to his youth, on the counsel of Medea cut him in pieces and "set him a boiling with I know not what herbs in a caldron." *Elements,* 2.9.15.178.

Chapter Seven

1. Richard Tuck, introduction to *Leviathan, or the Matter, Forme and Power of a Common-wealth, Ecclesiasticall and Civill,* by Thomas Hobbes (Cambridge: Cambridge Univ. Press, 1991), xxvii.

2. Maurice M. Goldsmith, "Hobbes's Ambiguous Politics," *History of Political Thought* 11, no. 4 (1990): 671–72.

3. The parliamentary debates are discussed in Blair Worden, *The Rump Parliament 1648–1653* (Cambridge: Cambridge Univ. Press, 1977), 225–32.

4. Andrew Marvell, "Horatian Ode on Cromwell's Return from Ireland," in *The Complete Poems,* ed. Elizabeth Story Donno (Harmondsworth: Penguin, 1978), lines 62, 21.

5. Goldsmith valuably explores some of the problems in determining the issues. See also Glenn Burgess, "Contexts for the Writing and Publication of Hobbes's *Leviathan,*" *History of Political Thought* 11, no. 4, (1990): 675–702, for a careful overview of difficulties in contextualizing the political arguments of *Leviathan;* hereafter cited in text.

6. Anthony Ascham, *On the Confusions and Revolutions of Governments* (1649).

7. There are several discussions of the frontispiece, but Prokhovnik (chap. 5) is especially helpful.

8. Brett, 178, discusses the similarity with the sixteenth-century scholastic Fernando Vásquez de Menchaca.

9. Quentin Skinner, "Thomas Hobbes: Rhetoric and the Construction of Morality," *Proceedings of the British Academy* 76 (1991): 1–61, esp. 59–61.

10. It is here that there is no doctrine of motivational irrelevance: the Hobbesian criterion for virtue is whether the action was aimed at peaceful living.

11. For the notions of separate absolutist and fallback positions see Hampton, 222–24.

12. Sheldon Wolin, *Politics and Vision* (Boston: Little, Brown, 1960) chap. 6.

13. J. G. A. Pocock, *Politics, Language and Time* (London: Methuen, 1972), chap. 5.

14. See Pacchi, chap. 8; Martinich.

15. Robert von Friedeburg, "From Collective Representation to the Right to Individual Defence: James Steuart's *Ius populi vindicatum* and the Use of Johannes Althusius' *Politica* in Restoration Scotland," *History of European Ideas* 24, no. 1 (1988): 20–21; Tuck, introduction to *Leviathan,* ix, citing the letter from Hobbes.

16. Conal Condren, "Liberty of Office and Its Defence in Seventeenth-Century Argument," *History of Political Thought* 18 (1997): 460–72.

17. Michael Oakeshott, introduction to *Leviathan,* by Thomas Hobbes (Oxford: Blackwell, 1946), vii-lxvi; and Johann Sommerville, *Thomas Hobbes: Political Ideas in Context* (London: Macmillan, 1992); Springborg, chap. 14.

18. George Lawson, *An Examination of the Political Part of Mr. Hobbs, His "Leviathan"* (1657), 92–94; for discussion, see Conal Condren, *George Lawson's "Politica" and the English Revolution* (Cambridge: Cambridge Univ. Press, 1989), 174.

19. The most systematic account of *Defensor's* subsequent use is Gregorio Piaia, *Marsilio da Padova nella Riforma e nella Controriforma* (Padua: Antenore, 1977).

20. Marsilius, *Defensor pacis,* ed. H. Kutsch (Berlin: Rutten und Loening, 1958), 1.i; hereafter cited in text.

21. For discussion, see Conal Condren, "Democracy and the *Defensor Pacis*: On the English Language Tradition of Marsilian Interpretation," *Il Pensiero Politco* 13 (1980): 304–9.

Chapter Eight

1. Abraham Cowley, "To Mr. Hobbes," in *Poetry and Prose,* ed. L. C. Martin (Oxford: Clarendon Press, 1949); hereafter cited in text.

2. Hyde, 1–3.

3. Skinner 1996, at length; Reik, chap. 6; see also Prokhovnik, chaps. 3, 6.

4. Reik, 158; more generally, Prokhovnik, 84–104.

5. Pennock, 101–16.

6. Paul Ricoeur, *The Rule of Metaphor,* trans. Robert Czerny et al. (London: Routledge, 1978), chap. 6.

7. Samuel Butler, "Notebooks," cited in David Farley Hills, *The Benevolence of Laughter* (London: Macmillan, 1974), 8.

8. Skinner (1996, 419) suggests this is the only occasion on which Hobbes uses the trope in *Leviathan* and does so with malice.

9. Donald Davidson, "What Metaphors Mean," in *Inquiries into Truth and Interpretation* (Oxford: Clarendon Press, 1986.), 245–64.

10. Leibniz to Hobbes, 13/23 July 1670, *Correspondence,* no. 189.

11. The most recent account of Hobbes's critics is Mark Goldie's excellent "The Reception of Hobbes," in *The Cambridge History of Political Thought, 1450–1700,* ed. J. H. Burns (Cambridge: Cambridge Univ. Press, 1991), chap. 20.

12. Conal Condren, "Confronting the Monster: George Lawson's Reactions to Hobbes's *Leviathan,*" *Political Science* 40 (1988): 67–83.

13. See Noel Malcolm, "Hobbes and the Royal Society," in *Perspectives on Thomas Hobbes,* eds. G. A. J. Rogers and Alan Ryan (Oxford: Clarendon Press, 1988), chap. 2.

14. Gilbert Burnet, *A History of His Own Time* (Oxford: Clarendon Press, 1823) 1:172, 322–23.

15. Martinus Scriblerus [John Arbuthnot and Alexander Pope], *Peri Bathous, Or The Art of Sinking in Poetry,* ed. E. L. Steeves (New York: Columbia Univ. Press, 1952), appendix.

16. John Arbuthnot, *The Art of Political Lying* (1712), 6.

17. Noel Malcolm, "Hobbes and Spinoza" in *The Cambridge History of Political Thought, 1450–1700,* ed. J. H. Burns (Cambridge: Cambridge Univ. Press, 1991), 545–57.

18. Leibniz to Hobbes, 1670, *Correspondence,* no. 189; Leibniz to Hobbes, 1674?, *Correspondence,* no. 195.

19. I am grateful to Dr. Ian Tregenza for discussing Smidt with me; for Oakeshott, see Ian Tregenza, "The Life of Hobbes in the Writings of Michael Oakeshott," *History of Political Thought* 18, no. 3 (1997): 531–57; on Collingwood, see David Boucher, *The Social and Political Thought of R. G. Collingwood* (Cambridge: Cambridge Univ. Press, 1989), 71–80.

20. Gauthier; Gregory Kavka, *Hobbesian Moral and Political Theory* (Princeton: Princeton Univ. Press, 1986); Richard Flathman, *Thomas Hobbes: Skepticism, Individuality, and Chastened Politics* (London: Sage, 1993).

21. Terry Pratchett, *Feet of Clay,* 2d ed. (London: Corgi Books, 1997), 209.

Selected Bibliography

Primary Works

The bibliographical details of the work of Thomas Hobbes are complex. The Clarendon edition of the works of Hobbes (general editor Noel Malcolm) is as yet incomplete. There are additional fragments of manuscripts printed in a variety of places. Although imperfect, the Molesworth editions of the works of Hobbes are the most widely available and make for the most economical bibliography. I have listed separately disputed or uncertain attributions indicated with a (?) and additional editions of works where I have used them instead of Molesworth. A number of Hobbes's texts in the *English Works* are translations from the *Opera latine*. I have not listed works from the *English Works* and the *Opera latine* separately. Unless otherwise stated, the place of publication is London.

The English Works of Thomas Hobbes of Malmesbury. Edited by Sir William Molesworth. 11 vols. 1839–1845.
Thomas Hobbes Malmesburiensis opera philosophica quae latine scripsit omnia. Edited by Sir William Molesworth. 5 vols. 1845.

Other Editions of Hobbes's Works

"Notes pour le Corpore" (n.d.). In *Critique du De mundo de Thomas White,* ed. Jacquot and H. W. Jones, appendix 3, 460–513. Paris: Vrin-CNRS, 1973 (redaction of two manuscripts, undated).
Short Tract on First Principles (?) (1630?). In *The Elements of Law Natural and Politic,* ed. Ferdinand Tönnies. Frank Cass, 1969.
Critique du De mundo de Thomas White (1643?). Edited by Jacquot and H. W. Jones. Paris: Vrin-CNRS, 1973.
Philosophicall Rudiments Concerning Government and Society (translation of *De cive*). 1651.
The Life of Mr. Thomas Hobbes of Malmsbury. Written by Himself in a Latine Poem. And Now Translated into English. 1680.
The History of the Grecian War Written by Thucydides. Translated by Thomas Hobbes of Malmsbury. Whittaker, Parker and Bliss, 1823.
"Love Poem" (untitled). In *Brief Lives,* 2d ed., ed. Oliver Lawson Dick, 237. London: Secker and Warburg, 1949; Peregrine, 1962.
"*Tractatus opticus*: Prima edizione integrale." Edited by Franco Alessio. *Revista critica di storia della filosofia* 18 (1963): 147–228.

"Sovereignty fragment." "Hobbes on Sovereignty: An Unknown Discussion," by Quentin Skinner. *Political Studies* 13 (1965): 217–18.

Behemoth, or The Long Parliament. Edited by Ferdinand Tönnies. Frank Cass, 1969.

The Elements of Law, Natural and Politic. Edited by Ferdinand Tönnies. Frank Cass, 1969.

A Briefe of the Art of Rhetorique. In *The Rhetorics of Thomas Hobbes and Bernard Lamy,* ed. John T. Harwood. Carbondale & Edwardsville: Southern Illinois Univ. Press, 1986.

Leviathan, or the Matter, Forme and Power of a Common-wealth, Ecclesiasticall and Civill. Edited by Richard Tuck. Cambridge: Cambridge Univ. Press, 1991.

The Correspondence of Thomas Hobbes. 2 vols. Edited by Noel Malcolm. Oxford: Clarendon Press, 1994.

Putative Works by Thomas Hobbes

De Motibus Solis, Aetheris et Tellursis (?) (n.d.). In *Critique du De mundo de Thomas White,* ed. Jacquot and H. W. Jones, appendix 1, 439–47. Paris: Vrin-CNRS, 1973.

Three Discourses: A Critical Modern Edition of Newly Identified Work of the Young Hobbes (?). Edited by Noel B. Reynolds and Arlene Saxonhouse. Chicago: Univ. of Chicago Press, 1995.

Secondary Works

Original publication place is London unless otherwise specified.

Arbuthnot, John. *The Art of Political Lying* (1712). In *Satire, Lies and Politics,* by Conal Condren, appendix C. Macmillan, 1997.

———, and Alexander Pope. *Peri Bathous, Or the Art of Sinking in Poetry* (1727). Edited by E. L. Steeves. New York: Columbia Univ. Press, 1952.

Ascham, Anthony. *On The Revolutions and Confusions of Governments.* 1649.

Aubrey, John. "Thomas Hobbes." In *Brief Lives,* 2d ed., ed. Oliver Lawson Dick. London: Secker and Warburg, 1949; Peregrine, 1962.

Bagshaw, Edward. *The Great Question of Things Indifferent* (1660). In *John Locke, Two Tracts on Government,* ed. Phillip Abrams. Cambridge: Cambridge Univ. Press, 1967.

Burnet, Gilbert. *A History of His Own Time.* 6 vols. Oxford: Clarendon Press, 1823.

Cavendish, William (Duke of Newcastle). "Advice." Clarendon MS 109, Bodleian Library, Oxford, England.

Cicero, Marcus Tulius. *De oratore.* 2 vols. Translated by E. W. Sutton and H. Rackham. Cambridge, Mass.: Loeb, Harvard University Press, 1942.

Cowley, Abraham. *Poetry and Prose*. Edited by L. C. Martin. Oxford: Clarendon Press, 1949.

Cumberland, Richard. *De legibus naturae* (1672). Translated by J. Maxwell. 1727.

Gillespie, George. *A dispute against the English-Popish Ceremonies Obtruded on the Church of Scotland*.1637.

Hale, Sir Matthew. "Reflections by the Lord Chiefe Justice Hale Criticisms on Mr. Hobbs His Dialogue of the Law." In *A History of English Law*, by Sir William Holdsworth, 5:499–513. 1922–1952.

Harvey, William. *Exercitatio Anatomica de motu cordis et Sanguinis in Animalibus* (1616). Frankfurt, 1628.

Hyde, Edward (Earl of Clarendon). *A Brief View and Survey of the Dangerous and Pernicious Errors to Church and State in Mr Hobbes' Book, Entitled "Leviathan."* 1676.

Lawson, George. "Amica dissertatio." In The Baxter Treatises, Dr. Williams's Library, London, 1, fol. 99–130b, item 9.

———. *An Examination of the Political Part of Mr. Hobbs, His "Leviathan."* 1657.

———. *Politica sacra et civilis* (1660, 1689). Edited by Conal Condren. Cambridge: Cambridge Univ. Press, 1992.

Lilbourne, John, et al. *The Leveller Manifestoes of the Puritan Revolution*. Edited by Don Wolfe. Frank Cass, 1976.

Marsilius of Padua. *Defensor pacis* (1324). Translated and edited by Alan Gewirth. New York: Columbia Univ. Press, 1956.

———. *Defensor pacis*. Edited by H. Kutsch. Berlin: Rutten und Loening, 1958.

Marvell, Andrew. *The Complete Poems*. Edited by Elizabeth Story Dunno. Harmondsworth: Penguin, 1978.

Milton, John. *Poems*. Edited by Helen Darbishire. Oxford Univ. Press, 1960.

Pepys, Samuel. *Diary 1660–69*. Bell, 1926.

Plato. *The Republic*. 2 vols. Translated by Paul Shorey. Cambridge, Mass.: Loeb, Harvard University Press, 1970.

Sidney, Sir Philip. *An Apologie for Poetrie*. 1595.

Warr, John. *A Spark in the Ashes: The Collected Pamphlets of John Warr*. Edited by Stephen Sedley and Lawrence Kaplen. Verso, 1992.

Modern Works on Hobbes

Brown, K. C., ed. *Hobbes Studies*. Oxford: Blackwell, 1965.

Brown, Stuart M., Jr. "The Taylor Thesis: Some Objections." In *Hobbes Studies*, ed. K. C. Brown, 57–72. Oxford: Blackwell, 1965.

Burgess, Glenn. "Contexts for the Writing and Publication of Hobbes's *Leviathan*." *History of Political Thought* 11, no. 4 (1990): 675–702.

Coltman, Irene. *Private Men and Public Causes*. Faber, 1962.

Condren, Conal. "Confronting the Monster: George Lawson's Reactions to Hobbes's *Leviathan*." *Political Science* 40 (1988): 67–83.

————. "On the Rhetorical Foundations of *Leviathan*." *History of Political Thought* 11, no. 4 (1990): 703–20.

Flathman, Richard. *Thomas Hobbes: Skepticism, Individuality, and Chastened Politics*. Sage, 1993.

Gauthier, David. *The Logic of Leviathan: The Moral and Political Theory of Thomas Hobbes*. Oxford: Clarendon Press, 1969.

————. "Hobbes's Social Contract." In *Perspectives on Thomas Hobbes*, eds. G. A. J. Rogers and Alan Ryan, 125–52. Oxford: Clarendon Press, 1988.

Gert, Bernard. "Hobbes's Psychology.", In *The Cambridge Companion to Hobbes*, ed. Tom Sorrell, 157–74. Cambridge: Cambridge Univ. Press, 1996.

Goldie, Mark. "The Reception of Hobbes." In *The Cambridge History of Political Thought, 1450–1700*, ed. J. H. Burns, 589–615. Cambridge: Cambridge Univ. Press, 1991.

Goldsmith, Maurice M. "Hobbes on Liberty." *Hobbes Studies* 2 (1989): 23–39.

————. "Hobbes's Ambiguous Politics." *History of Political Thought* 11, no. 4 (1990): 639–74.

————. "Hobbes on Law." In *The Cambridge Companion to Hobbes*, ed. Tom Sorrell, 274–304. Cambridge: Cambridge Univ. Press, 1996.

Grant, Hardy. "Hobbes and Mathematics." In *The Cambridge Companion to Hobbes*, ed. Tom Sorrell, 108–28. Cambridge: Cambridge Univ. Press, 1996.

Hampton, Jean. *Hobbes and the Social Contract Tradition*. Cambridge: Cambridge Univ. Press, 1986.

Hanson, D. W. "The Meaning of 'Demonstration' in Hobbes's Science." *History of Political Thought* 11, no. 4 (1990): 587–626.

Herbert, Gary. *Thomas Hobbes: The Unity of Scientific and Moral Reasoning*. Vancouver: Univ. of British Columbia Press, 1989.

Jesseph, Douglas. "Hobbes and the Method of Natural Science." In *The Cambridge Companion to Hobbes*, ed. Tom Sorrell, 86–107. Cambridge: Cambridge Univ. Press, 1996.

Johnston, David. *The Rhetoric of "Leviathan": Thomas Hobbes and the Politics of Cultural Transformation*. Princeton: Princeton Univ. Press, 1986.

Kavka, Gregory. *Hobbesian Moral and Political Theory*. Princeton: Princeton Univ. Press, 1986.

Malcolm, Noel. "Hobbes and the Royal Society." In *Perspectives on Thomas Hobbes*, eds. G. A. J. Rogers and Alan Ryan, 43–66. Oxford: Clarendon Press, 1988.

————. "Hobbes and Spinoza." In *The Cambridge History of Political Thought, 1450–1700*, ed. J. H. Burns, 530–57. Cambridge: Cambridge Univ. Press, 1991.

———— "A Summary Biography of Hobbes." In *The Cambridge Companion to Hobbes*, ed. Tom Sorrell, 13–44. Cambridge: Cambridge Univ. Press, 1996.

Moloney, Pat. "Leaving the Garden of Eden: Linguistic and Political Authority in Thomas Hobbes." *History of Political Thought* 18, no. 2 (1997): 242–66.

Martinich, A. P. *The Two Gods of "Leviathan": Thomas Hobbes on Religion and Politics.* Cambridge: Cambridge Univ. Press, 1992.

Oakeshott, Michael. Introduction to *Leviathan,* by Thomas Hobbes, vii–lxvi. Oxford: Blackwell, 1946.

Pacchi, Arrigo. "Una 'Biblioteca ideale' di Thomas Hobbes: Il MS E2 Dell'Archivo di Chatsworth." *Acme* (Milan) 21 (1968): 5–42.

———. "Hobbes and the Problem of God." In *Perspectives on Thomas Hobbes,* eds. G. A. J. Rogers and Alan Ryan, 171–87. Oxford: Clarendon Press, 1988.

Pennock, Roland J. "Hobbes's Confusing Clarity—The Case of 'Liberty'." In *Hobbes Studies,* ed. K. C. Brown, 101–16. Oxford: Blackwell, 1965.

Pocock, J. G. A. "Thomas Hobbes: Atheist or Enthusiast? His Place in Restoration Debate." *History of Political Thought* 11, no. 4 (1990): 737–49.

Prins, Jan. "Hobbes on Light and Vision." In *The Cambridge Companion to Hobbes,* ed. Tom Sorrell, 129–56. Cambridge: Cambridge Univ. Press, 1996.

Prokhovnik, Raia. *Rhetoric and Philosophy in Hobbes's "Leviathan."* New York: Garland, 1991.

Reik, Miriam. *The Golden Lands of Thomas Hobbes.* Detroit: Wayne State Univ. Press, 1977.

Rogers, G. A. J., and Alan Ryan. *Perspectives on Thomas Hobbes.* Oxford: Clarendon Press, 1989.

Sampson, Margaret. " 'Will You Hear What a Casuist He Is?' Thomas Hobbes as Director of Conscience." *History of Political Thought* 11, no. 4 (1990): 721–36.

Schuhmann, Karl. "Le 'Short Tract', première oeuvre philosophique de Hobbes." *Hobbes Studies* 8 (1995): 3–36.

Scott, Jonathan. "The Peace of Silence: Thucydides and the English Civil War." In *The Certainty of Doubt,* eds. Miles Fairburn and Bill Oliver, 90–116. Wellington, N.Z.: Victoria Univ. Press, 1996.

Silver, Victoria. "Hobbes on Rhetoric." In *The Cambridge Companion to Hobbes,* ed. Tom Sorrell, 329–45. Cambridge: Cambridge Univ. Press, 1996.

Skinner, Quentin. "Hobbes and the Proper Signification of Liberty." *Transactions of the Royal Historical Society* 40 (1990): 121–51.

———. "Thomas Hobbes: Rhetoric and the Construction of Morality." *Proceedings of the British Academy* 76 (1991): 1–61.

———. *Reason and Rhetoric in the Philosophy of Hobbes.* Cambridge: Cambridge Univ. Press, 1996.

Slomp, Gabriella. "Hobbes, Thucydides and the Three Greatest Things." *History of Political Thought* 11, no. 4 (1990): 565–86.

Sommerville, Johann. *Thomas Hobbes: Political Ideas in Context.* Macmillan, 1992.

Sorrell, Tom, ed. *The Cambridge Companion to Hobbes*. Cambridge: Cambridge Univ. Press, 1996.

————. "Hobbes's Scheme of the Sciences." In *The Cambridge Companion to Hobbes*, ed. Tom Sorrell, 45–61. Cambridge: Cambridge Univ. Press, 1996.

Springborg, Patricia. "Hobbes on Religion." In *The Cambridge Companion to Hobbes*, ed. Tom Sorrell, 346–80. Cambridge: Cambridge Univ. Press, 1996.

Stephen, Sir Leslie. *Hobbes*. Michigan: Univ. of Michigan Press, 1961.

Strauss, Leo. *The Political Philosophy of Hobbes*. Translated by Elsa M. Sinclair. Oxford: Clarendon Press, 1936.

Tregenza, Ian. "The Life of Hobbes in the Writings of Michael Oakeshott." *History of Political Thought* 18, no. 3 (1997): 531–57.

Tricaud, Francois. "Hobbes's Conception of the State of Nature from 1640 to 1651: Evolution and Ambiguities." In *Perspectives on Thomas Hobbes,* eds. G. A. J. Rogers and Alan Ryan, 107–24. Oxford: Clarendon Press, 1988.

Tuck, Richard. "Hobbes's Moral Philosophy." In *The Cambridge Companion to Hobbes*, ed. Tom Sorrell, 175–207. Cambridge: Cambridge Univ. Press, 1996.

————. "Optics and Sceptics: The Philosophical Foundations of Hobbes's Political Thought." In *Conscience and Casuistry in Early Modern Europe*, ed. Edmund Leites. Cambridge: Cambridge Univ. Press, 1969.

Index

Adam named the beasts in the garden; language is a tool for the creation of social order. This concept is central to Hobbes's thought. If language creates organization, then an index is in many respects a straightjacket. The fluidity of thought, the interaction of ideas are reduced to a list of terms, limited and inflexible. It is ironic that Hobbes, who so stressed the importance of definition, is so slippery when strained through the net; *Leviathan* is not drawn up with a hook, or easily bound in an index. Hobbes's works are used throughout the text and are found under their own names with cross-references and subheadings to indicate areas of conceptual and thematic importance. Because it is very difficult to untangle them, philosophy and science are listed under one term: philosophy/science.

The Author

Conal Condren is professor of political science and director of the Humanities Research Program, faculty of arts and social sciences, University of New South Wales, Australia. He is a member of Clare Hall and Churchill College, Cambridge, and is a fellow of the Australian Academy of the Humanities. Among his books are *The Status and Appraisal of Classic Texts* (Princeton: Princeton Univ. Press, 1985), *George Lawson's "Politica" and the English Revolution* (Cambridge: Cambridge Univ. Press, 1989), and *The Language of Politics in Seventeenth-Century England* (London: Macmillan, 1994).

The Editor

Arthur F. Kinney is the Thomas W. Copeland Professor of Literary History at the University of Massachusetts, Amherst, and the director of the Center for Renaissance Studies there; he is also an adjunct professor of English at New York University. He has written several books in the field; *Humanist Poetics, Continental Humanist Poetics, John Skelton: Priest as Poet,* and the forthcoming *Lies Like the Truth: "Macbeth" and the Cultural Moment* are among them. He is the founding editor of the journal *English Literary Renaissance* and editor of the book series Massachusetts Studies in Early Modern Culture.